THE BOOK OF LUKE

THE BOOK OF LUKE

★ ★ ★ ★ ★ ★ ★ ★ ★ ★ ★ ★ ★ ★ ★ ★ ★ ★ ★

MY FIGHT FOR TRUTH, JUSTICE, AND LIBERTY CITY

★ ★ ★ ★ ★ ★ ★ ★ ★ ★ ★ ★ ★ ★ ★ ★ ★ ★ ★

LUTHER CAMPBELL

Amistad

An Imprint of HarperCollins*Publishers*

FIRST EDITION

Designed by Suet Yee Chong

Library of Congress Cataloging-in-Publication Data has been applied for.

ISBN: 978-0-06-233640-8

15 16 17 18 19   OV/RRD   10 9 8 7 6 5 4 3 2 1

To my family—my wife, Kristin; my sons Blake and Brooklyn; my daughter Lutheria; and my two adopted sons, Devonta Freeman and Durell Eskridge. To my father, Stanley Campbell; my mother, Yvonne Campbell; my uncle, Ricky Stirrup; and my Liberty City Optimist Family. And to two of my best friends, Nikki Kancey and Tresa Sanders, who have always been by my side, through the good times and the bad; through the ups and the downs.

"So that you may know the exact truth."
—THE BOOK OF LUKE 1:4

CONTENTS

My father was a janitor. He worked at the same elementary school in Miami for twenty years. Before that he worked as a forklift operator at the Food Fair. It was a better job with better pay and better hours, but he was fired for insubordination, for being a black man who wasn't afraid to stand up for himself. My father wouldn't apologize to a manager who insisted that he'd done something wrong, something he didn't do. My father could have kept his head down and kept his job, but he refused. He left and took a menial, lower-paying job someplace else because he wasn't going to eat shit for anyone.

I am my father's son, and this is my story . . .

LIBERTY CITY

I was born on Miami Beach, at Mount Sinai hospital, on December 22, 1960. How I came out, what time I came out, I don't know. What I do know is that it was unusual for me to be born there. Miami was still segregated, same as the rest of America, and at the time black people weren't even allowed on Miami Beach except to work as maids and janitors at the resorts. If you were a black person working on Miami Beach, you had to carry an ID card. Get caught without your card and you'd be escorted off the island or taken to jail.

The greatest black performers in America, going back to Count Basie and Duke Ellington and all the way up through Sam Cooke and James Brown, they'd play their gigs at the Fontainebleau and the Eden Roc, but then after the curtain went down they had to cross the bridge to stay at the Charles Hotel in Overtown, Miami's original black neighborhood. It was the same for Muhammad Ali when he was training at Angelo Dundee's 5th St. Gym for the heavyweight bout against Sonny Liston. He'd come down to train at the gym, then he'd have to catch a bus back to Overtown at night.

In 1960, black people who wanted to be born were supposed to go to Jackson, the city hospital. But not me. Later on down the road, whenever I had issues with my club, Luke's Miami Beach, or when I got flack for trying to bring hip-hop concerts and conventions to Miami Beach, I'd always throw it in people's faces. I'd say, "Motherfucker, I was *born* here. I was born on Miami Beach. This is my city." It blows people's minds.

I never asked how she came to give birth to me at Mount Sinai. I can only figure they had some interns from the university, and they were encouraging blacks to come over so they could run experiments on them. Maybe I was an experiment. It was a pretty telling way to start the life of Luther Campbell: not even five minutes in this world, and I was already making noise someplace I wasn't supposed to be.

The history of black Miami is unique, different from any other major city in the South. There was no slavery here. Some landowners had tried to bring it down, before the Civil War, but the swampland was so brutal that for a long time every attempt to settle the area failed. The blacks who did come to south Florida were escaped slaves who'd fled from Georgia and Alabama to disappear into the Everglades with the Seminoles. Or they were Bahamians or other free Caribbean folk who came to fish and farm. White people didn't know how to live and thrive in the tropics. Bahamians did. They knew the agricultural practices to use, how to fish, how to use lime mortar to build houses. There would be no Miami if blacks hadn't built it.

When south Florida was a sleepy backwater, cut off from the rest of the state, it was an okay place for blacks to live. There was more equality. The black people here were fiercely independent, proud, hardworking, educated. We had our own thriving community and business district in what would become Coconut Grove. There was a high level of home ownership and civic engagement. When the city of Miami voted to incorporate in 1896, over 40 percent of the registered voters were black.

We were here from the beginning. This was our town. But then the railroads came. The railroads brought capitalism, and capitalism brought exploitation. Once Miami became a lucrative resort destination, all that black pride and independence was no match for the power of white money. White businessmen and real estate speculators poured into Miami and began buying it up and selling it off, piece by piece. Wealthy white tourists started coming. Miami needed blacks to dig the ditches and clean the hotels, but those blacks had to be kept out of sight and out of mind. Racial covenants and restrictive zoning started pushing us across the same railroad tracks that we'd built, into a neighborhood called Overtown. It got its name because it was on the other side of downtown from Coconut Grove, and you had to go "over town" to get there.

Miami began to take off, especially Miami Beach. It was the American Riviera, full of beautiful oceanfront mansions and art deco resorts. By comparison, Overtown was a slum, families living in wooden shacks with no city services and no sanitation. There were lots of houses without electricity or running water; people still used woodstoves and oil lamps. Despite how we were forced to live, the black community thrived in its own way. We built our own banks, our own hotels, our own restaurants and nightclubs. There were great movie houses: the Ritz and the Lyric and the Modern. Anything you could get in Harlem, you could get in Overtown. It was separate and segregated, but it was ours.

Second Avenue was the main drag. Friday and Saturday nights, men and women would step out in their finest to hear Hartley Toote's house band at Rockland Palace, or Count Basie at Harlem

Square Club. The big acts that came to town, like Ella Fitzgerald and Louis Armstrong and Bessie Smith, they'd play their gigs over on Miami Beach, get off around midnight, and then come back to the clubs in Overtown and play crazy, nonstop sets until the sun came up. There was dirt and disease right off the main drag, but out on the avenue, shit was jumping.

My mother grew up in Overtown, born and raised. Her father had come over years before from the Bahamas for work. She was Yvonne Galloway before she married my father, and she and her sisters were known as the most drop-dead-gorgeous women of Overtown, the Galloway girls. I don't know how my old man got in there, but he did, and after they got married they lived together with the two boys from her first marriage in an apartment right in the heart of Overtown.

Then they started kicking us out.

Overtown sits right down by the water, about two blocks from where the Miami Heat arena is today. As the city grew around it, it became some of the most valuable property in the whole south of Florida. Developers wanted the land for more condos and office buildings and hotels. At the time, the federal government was building the interstate highway system, and I-95 was going to be run straight down through the heart of Miami. Urban renewal, they were calling it. The original plan called for running the highway over the old Florida East Coast railroad tracks, which was already a transit corridor and would have caused little disruption. But the plan was deliberately shifted west to run through the heart of Overtown.

The community was destroyed, intentionally, to make way for white developers. Overtown's business district was gutted. They razed whole city blocks and started moving families out. The houses that weren't destroyed, the city went through and started evicting people. After years of forcing blacks to live in substandard housing, the city sent out inspectors and if they found any code violations (which they always did), they'd use it to evict us. In the years that followed, the population of Overtown dropped from forty thousand to ten thousand. Some people stayed, but the heart and soul of the community was being ripped out, and a lot of families moved away, including mine.

The other part of clearing us out was building someplace for us to go. Back in the 1930s, there was a white neighborhood just north of Overtown called Liberty City. Responding to the over-crowding conditions in Overtown, in 1937 the federal government had gone into Liberty City and built the Liberty Square Houses—it was only the second public housing project in the country and the first in the South. The white families in Liberty City were so pan-icked about all these poor blacks moving in that the city actually built a wall that ran down the middle of Twelfth Avenue, from Sixty-Second Street to Seventy-First Street, to separate the new projects from the white parts of town.

Liberty Square had modern kitchens, electricity, hot water, all these conveniences that were going to entice black families to move out of Overtown. The projects were very different than when I was growing up. By the time I was a kid, they were already falling apart. Same as with Overtown, they weren't maintained. There was no investment from the city to keep them nice. Eventually nobody called it Liberty Square anymore. Everyone called it the Pork N' Beans, because that's all the people who lived there could afford to eat.

Some black families moved out to take advantage of the new homes, but most black families wanted to stay in Overtown. Then the interstate came and black families started pouring out, spreading north into Brownsville and Caledonia and Carver Vil-lage. Sometimes the families moving in were met with protests, sometimes with dynamite. They kept coming because there was nowhere else for them to go.

My parents left Overtown when the interstate was built, moving first to an apartment in the Caledonia neighborhood. My father started looking for a house to buy with some of the money he and my mother had managed to save. He saw an ad in the paper for nice houses over in what was still the white part of Liberty City; my father being my father, he didn't care where the color line was. He was going to put a roof over his family's head.

These homes were being advertised for just $500 down, but when my dad showed up and the real-estate agent found out he was black, suddenly the down payment jumped to $2,500. He must have figured my father didn't have it, or maybe he was just trying to fleece us for as much money as he could get. My parents had to borrow a little here and there, but they came up with the down payment. Two years before I was born they moved into this little house at Eleventh Avenue and Fifty-Eighth Street. Within a few years, the whole area had flipped all-black.

When my father closed on the house, he read in the property deed that it could only be sold to whites. There are still people pulling that crap around here today. They just use code words for it now.

When I was really little, Overtown was still a fun place to visit. We used to go to the movies there at the old movie houses. On weekends, me and my brothers would go and stay by our granddaddy's house, stay by our uncle's house. We'd go there for holidays. But as the years passed, it was less and less. For half a century, Overtown had been the heart and soul of black Miami, but those days were over. The older I got, the more we identified with Liberty City. "We City," we'd say. That is the heart of black Miami now.

When I was growing up, our house was no bullshit. Island people are work, work, work. Everything was always about business and education and getting ahead. My father, Stanley Campbell, emigrated to the United States as a young man to look for work. He was Jamaican, a proud Jamaican. To this day, if you sat down next to him and called him an African-American, he'd say, "African-American? I'm *Jamaican*." Then he'd give you the whole history of the island, the people, the political struggles against the British, all of it.

My father worked as a custodian at Highland Oaks Elementary, and he co-owned a barbecue joint in the neighborhood with his friends. He worked the restaurant on the weekends and, during the week, worked the night shift at the school. He would always take me and my brothers to work with him and pay us to do odd jobs, help him out. He worked throughout the year, and in the summertime or anytime we had an off week, we would go over there and work with him; even if the kids have a week off, the janitors were still working. So instead of us sitting home, we would go with him. He never gave us an allowance. The only way we could get money was if we worked for it. "In the real world, money is at the end of a day's work," he'd always say. He and my mother opened us all bank accounts and made us save half of everything we earned. He was constantly teaching us about the need to have a good work ethic and make it on our own. He was always telling us to have self-respect and a sense of self-worth. He demanded that we be men and learn responsibility.

Everything my father did, he would think seriously about before doing it. He'd deliberate over all his options, then make a decision about what path to take. Once it was done, he'd stand by it. He'd never change his mind no matter what. His one quirk was that he could never say he was sorry, not for anything. Some people are willing to apologize even when they haven't done anything wrong, just to keep the peace. Not my father. He'd say, "Don't ever say you're sorry for something you didn't do just to keep other people happy." If you're going to do something, then stand by it. If he realized he'd been wrong, he'd change his behavior and do right going forward, but he'd never go back and apologize for the original decision.

I'm exactly the same way. I'm like my father in so many ways. I learned a lot from him. Unsurprisingly, we always butted heads. We didn't like anything that the other one liked. If he liked the Miami Dolphins, I liked the Dallas Cowboys. I loved and respected him, but we continually had beef with each other. My brothers used to call me a mamma's boy. My mother and I were so close. I called her "my old gal." I was the youngest, her baby, and she'd take me everywhere to do everything with her. I was her favorite, and she'd tell as much to anybody who asked. She was slow to punish me even when I probably deserved it. If I had a fight with my brothers or my dad, I'd go and hop in the car with her and ride off into the sunset.

My mom was every bit as tough as my dad, had that same island work ethic. She was a beautician, famous in the neighborhood. Her beauty salon was called Beautyrama, at Fifteenth and Sixty-Ninth Street. My godmother owned the place. I used to hang out around there a whole lot. My mother did hair standing on her feet all day, even when she got sick, and she was always getting sick. She had rheumatoid arthritis and her hands got worse and worse over the years but she never stopped working. Later on she got cancer and she worked through the cancer, too. I never once heard her complain. She gave me and my brothers chores around the house from the time we could handle them. She never wanted us to be unable to take care of ourselves. She taught us all how to cook, clean the kitchen, clean the bathroom. I know some guys can't even make a pot of rice without a woman there to do it for them. Thanks to my mom, I've always been able to handle things on my own.

Even though she was as tough as my dad, she had a softer side.

Where my dad was macho and prideful, my mom was understanding and trusting. She always had a hug for you and was always laughing. We were poor, but we never knew it growing up. We never went hungry, not even for a day. My mother made sure there was always a hot meal on the table for breakfast and a snack waiting for us after school. She fed the whole neighborhood. She always had a big pot of something going on the stove, and the door to our house was always open. If our friends came over to play and made the mistake of looking skinny or hungry around her, she'd feed them on up to full. If anybody came over smelling bad, she'd give them some soap and say, "Take your ass in there and take a bath."

Both my parents had a strong influence on me. Island people are a very family-oriented people. Everybody gets drunk on Friday, cusses each other out on Saturday, and gets back together for boiled fish and grits on Sunday. What's funny is that I remember them having this powerful presence in my youth, but the reality was that they weren't around all that much. My father worked the night shift, and being a beautician sometimes had my old gal working day and night. Their personalities were just that strong; the time I did get to spend with them left a huge impression. Day to day, I was mostly raised by my brothers. Our parents laid down the law, taught us good values, and expected us to take care of ourselves.

I was the youngest of five brothers, and we lived in this tiny house. It was two bedrooms and one bathroom, with all five of us boys living in one eight-by-ten room. I slept on the sofa most nights, just because I preferred to be on my own. The two oldest, Steven and Harry, were from my mother's first marriage to a man named Newbold. They were a lot older than the rest of us. When Steven left for Vietnam I was still in diapers. The three youngest were Stanley, Brannard, and me.

Everybody in the family had some sense. All of my brothers went to college. Steven did two tours in Vietnam so Harry wouldn't have to go; he knew if he reenlisted they wouldn't put two brothers in the same combat theater. Steven came home with a 95 percent disability rating because of the damage the Agent Orange did to his lungs. He became a clinical psychologist working with combat vets who have PTSD. Harry got a degree in chemical engineering and went to work for Monsanto—the company that made the Agent Orange. Brannard became an executive chef.

Stanley was the real genius of all of us. In college, he was one of the top aerospace engineering students in the state. He became a fighter pilot and later a test pilot for the navy. Stanley's real dream was to become an astronaut, and he blamed me when he got passed over for the program. "NASA don't want no 2 Live Crew brother in space," he said.

Growing up with five boys in the house, I had to learn to fight. I'd get teased. I'd get beat. We had other cousins who lived down the street, and they were boys, too. We all had to be tough, but compared to me, all my brothers were angels. You could say I was the problem child. I always had a temper. Once I lost it, I was out of control.

When I was four years old, Brannard played a trick on me. He traded me a toy of his for some candy I had. Once he finished the candy, he took the toy back. I told him to give me the toy, and he told me to kiss his ass. I went into the kitchen, took a cast-iron skillet from the cupboard, and walked up behind him and brought it down on his head. The neighbors used to say I had a demon in me, but Mamma told them I was just full of energy.

At the time, Liberty City was a poor, working-class neighborhood, but it was still a neighborhood, a safe and stable community. Me and my brothers and my friends, we'd play games in the yard, go back and forth hanging out at each other's houses, shoot fireworks at apartment buildings, and shit like that. Charles Hadley Park was the public park at the heart of the neighborhood, and we'd go there to swim, throw the football, just run around and do kid stuff.

When I was five I went with the rest of my neighborhood friends to Orchard Villa Elementary. Five years earlier, it had been an all-white school. Now it was all black. Our whole world was black. Before Miami was founded, the beach was just the beach. Nobody owned it. Anyone could go there, swim, fish, whatever. But then they wanted to turn the town into a resort, and starting in 1900 blacks weren't allowed on a single beach anywhere in Miami. To try and fix that, a black businessman named Dana Dorsey bought a huge chunk of Fisher Island, where Jeb Bush and Oprah and all these celebrities have houses today. Dorsey was going to try and build a private black resort, but he was forced out and lost the land. It was only in 1945 that the city designated Virginia Key beach as the colored beach. I remember my father would take us out to Virginia Key and me and my brothers would race to see who could swim the fastest. But I didn't know the history of black-owned business in Overtown or what that wall was doing running down Twelfth Avenue. I didn't know that when Charles Hadley Park was built in 1947, thirty-five black homeowners had been evicted to build what was supposed to be an all-white park. Then, as those white families retreated, the park turned black and the facilities were left to fall apart. I didn't know that during the New Deal, when our grandparents were living in slums, the city was sitting on $5 million to build affordable housing for blacks, but the appropriation wasn't being spent because there weren't any neighborhoods that wanted blacks to move in.

Like all black kids, it was only as I got older that I started to learn and understand more about race, about what it meant to be black and what it meant to be white. A lot of my education about race and the civil rights movement came from my uncle Ricky, God bless his soul. Between him and my dad, I learned all about the history of black Miami, all the racist games and things that happened. Uncle Ricky was very active in the civil rights movement. He was a painting contractor, one of the first black contractors in Miami to own his own business. I would spend my weekends at his house and my summers working for him, painting houses. He would talk to me about life, the things he went through, the things that I would go through. He would talk about politics, tell me stories about Malcolm X and the Black Panthers and H. Rap Brown.

At Uncle Ricky's house, he'd never let me watch cartoons. He'd make me sit down and watch the news. He'd say, "Turn the fucking cartoons off. Read the news. Watch the news. And when the news come on, pay attention to what you're going to see: you're going to see some black people doing some stupid shit, like robbing or killing. Then it'll be the weather, then sports, then some national shit about who we're going to war with. Then, at the end, the last thing they'll show you are some white people shopping at the mall or skipping through tulips or something. Like, 'Hey, look how great it is to be white!' They're not going to show you black people picking daisies in the field and talking about how great it is to be black. You're never going to see that."

I'd be sitting there thinking, *Whoa!* And he was right. I'd pick up a newspaper, and all I'd see was "Blacks are bad! Bad! Bad!" These were the images that the media was putting out there. Uncle Ricky would say, "Look at that. The black man in the orange jumpsuit on the news? To them, that's who you are."

He said I had to pay attention to what was going on around me. I had to learn about the world, because at some point they were going to come and put chains back on black men. He'd tell me that all the time. He'd say, "They gonna come for you with the chains. But they ain't gonna be the regular chains no more. They're gonna be the invisible chains, the ones you can't see. You're gonna be locked up and you're not gonna know you're locked up because you're gonna be locked up in the mind."

I was blessed to come from a good family, to be raised by people who prepared me for how tough my life was going to be. From my uncle Ricky, I got knowledge and the consciousness to think critically about the world. From my mother, I learned to be compassionate and dedicated to my community, to always put out a plate for a hungry neighbor to share a hot meal. From my father, I learned to work hard and be responsible and proud of who I am.

But pride can make you stubborn, and I was definitely that. I was young and cocky and I always held my head up high, and America has never been an easy place for a black man who doesn't know how to apologize.

MIAMI BEACH

Football was my thing growing up. If you're a young guy in Miami, you almost *have* to play. It's a rite of passage. You have to play if you want people to think you're any kind of real man. I was a football junkie, and it was all I wanted to do. It was how I was gonna make it big. Miami is a football town. It treats football the way the Russians and the Chinese treat gymnastics. It's serious. South Florida produces more NCAA Division I recruits per capita than any other part of the country. Our high school games look like college games. A few years ago, a regular-season game between Northwestern and Jackson brought forty-six thousand people to the Orange Bowl. *For a high school game.* That's how serious football is down here.

I was a Miami University fan above all else, and followed them religiously. My brother took me to all the games. Back then, the team was so bad, they would give tickets away. Anyone could go to Burger King and get free tickets with the hamburgers. We would go to the game, sit up there, nobody in the stands, and we'd watch the team get slaughtered. They got tore up every year, but they were still my favorite team.

I was a Dallas Cowboys fan. I used to dream about growing up to be Bob Lilly, who played defensive tackle for the Cowboys. I liked the fact that Tom Landry drafted Bob Hayes from Florida A&M to play for the Cowboys. Landry was like Bear Bryant. He'd recruit black players and he'd give them a fair shot on the field. He was the first pro coach who was out getting these guys from historically black colleges. I liked Landry for that. The Dolphins, I would watch the games and they would have Mercury Morris, the black guy, run the ball all the way down to the goal line. Then they would bring in Jim Kiick, the white guy, and he'd run it in for the touchdown and get all the glory and praise. Everybody around here would talk about how fucked up that was. So I was a Cowboys fan and didn't like the Dolphins.

I wanted to play organized football, even from elementary school, but we didn't have that in Liberty City. Youth football started for real in Miami in the early 1970s. They had several Pop Warner little-league teams coming up, most of them sponsored by the Optimist Club or some other youth charity. All the teams were based out of different city parks, and the parks, like all the public facilities, were segregated. The parks in the white neighborhoods, they all had teams. But the parks in Overtown and Liberty City—Gwen Cherry Park and Charles Hadley Park—they didn't have facilities, didn't have money for programs. The best we got in black neighborhoods was kids playing pickup games, sandlot ball. There was no Optimist Club, no Pop Warner, none of that. Not for the blacks. But the coaches at the white parks, they wanted to win. They saw all these talented kids living in these black neighborhoods with no programs. We were an untapped resource. Maybe they didn't want us living over where they lived and joining their country clubs, but they wanted us to play ball. So they started recruiting us—recruiting kids out of elementary school to play football, that's Miami right there.

At Orchard Villa Elementary, in the fifth grade they gave us this Presidential Fitness Test. We were being recruited based on the results of this test. We had to run fast, jump high, do all kinds of wild stuff. I did that, and I was real good at it. Me and my friends, we were very athletic. The coaches from the youth football programs across the city, they were scouting all the top athletic kids out of Liberty City to go and play ball to make their programs better.

All this was happening in the middle of the fight over school desegregation. My two oldest brothers, they'd gone to Northwestern, which was down the street from us, back when it was still segregated. Then the whole school-busing thing started. My third-older brother Stanley, the rocket scientist, he was in one of the first waves of black kids to go to school on Miami Beach. Then Brannard, and then me. I got bused over for the start of sixth grade at the same time I got recruited by the youth football team. They had it all set up that way. It was worked out so that the kids getting bused for the desegregation program were also the kids who were the most promising athletes. They'd bus kids from Liberty City and Overtown to Miami Beach schools to make sure we were available for football.

I could have gone to school right down the street, but they wanted me on that bus. They pulled that thing up right on my street and made sure I got on it. Not that they had to pressure me much. I wanted to go. My parents supported it, too. Some kids didn't like the idea of leaving Liberty City, but I wanted to do it. I knew it was my shot. The Liberty City schools, they had athletic programs, but they weren't really good because they had no feeder system, no youth league to teach kids the fundamentals. When I played for Beach High, we used to beat the shit out of em. It was a joke. We beat em like they stole something. So when I was offered a chance to go to school on the Beach, I took it—I took it and I ran as fast as I could.

For the first thirty years of Miami's history, there was no black high school at all. Public education for blacks didn't go past the eighth grade, because they didn't want us to be educated. Not too many kids are taught in American history what actually went on, about where they came from, what they own, or what they should be proud of. They might hear a few things about Martin Luther King or Rosa Parks, but that's about it. Black kids in Miami never learn the history of black Miami, because if they knew their own history they'd want their piece of Plymouth Rock.

Back in the day, Bahamian families had to send their kids back to the Bahamas to live with relatives if they wanted them to go to high school. In 1927, they opened Booker T. Washington High. That was ours. That school was the heart of Overtown. It gave us our own place, our own institution, something that we controlled, that gave black Miami a sense of pride, of empowerment. But in many ways it was an illusion. It wasn't real power. Because once *Brown v. Board* came along and they started trying to desegregate the city schools, we didn't have any control over how it played out.

The desegregation actually started at my elementary school, Orchard Villa, in Liberty City, which back then was all white. In the 1950s, after *Brown v. Board*, more black families like ours were moving into the area, and black parents sued to get their kids into Orchard Villa. The city fought it as long as they could, but eventually they lost and finally they announced that the school would integrate in the fall of 1960. By the time classes started, there were only a dozen white kids left. By Christmas it was all black. Pretty soon they were putting us on buses to go off chasing integration at some other white schools. The wealthy white neighborhoods, they were protected. They had the political clout to make sure their kids didn't have to go anywhere. It was only the average, working- and middle-class whites who had to deal with us coming in. And the black community—once desegregation started, we didn't have the clout to protect what was important to us.

In 1967 they shut down Booker T. Washington High and turned it into a middle school. All its kids were being separated and bused across town. It had a devastating impact on the community. Right there it set off a lot of the hate and the mistrust. I didn't understand it at the time, but my parents would talk about it and later I saw it as an adult. It started when they plowed Interstate 95 through the heart of black Miami, but then when they closed Booker T., that was the last straw. It was like, "What are y'all trying to do? Y'all fuckin the 'Town. Y'all just stuck a fuckin expressway through the middle of our neighborhood, and then you close up the number-one black high school?"

There were a lot of people from Overtown who felt like they were displaced. Their pride was destroyed. It became really, really heated among blacks in Miami. Many angry black people were moving into the white areas of Liberty City, and they were mad because they didn't want to be there. Just talking to my mom and dad, they'd say that's when the hate and the venom really got worse, going both ways between blacks and whites. We initially felt all right as long as we had our little area: at least we had pride in having our own thing. Then they started taking shit away from us, and we didn't feel like we were getting much in return. After everything they promised us with the civil rights movement, they were closing down our institutions but they weren't really opening the door to their side of opportunity. All-white private schools were springing up everywhere. By 1969, we'd lost Booker T. Washington High, but 42 of the 217 public schools in Dade County were still all black.

Whites were fighting us in court. White parents on Miami Beach sued to stop their kids from being bused out into black neighborhoods, but they didn't fight us being bused over there.

Miami Beach was nothing like what you see today, the boutique hotels and million-dollar condos and beautiful women on every corner. The glory days of Frank Sinatra and Count Basie playing the big hotels, those days were long gone. The big acts had gone to Las Vegas. In the late eighties *Miami Vice* happened and the gays came and they created a little industry. The place took off. Then Disney World opened, and that was the new thing for families going on vacation.

If you watch *Scarface*, the scene in the beginning where the guy gets cut up with a chainsaw, that's what the Beach looked like when I was going to school. Miami Beach was dead. Those old hotels on Ocean Drive were all falling apart, paint chipping, a bunch of old Jews sitting out on the porch in aluminum folding chairs. A lot of those hotels had gone bankrupt. They'd been carved up into efficiency units and SROs for these old folks on fixed incomes—a lot of retired Jews, immigrants, and refugees. They would just hang out on the sidewalk, didn't have any air conditioning, nothing but a hot plate to cook on. Half the buildings down here were zoned for demolition. The art deco preservation, none of that had started. The whole place was run-down.

Before I was bused to Miami Beach, I had no experience with white people. None. I don't know if I'd ever even talked to a white person before I went over there. The doctor, maybe. That was it. But I was never worried, because my brothers were already over there. Stanley, being in the first group to integrate the school, it felt like he started changing, started acting more like he was white. We would pick at him. My old man had a problem with it. They would argue about that. A lot. I guess that was a phase he went through, being the first to go over there. Not me. I saw that and I never got caught up in it. I didn't change at all. I was still the tough guy. I was the bad guy. I was a really, really bad guy.

Busing all these kids from different backgrounds into the same school was like starting a turf war. It was some territorial shit. It was wild. It was rough. My first day at school, it was literally an all-out brawl. Miami Beach police in the hallways. It was the Cubans and the blacks and everybody fighting each other. I was right there in the middle of it, and I had to fight. It wasn't so much the white kids, because it wasn't straight white folks over there. The white kids on Miami Beach, they were mostly Jewish. They were cool. They weren't really as confrontational. We'd hang out. It was mostly blacks and Cubans doing the fighting. There were Cuban guys coming to school with chains like it was fucking prison.

Race and desegregation and all that played out differently in Miami than anywhere else because of the Cuban thing. I got to the Beach right as that was happening. A lot of my classmates were named Gonzales and Almodovar. Fidel Castro took over in Cuba in '59, and hundreds of thousands of Cubans started flooding into Miami. The government just waved them on in. The tension between the blacks and the Cubans at the school, it settled down after a couple years, but in the beginning it was bad. I was more likely to be friends with a Jewish kid than a Cuban.

School was fine, but it wasn't at all what I was focused on at the time. I was on the field. We played Pop Warner in Flamingo Park, which was like a second home to me. Every day after school I was at practice. Practice, practice, practice. Running drills in the heat, sweating my ass off. I'd be out there all afternoon and sometimes into the evening before catching the bus back to Liberty City. They had metro buses dropping us off. It wasn't school buses. It was the city bus. Didn't have no air conditioning. I'd never get home earlier than eleven o'clock at night. I didn't really get to see my friends.

I played linebacker and defensive end. I hated the offense. I didn't want to get hit. I liked to do the hitting. At the youth level I was very successful. We didn't keep stats or anything like that, but I knocked the shit out of everybody I played. The only stat I probably kept was how many times I got thrown out of games. I played with a chip on my shoulder, an attitude. I'd get thrown out for fighting, cussing the ref, all kinds of things. I got thrown out this one time on the ninety-five-pound team, playing at Suniland, one of the suburban teams we used to play. This guy hit me in the back, speared me. I told the ref, "Hey, this guy just hit me in the back, and you're standing right there. You didn't see?"

Ref didn't make a call. Then, I guess I was just having a bad day. This same guy, my finger got stuck in his helmet and got dislocated. I went to the sidelines, sat there a minute, and I said, "Fuck it." I pulled my finger back into its socket. Coach looked at me like I was crazy. I went back out, got on the field, guy speared me again. Ref didn't say nothing, again. I cussed the ref out, told him bout his ass. He threw me out of the game. I sat on the bench for a minute, started thinking about it, said, "Fuck this. This referee is an asshole." I went after the ref with a bottle—a Gatorade bottle. This was a *glass* bottle. I ran after the ref and threw it at him, right at his head. I didn't hit him. I missed, but I still got suspended for a couple games.

I was probably about twelve when that happened. The next year I moved up to the next weight division, and I got with Coach Medina. Alex Medina. He was a tough coach. He would've killed me for throwing Gatorade. He'd have cussed me out all the way across the field. He was a tough guy, but it was this real tough-love kind of thing. He'd cuss our asses out because he wanted us to be better, to not settle for less in anything in life, whether it was school, education, football, whatever. A lot of kids couldn't play for him. They'd wash out. I was a hard-ass. For the most part we were cool because I was one of his toughest players on the field. We'd butt heads a lot since he knew I was one of those asshole players. The way we'd go at it, him cussing me out, he was really breaking me down.

He was very disciplined, but he loved us at the same time. He'd cuss my ass out and then drive me home and I'd be cool with him the next day. Coach Medina and his wife were some of the best people in the world. They loved us like their own kids. There was this little amusement park, Funland. After football practice sometimes they'd take us down there and we'd ride the rides and play games. If there was a late practice, or a team member couldn't make it home, he would sleep over at his house. Medina was a good guy. And our team was good. We won championships. There wasn't a Pop Warner Super Bowl in Orlando or anything like that back then. That came later, when Pop Warner really took off nationwide. But back then they had regional bowl games, the Coconut Bowl and stuff like that. We won all of em. And the perks you got for playing on the Beach? If you were a black kid from Liberty City, it was like being in the NFL. If you came over here to play ball, you'd be taken care of. There was this one sporting-goods store. They'd tell us, "Go over there and you can pick up any cleats, socks, whatever you want. For free." The store owners, they knew all the black kids who played on the team. "You're playing for the Optimist," they'd say, and they'd hook us up.

Whatever we wanted to have during the week while we were playing ball, they'd take care of us. There was a grocery store across from the park. Whatever we could fit in our football helmets, we could take. That was the deal, they told us. So we'd go in there and we'd grab baloney and turkey and steaks and shit, piling it up in our helmet. Then we'd take it home and we'd eat.

It was a racket. They knew the black kids from Liberty City didn't have much, couldn't afford all the gear or even the food we needed to get through all those practices and games. They weren't doing anything substantial to help the black community in Liberty City, but if they picked us out and could use our talent playing ball, they'd give us a pass, bring us along, invite us into the club—or at least make us feel that way.

In the summer, once school was out, we had jobs waiting for us, too. If we played ball, we made money. I worked at the golf course one year as a caddie. Another I worked cleaning the tennis courts at Flamingo Park; they were clay courts, so I had to pull up the lines, smooth everything down. One summer I worked on a sanitation truck, riding around picking up trash. That was the job where I really got to see everything on Miami Beach, driving through all those back alleys, seeing all those convalescent homes, all those old people just sitting there. I also worked at the convention center. Got that through playing football, too. Whenever an event was coming up, they'd say, "Hey, we need some kids to work." Okay. No problem. I'm there. When they had wrestling, Ringling Brothers, the Harlem Globetrotters, I was out there, selling hot dogs, making a little extra money.

I'd do anything for work when I was little. I worked my ass off. I was a hustler. During the week, I'd work on the Beach, after school and in between practice. On the weekends, I'd go and work at the barbershop in the neighborhood, sweeping up hair. One summer I was a paperboy, throwing newspapers. I'd take our crappy old push mower and I'd stalk the streets looking for lawns that needed clipping. I put together a kit and washed windows till my arms practically fell off. I did everything. I was a workaholic. My old man was all about that. He never gave us an allowance. If we didn't work, we didn't have money to spend. So all of us worked.

I didn't just have jobs. I didn't just sit around, filling out applications and waiting for people to call. I was an entrepreneur before I even knew what that word was. I started in high school when my mom got us a stereo. She hit the jai alai combination using some numbers that came to her in a dream—that was the start of Luke Records and the Miami hip-hop scene right there. With the money she won, she got the family a component system with a turntable, cassette deck, and speakers. In the summer, when she was still at work, I'd turn those speakers out on our front yard to make it into the cool spot for all the neighborhood kids. We'd play music and sell lemonade and ice cream and frozen cups out of the kitchen. When Pac-Man first came out, I went to a video-game distributor and convinced him to rent me a Pac-Man game. Pac-Man was the shit in those days. I hooked it up in the utility shed in the backyard. All the kids from the neighborhood came to hang out in our yard and drink lemonade and play Pac-Man. The distributor told me that Pac-Man game was the single most profitable machine he had in all of Miami.

That stereo was also how I got started selling weed. I met the guys who lived across the street from us. They were Jamaican Rastas. Like, *real* Rastas. They'd give me their reggae LPs, and I'd make tapes for them, eight-track tapes, putting all the good shit in a row. In exchange, they'd give me a bag of weed. I'd take the bag of weed, roll me up some dollar joints, take em to school, and sell em. That was my little money I was making. I'd be at the back door of the school. Kids would knock on the door a couple times. They'd slide the dollar out and I'd slide them the joint up under there and they were good to go.

I didn't smoke much myself. I couldn't. I was getting in too many fights. What made me stop was one time I'd smoked some of that shit, and some guys were getting ready to come and fight me and my friend. Because I was high, those motherfuckers were moving in slow motion. I was trying to hit them and all my timing was off because it felt like they were moving so slow. I said, "Man, I'll never smoke no weed again in my life. Fuck that." I didn't have time to slow down like that. I'd just sell a little here and there. I'd make my money, go down to the dice game, and shoot some dice. Make some more money and keep it moving.

I was a businessman and I was a football player, but I was not a good student. I should have been. Looking back, I wish I had been, but even with all the talks I got from my father and my mother and my uncle about education and knowing politics and history, it just didn't stick with me. I didn't have the patience to sit in a classroom; that was never me. I was selling weed out the back of the high school, skipping class. I always had to be moving. By high school, I had skipping down to a science. I knew I could miss up to nine days in any class and not fail. I would use nine days up in every class, strategically, here and there. I'd skip first period one day, then class after lunch another day. A morning here, an afternoon there. My Jewish friends, they all had houses on the Beach, on Star Island. Their families had boats and Jet Skis and shit. We'd go out on the water and ride around. We'd skip school, go to their houses while their parents were at work, and hang out. We'd go to the park, shoot dice. We'd go down to the beach and it was topless girls in thongs, going for a swim. Stuff like that.

Back then it was mostly Orthodox Jews around here, and those guys were pretty cool with black folks. I didn't have no problems with them, with the everyday people. But what we did have was the police, who were racist motherfuckers. Black kids walking around on the Beach were regularly stopped and hassled by the cops. The little white kids I hung out with, they all had cars. We'd get in their car and go and as long as I was with them, at their houses or out on their boats, the cops never bothered me.

A couple times I got harassed, just like any other black kid in the city. If some black kid did ever go and do something, if there was any crime committed by any black person anywhere on Miami Beach—rob a purse, anything—they'd shut that motherfucker down. They'd close up all the bridges, block the causeway, and pull the Venetian bridge up. Then they'd come pull our bus over and search the bus. But that was only every now and then. For the most part, during my football days, I was living the life on Miami Beach, and I thought I had it made.

My whole world at that time was one thing: football. I wasn't thinking about school. My whole world was just: "I'm a bad motherfucker, and I'm going to the NFL. Football is what I do." In eleventh grade we got a new coach, I think his name was Coach Norton. He'd been in the NFL for maybe a season and he'd blown his knee out and now he was back coaching high school. He started telling us all these horror stories. Guys getting cut. Guys going broke. He told us, "Look, one percent of y'all might make it to the NFL. And even if you make it, you ain't gonna last but two or three years."

When he came straight out of the league and told us all that? It gave me a reality check. I just quit football completely. I was coming off JV, and they were expecting me to come up and be the man on varsity, but I just said, "Fuck it. I'm gonna stop. I gotta do something with my life." I didn't want to be one of those washed-up shade-tree athletes in Liberty City, reliving the old games and passing the joint out on the corner.

At that point I changed my whole attitude. I quit football and I started focusing on "Where am I at, education-wise?" At that moment I realized how much I'd fucked up. I was in the eleventh grade, and I was probably reading on a fifth-grade level. My writing was horrible. My math was horrible. Once I really started to look at my academics and my grades, I started thinking about what was going on around me. I realized, These people are just passing me in this place. I'm just over here to play ball for em. They're not educating me.

I started thinking about the classes I was in. My classes were filled with all black guys. Everybody in the class looked like me. I remember I walked down the hallway one time, thinking, Something ain't right about this shit. I looked through the door's window into this one class and saw nothing but white kids. I went to another door, nothing but white kids. After all this talk about "integration," the only time we were integrated was when the bell rang and we were all in the hallway at the same time. The white, Jewish, and Cuban friends I did have were all through the youth football program, never the classroom.

Our teachers were different, too. Our teachers were bullshit. They were joke teachers. They'd take some burned-out motherfucker who didn't give a damn, put him over with the blacks. I had this one teacher, he would leave class and go to the horse track. "Hey, y'all chill out. I have an appointment I have to go to. Just don't go in the hall." He'd go and haul ass to the horse track in Hialeah. The white kids, they got the real teachers. I asked my counselors about that, about all the black kids being off in one room. They had no explanation. They'd just say, "Well, that's how it is. There are different classes for students at different levels."

That's when the talks with my dad and my uncle Ricky really started to click for me. I'm painting houses on the weekends, listening to him preach all this pro-black stuff about those invisible chains they're going to put on my ass, and I'm looking at this situation over at Beach High and I'm like, Oh, *fuck*. This is a fucking setup. All of us are dummies. Nobody's worried about our education. They've just got us over here to play football. I'm over here with all these black kids and all they're doing is clowning up in here and the white kids are the ones getting all the information.

Without the NFL, my next option was going to college. I started hitting the books. I got with this lady named Ms. Burke, a tutor, to help me with my grades. But by the time twelfth grade started,

I had to admit to myself that I just wasn't college material. I didn't have the grades. I'd waited too long. I didn't know what I was going to do; I just knew I wasn't smart enough to get into any kind of decent school. I just knew I was going to have to go and get a job and start working.

As soon as I finished school, I started as a cook at Mount Sinai hospital on the Beach. But even as I took the job, I was like, "What the fuck is my life gonna be about if I'm making seven bucks an hour? What's seven times eight? Fifty-six dollars. That ain't gonna cut it. If that's all I can make in a day, I need to go put some cement on my feet and jump in the water right now. How I'm gonna live a life on that? I've got to do something better with my life." So I said, "Okay, I'll hold my little job at the hospital and I'll make my money on the weekends, go hustle and make me some more."

Being on Miami Beach, even though the school was using us and just passing us along, I still got an education in how the world works outside the ghetto. Most of the guys from my experience, the guys who never left Liberty City, they didn't learn the same things I did. Those guys are off working for seven dollars an hour somewhere, because they didn't learn anything. They didn't see how to transform themselves into something more than that. I did. I credit my parents for that. My brothers, all of us are entrepreneurs. All of us are self-made. It was always instilled in us to get our own. Our parents taught us to have common sense and think for ourselves.

Going to Beach High also helped me realize that all white people aren't bad. The system is bad, the game is rigged, but not all people are bad. By going there and playing with white friends, Jewish friends, Cuban friends, it just broadened my horizons. There are good and bad people in every walk of life. There are racist white people and prejudiced black people, and every individual is his own person.

I was exposed to the bigger picture. I saw glimpses of how the system really works, what the rules of the game really are. What I saw, when I really boiled it all down, was money. I saw that it's money, not necessarily a college degree, that's important for getting ahead. I'm not talking about money in terms of being materialistic; I wasn't about getting money to have more stuff, flashy cars and jewelry and all that shit. I never gave a damn about any of that. I'm talking about money as leverage, as power. Who owns what? Who controls who?

Without money, the blacks in Overtown, they didn't own their own land, and so they were powerless to stop the interstate from coming through and destroying their community. Without money, I knew I'd spend my life dodging bullets in Liberty City, on the corner, going nowhere. For kids from the neighborhood, the only way they felt they could get any real money was selling dope, but even when I was doing a little of that, I could already see that it was a dead end. Drug money don't stick to nothing but a good time. I didn't want to just sell dope, and I knew I couldn't make any real money working for someone else. To get rich I had to have people working for me, even when I was asleep.

So I took a whole different direction from my brothers. I aspired to do different things and be my own man. I felt I could start my own thing. I had no idea what that was going to be, but I felt like I could. I got a lot of that attitude from my uncle Ricky. He owned his own business because he felt like, as many black men do, that he couldn't get a good job because he was a black man. "It's about owning your own shit," he'd say, "not waiting around for nobody to give you a job." He used to preach that all the time. "You don't gotta work for nobody—you can own your own self."

GHETTO STYLE

When I got out of high school, I had all these ideas about what I was going to do, this great success I was going to be. But I quickly learned that nothing in Liberty City is easy. I had to go a ways down the wrong path before I found my way to the right one.

Once I gave up on the NFL, what I decided was that I wanted to be a DJ. It was my new dream, to be the best DJ in Miami. I loved to throw parties. I'd have those house parties after school while my mom was still at work. We'd shake the walls of the neighbors' houses up and down the street, then have the whole house put back together by the time either of my parents got home from work. I always knew how to throw the best parties, how to get everyone having a good time. It was something that came natural to me. I just hadn't figured out how to make a living off it.

Back then, DJ groups were hot. There were a bunch of groups all over south Florida, maybe eight major ones between here and

Fort Lauderdale and West Palm Beach. There was the South Miami DJs, the Soul Survivor DJs, the International DJs. The Jammers were real hotshots. Those were the big crews. Those guys were my idols. I'd hear them on the radio, see them playing in the park on the weekends, at high school dances, girls all over them. The Ghetto Style DJs was one of these groups. They were small-time. They were the little guys aspiring to be like some of the better-known groups. I ended up hooking up with them. I used to go to the park, hang out, and listen to them spin. They ended up inviting me to join because I had a van and I could drive all the equipment around. It wasn't the most professional operation at that time. All they had was a couple of shitty speakers. They'd play in the park for free, mostly to have fun and meet girls. They might do a high school dance here or there, pick up a little money, but they didn't treat it like a real business.

Two of the main guys in the group were Sam and his brother Ricky P. They were the ones who originally bought the speakers and started the group off. There was Dewayne Kemp, Jerry Parker. Jerry was the guy who fixed the speakers. Kemp was a good DJ. Sam was a good DJ. This kid named GI Joe, another guy named Bean. At some point we had close to twenty guys, which was way too many fucking guys. Only about five of us were actual DJs, but we wanted to have a crew behind us. You had to have the gift of gab to get on the mic, but if you didn't, you would ride on the truck, help out with the speakers, get you a T-shirt, just to be a member of the group.

Everybody in the neighborhood had a group. It was like a club. We prided ourselves on not having "real" gangs, which was more about blocks. The Ghetto Style DJs, people might consider it a gang, though. We'd fight together if we had to because somebody messed with one of our guys. If we went to the club and somebody tried to beat down one of our friends, we'd all step up and fight with him. But it wasn't a real gang. We just hung out with our crew. It wasn't like the Crips and the Bloods, with initiations.

Most nights folks hung out on the corner, at the corner store. That's life in the ghetto. Everybody hangs out. When we were little kids, we were on our block playing in the streets. Sun went down, streetlights came on, we went in the house. As we started getting older, sixteen, seventeen, we started hanging out on the corner, outside the store. There'd be a carton, a milk crate. We'd sit the milk crate down, have a seat, and talk shit all day. Every now and then a dice game would start up. Once in a while girls came by: "Hey baby!" Next night, same thing. All we did was hang out because that's all there was to do. We could either go home or we could hang out on the corner. There's no movie theaters to go to, no mall to go to. Liberty City didn't have any of that. Wasn't a whole lot of jobs to be had, so we hung out.

On the corner, I learned about the world. Everybody out there, talking about life, telling stories. We'd get these older guys sitting around talking shit, talking about, "I was the *man*. I was the baddest football player in the world. I was this. I had that. I was the shit." And now he's on the block, selling dope, because he's confused and doesn't know where he is going. These corner boys, that's all we would hear about: what they did, when they did it, how they lost it, when they got on the drugs, how they got off the drugs. I'd listen to this stuff, and I'd get something out of it. I learned a lot about what to do, what not to do.

That's what most rappers do. They learn about life by hanging out on the corner. Most rappers ain't been in no gangsta shit. They ain't been in no shootouts. They ain't got a criminal record. Most of them dudes are squeaky fucking clean. What they do is hang on the block and hear these stories. "Jason, man. Jason used to sell this and sell that. Jason killed bout five motherfuckers." And before you know it, we hear a rap song about it, about how this rapper used to slang kilos. He's buying bricks. He's flying them in to Miami from Colombia. We hear that and we're like, Damn, this guy, he's a tough guy. He's trapping. He's got a chopper in his car, and all that. These rappers, they get their stories from the guys who lived that life, who came off the block. It's like folktales that get passed along, the folktales of urban life.

I had no intention of getting caught up in all that, but we needed equipment for our group. When you DJ, if you ain't got speakers, then you ain't shit. Being the best DJ, it's about knowing the right music and having the best and biggest system. If you don't have that, some other group will take you out. We used to battle for street cred, for the right to play the parks. You'd be out there spinning records and some other DJ group, they'd see you with nothing but two shitty little speakers. They'd set up on you and turn their shit on and blow you away. Nobody would be able to hear you. They'd shut your ass down, make you pack up and leave. Then they'd take away your gigs.

That's how DJ groups would claim their turf, same way a gang would. It was a kind of fight. Sometimes it would turn into an actual fight, and we had to do that, too. We had to battle for our turf. There were times when we battled other groups and we beat them and took their T-shirts and burned them. We'd set the shit on fire and say, "This is what we think about these fucking pussies!" Some of the battles were honest. Some of them got real dirty. Our group was more hard. We'd fuck around and we'd beat your ass. A lot of other groups didn't want to battle us because they thought we'd get mad and start fighting if we lost. If anybody in the audience voted against us, we might beat their ass, too. I'm one of the sorest losers you'll ever meet.

To get a bigger audience and to win more battles, we had to

build ourselves up by buying more speakers, and around here there wasn't but one way to get enough money to get the equipment you needed: selling drugs.

At the time, most of us were selling marijuana to make some money to buy our gear. I was selling a little here and there. The other guys in the group, some of them were slinging, too. That's what we did. But along with that comes the bullshit. In the back of my mind, I knew I didn't want to be a dope dealer. I knew it would leave me on the corner like these other guys, talking all about what I had and how I lost it.

I was telling myself I could just sell a little here and there and use that money to do my music. But that ain't how it works. You get in that life even a little bit and it starts sucking you in. You get stuck. I was getting sucked into playing the part of a goon. I was working for my friend's brother. He was just out of prison, and he hired us to sell his shit. Somebody owes him money, now I got to go collect the money. When we go to collect, if the debt holder didn't have all the money, we had to make sure we get the money. So now I'm a tough guy. I'm hanging out with tough guys, and I'm one of the toughest guys. Police are starting to know who I am. I'm not a gangster. I'm just another one of these kids on the edge of the life.

I was on a bad path. My mom knew I was hanging out with the wrong crowd, the wrong type of people. I wasn't really working much, but I was bringing home money. I'd get chastised: "Where the fuck you getting this money from? You don't need to be hanging on the corner with them motherfuckers ain't doing nothing with their life!" She knew I needed to get out of Liberty City. She wanted me off the streets, so she sent me to DC to spend some time with my brother Stanley, who was working in the defense industry as a test pilot and an aerospace engineer. He got me a job working at his office.

I was only there for maybe six months, but it changed my whole outlook. It was a big eye-opener. I was sitting up there, seeing black people with suits on, being professionals, riding around in Mercedes. They were running shit, working with computers. It was completely foreign to me. All black people did in Miami was janitor, yard man, bus driver, jobs like that. I didn't see black executives. I went to a black restaurant in DC, and black people owned the shit. I never saw that in Miami. Black people in Miami were in the back in the kitchen. We weren't even the damn hostess at that time. Not even the waitress.

I was looking around DC, thinking, Ain't this some shit? My whole life changed. It totally straightened me out. Out on the corner, the focus was always about kill or be killed, but now my eyes were open to the world beyond that. I got myself together, got my mind right. I said, "I can do better. I'm smarter than this. I don't need to be out here selling no weed, doing all this wild shit. Let me put my mind toward something that can be beneficial in the long run." After those few months up there, I told my mom and my brother, "Look, I'm straight. I get it. I see what you're talking about."

I'd always known I wanted to do my own thing, but in DC I saw *how* to do it, that I was capable of doing it. I also recognized that there was the potential to do it with what I already had going, in music, in DJing. Kids in our neighborhood didn't have anything to do but hang out on the corner. There was a need for organized entertainment. We could be putting on dances, playing roller rinks and teen discos, selling tickets, selling drinks, selling food—making real money. I went back to Miami and I told my guys, "Shit's changed. We're gonna raise up our own money and do our own thing. We can make this a real business, booking real gigs. We can turn this into something. We could maybe even open our own club."

All my guys were like, "The fuck you talking bout?"

And I'd say, "No, no. Listen. We can do this."

After seeing all those black folks in DC going to work with briefcases, that just turned me on. In Miami, I went back to my job at Mount Sinai hospital, working as a busboy and later as a cook, and I built my own thing on the side. I wanted to learn more about how music worked as a business, so I got an internship at a radio station, 99 Jamz. I started taking the Ghetto Style DJs in the direction I wanted it to go. They'd originally brought me on because I was the guy with a van who could haul the speakers, but pretty soon I was the brains of the operation. When I came back home, I got myself a briefcase. I was a twenty-year-old DJ going around Liberty City with a briefcase, people looking at me like I'm crazy.

The DJ groups were playing in the park—for free, as it was about having fun and meeting girls. Parks in the ghetto, they didn't have programming or events or anything. We never had permits, and a lot of the parks didn't even have outdoor power outlets. We couldn't power up because we weren't really supposed to be there in the first place. What we'd do was go to the hardware store and purchase outlets that plugged into a lightbulb socket. We would get those and go to one of the apartment buildings next to the park, unscrew the lightbulb from one of the outdoor lights of the building, screw our outlet into there, and then we'd be able to run the juice out of there and plug in our amplifiers. Once we got the juice we could fire up. Fire up. Turn the shit on. Have a big event.

DJing in the park was mostly about building up our fan base. We were going out in the park on Sunday and jamming. People were liking us and became familiar with us. They liked our vibe, they liked our group. They liked the color of our speakers. They liked our swag and all that. It was pretty much the same as what was going on in New York, in the South Bronx with Kool Herc and Grandmaster Flash and Afrika Bambaataa and those guys. You'd do call-and-response, do little rhymes over the microphone. At the time, we had no idea that those guys were doing the same thing in New York. I later learned that the difference was in New York they were mixing, mining records for the breaks and scratching and all that. Down here we were just spinning records and talking on the microphone. What we'd nowadays consider a hype man at a concert, the guy who's talking the good shit to get people revved up, pumped up. That's how we DJed. We were creating our own sound.

The thing that really made a group stand out in Miami was how much bass it had. Other than being a person that had the gift of gab, you had to have a lot of bass. It was expected that each group would do a bass check in the middle of a set. It's what people wanted to hear. People wanted the *shzzz, shzzz,* that hard bass, and that's what made one DJ group more popular than another. We'd set up and start talking shit on the microphone, "Hey, we got more bass than all you motherfuckers!" We'd put a record on the turntable, hit the button, and that shit would *drop.* It's what would really get the crowd moving. So when you were building out your gear, you'd do everything you could to enhance the bass: bass bins, bass cabinets, bass speakers, bass enhancers, bass equalizers. Anything that would get you more bass.

Miami's a melting pot. It's Cubans, Bahamians, Jamaicans, Haitians. It's all island music, all Afro-Caribbean influenced. The Bahamians laid the foundation, bringing over the Junkanoo parade and traditional goombay music. Then we had calypso from Trinidad, méringue from Haiti, the mambo out of Cuba, reggae and rocksteady music from Jamaica. It was all these different musical styles coming together. They're different but they're all related, and they all share that rhythm, that bass-centered rhythm that gets the gyrations in the dancehall. There was the Latin influence coming in on top of that. The congas and the hi-hats and all the up-tempo stuff coming out of South America and Latin America and mixing with the Afro-Caribbean sound. Mix all that bass with the up-tempo percussion, and that's booty-shakin' music. It's a very sexually oriented music.

There were all these musical influences around Miami coming from all these immigrant populations. My biggest influence was reggae. The Jamaican dudes across the street, the guys who had me putting all their reggae vinyl on tape in exchange for a little weed, I'd be listening to those albums while I was dubbing them and I'd be like, "Man, this is all right." Reggae has that bass sound, that Jamaican bass line. When I started DJing, knowing DJing is all about who has the most bass, I went back to those records. I was like, "Oh, man, these fucking reggae records got more bass than anything." I started going back to the songs I'd recorded for these guys. I would take those songs and put them in my mix when I would DJ. I'd play a mix of music. I'd play the hot popular American dance stuff, but then I'd sample a stupid amount of bass from these obscure reggae songs that nobody'd ever heard of. That gave the Ghetto Style DJs a unique sound.

We started getting groupies, which was why half the guys were in the group anyway. Women love DJs. The girls in the neighborhood, they thought DJing was glamorous. It isn't. Like anything else it's just a job, a lot of hard work. Me and my boy Kemp, we had a hookup at a hotel near the park. Back then, the going drug was quaaludes. The guy behind the desk at the hotel, we'd get him a bag of weed or some quaaludes and he'd give us a room; it was already late, after hours, and nobody else was going to be checking in that late. After we'd DJ in the park, we would take us a bunch of girls to the hotel to get with the guys. We'd stay in the room all night. Next day, get up and go home. As our popularity grew, all the girls wanted us. Our whole thing started to be about how fast we could talk the girl into taking her clothes off. It was wild.

I started to go talk to the people at the high schools, at the junior highs, about playing their dances. I was a great salesman, but these other DJ groups had the market all locked up. The student councils had to vote on who got those gigs, and the older DJ groups had relationships with all the student-activity directors; they were giving those kids kickbacks to lock up the gigs. I tried to beat them on price, but I was still locked out. I went over the kids' heads. I went straight to the coaches in charge of the athletic events and pitched them and gave them the kickbacks. Pretty soon, the kids were being overruled by the faculty, and we were doing all the dances at the area schools. I knocked out all the other crews before they even knew what happened.

We'd do gigs anywhere, at a junior high cafeteria, the opening of a car wash, you name it. With my internship at the radio station, I was able to learn how all the other local bands and DJ groups were promoting themselves, and I copied what they were doing. I could even slip some promos for my own gigs on air for free during some of the station breaks. It took a couple years, working in the kitchen at Mount Sinai, hustling every possible gig on the side, but eventually I'd built us up into a solid little business. Along the way I picked up my DJ name. *Star Wars* had just come out, and since I had the touch that was making everything work, guys said it was like I had the Force. They started calling me Luke Skyywalker.

Negotiating every gig as a one-off thing was a hassle. It wasn't terribly lucrative, and I couldn't count on it as a regular thing. One day it came to me that we should be organizing and promoting our own gigs, rather than waiting around to take what we were offered. I started looking for other angles. There was a skating rink called the Sunshine Skating Center out on 199th and County

Line in Homestead. It was a nice place in a nice neighborhood, and I knew the kids in Liberty City wanted places to go. They'd say, "We in the hood every day. Let's go someplace nice." They wanted something to do to make it feel like a real night out instead of just hanging out on the same old corners. Nobody was doing anything really fun and uplifting for those kids. I talked to the guys who owned this roller rink and there were a couple of nights a week that they didn't have anything going on. My plan was to rent the place out, promote it on the radio, put up fliers around the hood, and have a big party. The nights we rented it out we called it the Pac Jam Teen Disco. Wednesday night was Soul Night. Thursday was Reggae Night. We charged seven dollars to get in, and we were packed.

The cops hated that we were bringing so many blacks into the area, but we were making so much money for the owners, they couldn't stop us. Cops were looking at all these black kids coming in, scared there was going to be some violence. We policed our own shit. We had a reputation for being tough. People knew the Ghetto Style DJs would beat your ass, but it was only because we were trying to keep the bad element out.

When you're from the ghetto, even when you try and get out and go someplace nice, the bullshit follows you, that street attitude: "I ain't no punk." Guys always ready to fight over some kind of shit: you disrespected them, you're on their turf, they're jealous about some girl. One guy from our group, he would go to a party and somebody would jump him. Who jumped him? The 22nd Avenue Players. Okay, so we gotta go to where they hang out and we gotta jump them, beat their ass. We'd go to a dance over in Hollywood and all the Hollywood dudes, because we touching up their girls, they get mad, so they jump us and now we gotta fight over there. Macho bullshit. Dances would turn into all-out fucking brawls.

At the Pac Jam, I decided I had to clean all that up. We couldn't be known as the guys throwing the party where you were going to get the fuck beat out of you over some bullshit. I would get on the mic and say, "Look, we trying to be peaceful. If you come to our party, you going to be safe. But if you trying to start shit up in here, you gonna get fucked up by some Ghetto Style DJs. Simple as that." When people came into our party and tried to fight, we beat the shit out of them, threw them out. So people knew it was safe to come to our party. We started getting more and more popular. Pretty soon we were the big-time DJs around the neighborhood. If you wanted the dopest party with the finest girls in Miami, the Pac Jam with Luke Skyywalker and the Ghetto Style DJs was the place to be.

Starting the Pac Jam, that was the difference between how I ran the Ghetto Style DJs versus a lot of these other groups that you've never heard of. Most people take the opportunities that are presented to them, and in the ghetto the opportunities put in front of you aren't worth shit. Me, I was always on the make, always looking for new opportunities. I didn't have time to sit around waiting for shit to happen. I wanted to make shit happen.

RIOTS

Everything changed for Liberty City and black Miami on December 17, 1979. That night, a black insurance agent, Arthur McDuffie, left his girlfriend's house around one in the morning. He was riding his motorcycle home along North Miami Avenue. A Dade County policeman in a patrol car says he saw McDuffie pop a wheelie on the bike and blow through an intersection. Cop threw on the lights and went after him. McDuffie took off.

Pretty soon it was a high-speed chase, a dozen cop cars running this guy down. McDuffie finally pulled over around Thirty-Eighth Street. The cops swarmed in—all of them white cops, of course—with their guns drawn, pulling him off the bike. This is where one of the cops says McDuffie took a swing at him, if you want to believe that. The cops pulled him to the ground, cuffed him, and started beating him with their Kel-Lites, those industrial metal flashlights that cops use. Three minutes later, McDuffie was unconscious on the pavement, skull cracked open. They took him to the hospital, he fell into a coma, and he died four days later.

The cops tried to cover it up. They filed a report said that McDuffie was injured being thrown off his motorcycle. The cops even backed over his bike with a patrol car to make it look like it had been in an accident. But his injuries were far too severe for that. The man's head had been bashed in. The medical examiner said his injuries were consistent with falling off a four-story building and landing on concrete face-first—and he was handcuffed the whole time they did it to him. On December 29 they buried McDuffie in full dress uniform; he was a marine, had served his country. The whole city was on edge while we waited for the case to go to trial. White folks were terrified that we were going to burn the place down. And black folks, well, let's just say none of us expected the verdict to go our way.

Shit's bad between cops and the blacks everywhere, but in south Florida it's different. It's a different history. In the early days, Miami was growing so fast they had to bring in Bahamian labor to build the roads and dredge the beaches. The city also needed more cops to patrol the streets, but they weren't about to hire a bunch of Bahamians to be cops. To build up the police force and the fire department and organizations like that, the city fathers went up and got a bunch of white guys from Georgia and Alabama hick towns. They recruited these ignorant white rednecks, brought them down to Miami, gave them badges and nightsticks and shotguns, and made them policemen.

Their main job was to keep the blacks in line. These Georgia and Alabama boys, they were used to dealing with former slaves, blacks that knew how to stay in their place, knew how to say, "Yes, boss," and all that. But Bahamians are proud people, independent people. They weren't used to shuffling down the street, averting their eyes from white women, being called *boy* and *nigger*. They didn't just bow down and lie down for the cops. That Bahamian independence had to be beaten down, broken.

It was brutal. Young black boys were shot in the back for shoplifting bread or eggs, trying to get something to eat. Black men would be accused of raping white women and then just disappear in the night. To get confessions, they would actually torture us. They had a torture room in the Miami police headquarters, just for blacks. They'd chain people up for days, beat them on the soles of their feet with metal rods. They had an electric chair, and they'd shackle you down, put the clamps on your genitals, and shock you. They'd tie black women to the chair, naked, and hit them with the current and watch them shake and convulse. For fun. Anytime blacks tried to organize or protest, if there was any kind of disturbance in Overtown, a hundred cops and Klansmen would ride in together on horseback with torches and dogs—"nigger hounds," the sheriff called them—to keep everyone in their place.

The only difference between what happened with McDuffie in '79 and what happened back then was that back then they didn't even bother to cover it up. Black bodies could be found out by the train tracks. There'd be no investigation. Cops would just say the man jumped and rule it a suicide. By the time I was growing up, the cops had cleaned up on the surface. They made things look better, had hired a few blacks to work patrol, but day to day it wasn't much different. Cops would stop black men on the sidewalk. "Hey, nigger. Over here." They'd make us show ID and tell them where we were going. If they didn't like the answer, they'd pick us up on a vagrancy charge. Cops would come through Overtown just to harass and intimidate, crack some heads on the pavement.

The civil rights movement woke people up. Black folks started to fight back. We tried sit-ins and nonviolent protests. Later we had Bobby Seale and Huey Newton saddled up with shotguns, defending their homes, standing up to the police. This was followed by the riots: Watts, Detroit, Newark. Cities going up in flames. The first big riot in Miami happened in August of '68, during the Republican National Convention. Blacks were holding a political rally at a community center in Liberty City, hundreds of people standing around in the heat waiting for this thing to start. Some asshole drove by in a car with a "George Wallace for president" bumper sticker on it. People started throwing rocks and bottles at the car. Car stopped, they dragged the driver out, flipped the car over, set it on fire. Pretty soon it was riot cops and tear gas, black kids looting stores, National Guard coming in. Whole thing lasted for days.

In most American cities, once the sixties were over, the riots died out. Thanks to affirmative action, we gave out enough jobs and put enough black kids in college that most folks were willing to settle down, go along, see how this whole integration thing played out. Not in Miami. Down here, the riots never stopped. It wasn't full-out, citywide riots. It was more like at the end of the movie *Do the Right Thing*. There'd be some incident. A white cop would pull some shit, a bunch of blacks on the corner would be watching because they didn't have anything else to do, they'd start throwing rocks and bottles, and the whole block would erupt, windows smashed, a car set on fire. We had shit like that go down at least a couple times a year. Sometimes it would last a few hours, sometimes a few days. It didn't take much to set off a riot in Liberty City.

The year running up to McDuffie, it was even worse than usual with the cops. In January of '79, some white cop picked up an eleven-year-old black girl, molested her in the back of his patrol car. She reported him. He got off with three years' probation. No jail time. Not even a month later, a bunch of cops were making a drug raid in Overtown. They busted down the door of the wrong house. The guy who lived there was a junior high school teacher. He ran, hid in his closet, called 911, and said he was being invaded. Cops busted into his bedroom, pulled him out of his closet, and pistol-whipped him, yelling, "Where's the drugs? Where's the drugs?"

They tore up his house looking for drugs that weren't there. They put that man in the hospital; he was pissing blood from the damage they did to his kidneys. Then they charged *him* with resisting arrest. Later the truth came out. Wrong house. Innocent teacher. But the cops who beat him? No arrests. No indictments. A slap on the wrist, and they were back on the street.

That fall, a few weeks before McDuffie, a black kid was driving through Hialeah with his sister late at night and he pulled over on a deserted street to take a piss. Some white cop rolled up and got out, sighting a "suspicious" black male. This cop had a gun on the back of the kid's head while he was frisking him, and the gun went off: a black kid shot dead in the street for taking a piss. His sister watched the whole thing go down. The city ruled it an accident. The cop wasn't even suspended. He was given paid leave. Two months later, he got a promotion.

You shoot an innocent black man in the back of the head and you get a promotion? And people wonder why McDuffie ran. People say he ran because he was driving on a suspended license.

I never got beat by the cops, just arrested. Everybody got arrested. It was every day. Every fucking day there were little pockets of bullshit going on. There were many stories. "Oh, man, police arrested so-and-so and he ain't even did nothing." It started to build up.

I was arrested at least twelve times. If one guy shot a gun in the air and ten guys were sitting around, the cops would lock us all up to get somebody to tell them who did it. Even if you never did anything it's on your record that you got pinched for gun possession. Sometimes we'd just be sitting there on the corner and the cops would roll up and say, "Y'all get the fuck off the corner or we're gonna lock y'all up." Sometimes they'd throw us in the car without a charge, just to try and intimidate us because they thought we knew something.

Worst I ever really did was sell a little weed, but if you looked at my rap sheet you'd think I was a gangster. Some of it I did. Display of firearms? Yeah, I did that. But the majority of the stuff was just police harassing me, throwing me in jail for no reason. I've always been self-employed, so it never affected my career, but a lot of guys pile up these bullshit rap sheets and they go and apply for jobs and can't get them. It follows them around their whole lives.

Right before I went to stay with my brother in DC, I got busted for marijuana while driving in my van. I was busted by a crooked cop, this white guy named Bachmann. Everybody in Liberty City knew about Bachmann. Cops like him were everywhere. They'd bust you, but they wouldn't take you in. They'd confiscate your weed and take whatever money you had on you. Afterward they'd turn you loose, knowing you couldn't do anything about it. Sometimes Bachmann would stop you, take your weed off you, and smoke your shit right there. Everybody knew he was a dirty cop. He'd come around the corner, and we'd say, "Oh, here comes Bachmann." He'd just go into people's houses like he was a warlord or some shit, like he was the gestapo.

That's the world we were living in when the McDuffie trial started in March of 1980. Everybody followed it on the news. We had to follow it on the news, because they'd moved it to Tampa. The Miami judge said the case was a time bomb, and he didn't want it going off in his courtroom. The judge was wrong: the

McDuffie case wasn't the time bomb. Miami was the time bomb.

The economy was in a terrible recession. No jobs. We had the cops harassing us and killing us on one side, and on the other side—the thing that makes the black situation in Miami unique—on the other side we had the Cubans taking over, pushing us out. At that point, shit between the blacks and the Cubans was bad. It had been getting worse for years. Thousands of wealthy Cuban families flooded in right after Castro took over, and a couple hundred thousand more came in the years after that. Under Jim Crow, Florida was always trying to pass laws to restrict the number of Caribbean blacks who could come over. Jamaicans, Dominicans, Haitians, they had all kids of visa requirements and hoops to jump through. Not the Cubans. Immigration just waved them on in. Political refugees. The government gave them a free pass—but only some of them.

The island of Cuba is predominantly black. You go over there, look around, that shit is *black*. But that's not who came over, not in the first wave. It was just the white Cubans they let in, immigrants who looked like the people in power so they could keep the power. White folks in Miami said, "We've gotta get some people who look like us, who think like us. Conservative-type people. We can sit down with them. We can break bread with them."

That's how black people lost Miami. Malcolm X and Stokely Carmichael and the Black Panthers, their whole message was about economic self-sufficiency, about how blacks needed to own and patronize our own businesses, to lift up and take care of ourselves. And I believe that. The problem was that the government had denied us our property rights for so long that we didn't have much to work with. The small value of what we did own, our business district, they destroyed that when they put the expressway through. Most blacks didn't own any assets or property to borrow against. Banks discriminated, so we didn't have access to business loans or financial capital that you need to run a business.

But the Cubans, a lot of the wealthy Cubans brought money with them. They also had La Lucha, "the struggle," the fight against Castro. They said they were only here in Miami temporarily, that if the US helped them take down Castro they'd be going right back. So all the resources that blacks have been denied the government gave it to the Cubans. Just gave it to them. That shit didn't stop with the Bay of Pigs. If you said you were an anti-Castro group, an anti-communist group, the federal government would pretty much write you a blank check. The CIA had this training center at the University of Miami, hundreds of agents, the largest CIA facility in the world outside of the headquarters at Langley. They were pumping millions of dollars into these anti-Castro programs. They were running a secret airline, buying boats, planes, guns. They financed camps out in the swamps, where all these freedom fighters were training to overthrow Fidel.

All of that money and those resources went into Cuban hands. At the same time Overtown was being destroyed, Little Havana was being built up. It was mostly Cubans, but it wasn't just Cubans. Feds were scared of communism spreading all over Latin America and South America, and there were exiles from all of those countries, Nicaraguans, Panamanians, Argentinians, Bolivians. They all set up shop in Miami to organize and try and take down this dictator or that dictator, and the boys in Washington made sure they were taken care of. That's the mistake that blacks made. We should have been an anti-communist group. Then maybe white folks would've given us some of that covert money. The only oppressive government we wanted to overthrow was our own, so we didn't get shit.

Not only did the Cubans get taken care of by the government, they also got in on the programs that should have been ours. Civil rights marchers fought to get things like affirmative action and access to minority loan programs. That's what we had coming to us as a people who had worked for more than 250 years for free. But anybody who was a minority could qualify, not just blacks. Of all the small-business government loans made in Miami in the 1970s, Hispanics got 47 percent. Blacks got 6 percent. All the new affirmative-action laws about how minority-owned businesses were legally entitled to a share of government and municipal projects, we got shut out of most of that, too. Pretty soon, over 50 percent of the minority contracting in Miami-Dade was going to Hispanic-owned companies. Black-owned companies were barely getting 10 percent—and we're the ones who fought and died in the streets to get those programs put in place.

That's pretty much how it went down, in Miami. The Cubans came in, the blacks got displaced—and there was a lot of anger at the ones who displaced us. A lot of people believe that white folks brought the Cubans in because they *wanted* a power struggle with the blacks. In the beginning, it was the blacks cleaning all the hotel rooms. Now it was the Hispanics. Under Jim Crow, they had us doing all the work. We got domesticated, comfortable, Americanized. We started to say, "We don't need to do this shit." They let in the next group. They're always looking for the new nigger, as we say, to do the work.

But all that blew up in white folks' faces with the Mariel boatlift. First blacks were displaced, now whites started to get displaced, too. The same week the McDuffie trial started, Castro opened the port at Mariel to get rid of all the political protesters giving him headaches. He'd dump them on the US and was done with them. Pretty soon anybody who could get on a boat was on their way here. *Marieletos*, we called them. Only this time it wasn't the wealthy, middle-class Cubans coming over. It was the poorest of the poor, the lowest of the low. Castro said he wanted to flush his toilets, empty his jails. He sent criminals, mental patients, all kinds of people. Over 125,000 showed up in just a few months. We had tent cities going up under the freeways.

Meanwhile, over in Haiti, there were all these poor, exploited people, and they saw the US opening its door to all these Mariel Cubans. So tens of thousands of Haitians, they started piling into ships and coming over, too. Only America didn't let them in. They were "economic" refugees, not "political" refugees, so Washington said they didn't qualify. Of course, the truth of it was that Haitians are black. This is how it went: you've got two boats in the water, both rowing over for freedom. Cubans jump off, they've got one wet foot, one dry foot. They're okay. As long as they're on the beach. Haitians do the same? Nah, you've got to go back. You're going to jail. We'll send you to Krome down the street to get deported.

The Krome Detention Center was this shithole on the edge of the Everglades. You had thousands of Haitians crammed into this prison built for a few hundred people. Like a concentration camp. Cuban criminals got government-funded refugee camps while innocent Haitians went to jail. So with the Haitian thing on top of the Cuban thing on top of the McDuffie thing on top of getting fucked with by the cops for the last hundred years, Miami was a big fucking time bomb. The whole place was ready to explode.

When the McDuffie case went to trial, the facts of the case were plain as day: a defenseless black man in handcuffs with his skull bashed in and a bunch of white cops standing around with bloodstained flashlights in their hands. Unfortunately, the prosecution put all the cops on trial together, rather than as individuals, and every cop who testified covered his own ass by pointing the finger at somebody else. This cop saw that cop deliver the fatal blow. That cop saw a different cop do it. All the cops were guilty, either of making it happen or letting it happen, but the prosecution couldn't give a clear picture of who did what.

The real problem was the jury. Down here in the bullshit Florida judicial system, they have this thing in selecting juries called a "peremptory challenge," which means either the defense or the prosecution can strike a certain number of potential jurors from the jury pool without giving any justification whatsoever. All of these cases of white cops molesting, beating, and killing black folks and getting off had all-white juries. Every. Single. Time. Any black juror who came up? "Your Honor, we'd like to dismiss this juror." Gone. No questions asked. That's how they did it, and it was completely legal. And that's what they did on the McDuffie jury, too. They'd dismissed every black juror who came up until they got a nice, all-white jury, guaranteed to acquit.

It all came down on May 17, 1980. The jury spent less than three hours deliberating, and came back with the verdict: Not guilty on all counts. Not guilty of murder. Not guilty of evidence tampering. Nothing. A black man beaten to death for a traffic violation, and all twelve perpetrators walked free.

I watched them announce the verdict on TV. When we heard "not guilty," that just lit the fuse. It was like all this shit had been building up, all these years of getting fucked with by the cops, having our communities destroyed, being displaced by all these Cubans coming in. We just blew the fuck up. The Liberty City Riot was on.

Folks started to gather in crowds along Sixty-Second Street, near African Square Park. Pretty soon everybody was shooting, throwing rocks, setting fires, looting. People were taking shopping carts and walking them down the street with color TVs and shit in them. They had couches balanced on them, walking that shit home. We had this little shopping mall down the street from my house, man, people just tore that place up. I think it might have been a Sears there. They went through it. Didn't leave nothing. My homeboys mounted up. They were like, "Man, we gotta go and get some of this shit." Me, I wanted no part of it. My old girl, she told me, "Don't bring that shit in my house. Don't bring no groceries, nothing." I mainly walked around, watching.

The whole thing was wild. I mean, people burned the fucking place down. Storefronts smashed in. Buildings on fire. The police shooting tear gas. The people who owned the shops and stores, they were getting thrown out in the street while the stores were looted. It was supposed to be just the white-owned stores that got looted, but they hit everybody. Some of our best black-owned businesses were completely destroyed. It was horrible.

Downtown, outside the metro justice complex, the NAACP tried to hold a peaceful rally. They started out marching and singing "We Shall Overcome," but pretty soon the whole group just turned into a mob. They were smashing down the doors of the city government buildings. They were taking official Dade County vehicles, flipping them over, shoving gas-soaked rags in the tanks and setting them on fire—and this was respectable, middle-class black folks doing this. Imagine what it was like in the ghetto.

In all the riots from the 1960s, young blacks were venting their pent-up anger and frustration, setting fires, smashing windows, looting. The difference in Miami, what had never happened before, was that black anger wasn't just directed at destroying property. It was directed at white people, at individuals. For three days, any white person caught in the wrong place at the wrong time was killed. Some white college kids were driving the wrong way through Liberty City when the riot started. A black mob pulled them from their car and beat them and stabbed them to death with fucking screwdrivers. There was this one white lady, elderly woman, they stopped her car and smashed it with rocks and then set it on fire with her in it. Burned her alive.

Eight white folks were killed that week for no reason other than black people were fed the fuck up. And if blacks were killing whites, for whites it was open season on blacks. These crazy rednecks were driving through Liberty City, picking us off from the back of pickup trucks. The cops and the National Guard, they were coming in like it was a war zone, shooting at anything that moved. By the time it was over, dozens of people were dead, hundreds in the hospital, half the businesses in Liberty City had been burned to the ground, and Miami was never the same.

Our community was destroyed. The riots killed everything. The total damage was something like $200 million. All these plans and programs were set up to help us rebuild, but we even got fucked on that. That's how it always goes. The government sets aside all this money to invest in the ghetto, to create "empowerment zones," but somehow nothing ever gets built but chicken shacks and check-cashing joints. There were millions of dollars set aside for rebuilding the stores and the businesses in Liberty City. Over 90 percent of that money went to whites and Hispanics, because they were the business owners, the property owners. Almost all of them used the money to get out, to relocate. The grocery stores were gone. The tire factory closed. The gas station on the corner never came back. Even some of the black-owned businesses that got some of those funds, they left, too. They moved out to the suburbs, over to Coconut Grove, left the community.

To this day right now, Liberty City is still fucked up behind those riots, because after that nobody would insure new businesses there. For years after, the only businesses were the corner store, the wing joint, the fish joint. And those establishments were barred like a fucking fort. Everything behind plexiglass. No place to sit down. They just wanted you to order your shit and get out.

That was the world I lived in. I was a DJ, with no real thoughts or aspirations of being more than an entertainer in the neighborhood. With the whole neighborhood gutted like that, groups like the Ghetto Style DJs became even more important to people. There were no real restaurants, no good bars. Our dances were the only entertainment lots of people had, the only thing to lift people's spirits. We'd play gigs in the park, and thousands of people would come, dance, let off steam. For some of them, it was the highlight of their week. But even after hassling us for years and nearly destroying the whole neighborhood, the cops still wouldn't leave us alone. They prodded and provoked us until one night I ended up starting a riot of my own.

It was March of '83, a Sunday night. The Ghetto Style DJs were playing a free gig in African Square Park like always. Park was packed. We were jamming with about a thousand people in the pit, everybody dancing, having a good time. It was pretty late at that point, getting dark out, when I saw the red-and-blue lights coming from up on the street. Cops started making their way through the crowd to talk to me at the turntables. One of the cops, a black guy, asked me to turn the music down. He said, "It's late. Some of the older residents are complaining."

I said okay, and I turned the music down. I wasn't stupid. I knew how this went. We were out there late, didn't have a permit or anything like that. I just wanted to play it straight. I'll take the party down a notch, and everything will be cool. But the other cop with this black guy, the white cop, was that asshole Bachmann: the same crooked, gestapo motherfucker who'd been fucking with the neighborhood for years. We were down in the pit of the amphitheater, and Bachmann was up a little hill on the sidewalk with his flashlight shining down on everybody. He didn't even give us a chance to quiet things down. He just yelled, "Y'all can't be out there. Y'all niggers cut that shit off and get the fuck out of the park!" I was like, Hold the fuck on. Who the fuck is he talking to? And he just kept yelling, "C'mon! Y'all niggers out the fucking park."

Back then, my fuse was short. My head was already on a Black Power trip thanks to my uncle Ricky. He'd been training me for something like this, and Bachmann was a guy who'd already pissed off everybody in the community. At that moment, all the tension that had been building up between us and cops like him, it just snapped. He was flashing the light in my eyes and I cut the music off and I yelled out, "You want us out the park, bring your mother-fucking ass down here and do something about it. *Fuck you!*"

The whole crowd chimed in yelling, "Yeah, fuck him! Fuck you! Fuck you!" The rocks and the bottles started flying. Everybody in the pit was hurling shit at this guy. *Bam!* It was a full-blown riot. Sirens went off. Dozens of cops flooded in. People were throwing shit. Cops were beating them down. When the sun came up the next day, the shit was still going. It had spread. By the time the whole situation was defused, nobody had been killed, but a few hundred injured and something like thirty people arrested.

It made the front page of the city section of the *Miami Herald*. Later that week, the city sent in these Community Relations Board representatives. This group the city kept on their payroll. They always got sent in to patch things up whenever there was an incident between the cops and the blacks. Their job, basically, was to get us to shut up, to smooth things over so we wouldn't burn the motherfucker down like we did with McDuffie. This time it was just about a bunch of ghetto kids playing our music too loud, so they probably figured they could quiet us down without too much trouble.

They arranged a meeting with representatives from a lot of the different DJ groups that played in the parks. Me and a couple of the Ghetto Style guys went. The guy they sent to meet with us was this black dude from some kind of community relations board. He sat down and started talking all this shit trying to get on our side. He came in telling us, "Yeah, I'm gonna fight for y'all. We gonna make things right." He put on this big show about how he'd been harassed by the cops before, too, and those white motherfuckers had sent him to jail on some trumped-up bullshit, so he knew what we were going through. But now he was in this position and he would make things better if we just worked with him.

But me, being smart, I was just sitting there, thinking, The fuck you talking bout? You work for the city. How you on our side? I sat there listening, because that's what I'd learned how to do in business negotiations. If you're arguing with someone and talking over them, you think you're making your point, but you aren't learning what the other guy is about, what his agenda is. I like to sit back and just let people run on at the mouth so I can hear what's coming out. You listen to people long enough, eventually they'll reveal what their angle really is. They'll let it slip.

There was this one kid in the meeting, kind of a hanger-on, a wannabe, a guy always trying to get in with us to be a part of our crew. He was a nobody, but the guy from the city was making this big effort to rope him into the discussion. Once I saw that, I knew exactly where all this was heading. Long story short, a couple of days went by and all of a sudden, this guy, this hanger-on, he's riding around in a city car with the community relations dude. The Ghetto Style guys, we were all on the corner, and we saw them roll by. What the fuck is he doing? He's down with them.

White folks been doing that shit for years. They find the strong black guy and they find the weak black guy and they prop the weak black guy up, make him important, put him in their pocket, make him the HNIC, make him a spokesman or some shit so they can keep it looking like the situation is taken care of. That was exactly what happened. They took this weak guy out of the group, gave him a position with this community-outreach thing, and they made him feel like a big shot, like he's gonna be the liaison with the city and get the concerts going again and he'll be a hero.

Over the next couple weeks, the city said they were working on settling the issue. Next thing you know, the city called this big press conference. He got all the local reporters and a bunch of DJ groups and cops and community leaders out in the African Square Park amphitheater. I showed up to see what the fuck that nonsense was going to be. They had this chump up there at the podium, talking like he was a representative of the DJ groups. He was reading off this prepared statement, saying shit like "We, the youth of Liberty City, would like to say that we know what we did was wrong. We disrespected the police. . . ." And blah blah blah, all this shit. He said that the park was going to start doing official daytime concerts. Not with us. Not with Ghetto Style. They're going to bring in these soft soul and R&B groups that the city approved, and they were using this kid to make it look like the DJ groups had agreed to be a part of this settlement.

"Hold on, hold on. What the fuck?" I got up and said it right in front of the whole press conference, right in front of all the news cameras. "Hold the *fuck* up. We ain't had nothing to do with writing this shit. I didn't agree to this shit." I pointed at the community relations guy and then at the chump. "*That* motherfucker wrote this shit for *this* motherfucker. This motherfucker, he ain't even in our group. Y'all done paid this dude off so now he's the spokesman for us? Y'all lost y'all fucking mind. Y'all crazy. Y'all full of shit."

I walked out of the press conference. The *Miami Herald* wrote the whole thing up. "Luther Campbell of the Ghetto Style DeeJays erupted in an angry stream of obscenities before stomping out of African Square Park's outdoor amphitheater. . . ." That was the day Luther Campbell started becoming a name in Miami. That was the day I set off on the road to becoming public enemy number one. You tell me I can't do something I have every right to do? I'm just gonna do it more. I'm gonna do it bigger.

From that point on, my focus became making the group bigger, doing bigger things, branching out, moving up. I wasn't gonna make some deal with the city to use the park on their terms. There was no way I was going to let them tell me where I can go and what I can say and what music I can play. Fuck that. "I'll start my own club where I can do everything on my terms, where I don't have to answer to nobody." I wanted to be big enough, have enough money, and have enough leverage that the cops and the city couldn't mess with me anymore. I'd be in control of my own thing.

I'd tell my guys what I wanted to do, where I wanted to go, and they'd say, "Man, you talking crazy."

I'd say, "Nah, motherfuckers, we gotta think big. It's time to think about starting our own club. It's time to think about promoting our own concerts. It's time to think about blowing this shit up."

LUKE RECORDS

When I started up with the Ghetto Style DJs, my goal was to be the best DJ in Miami. At the time I thought that was just spinning records and having the gift of gab and throwing the best party. As I got older, I would go to this club, Big Daddy's, on Seventy-Ninth and Biscayne Boulevard. This guy DJ Frankie Hollywood used to be in there and he would spin, talk over records, rap all the good shit women wanted to hear. He would also talk up the best records: who was the hottest group, the new sound. At his club it wasn't about speakers or having the biggest bass cabinets, it was about the music that was playing. It was about breaking songs, making hits, telling people, "*This* is the shit that you should buy and you should listen to."

Not everybody can break a song. You have to be able to get control of the crowd. People have to believe in you and respect you so when you stand behind a song they'll go with you and embrace it, buy the single, and make it a hit. The crowd respected this DJ at Big Daddy's. If he stood behind a song, pretty soon you'd hear it blowing up on local radio, people calling in and requesting it. I realized that's what I needed to learn to do. You ain't a DJ unless you're breaking songs. Most guys just spin. Wedding DJs spin. Real DJs break shit.

Up to that point we'd been doing most of our shows either out in the park or at the Sunshine Roller Rink, renting it out on slow nights and calling it the Pac Jam Teen Disco. I figured we were leaving a lot of money on the table paying the owners of the roller rink to be there, and I was tired of being hassled by the cops on other people's turf. We started looking at opening our own club. There was this empty one-story cinder-block building at the corner of Fifty-Fourth Street and Twelfth Avenue in the heart of Liberty City. We saved up some of the money we'd made and rented it out. We decided to make it a teen disco—a teen club, not an adult one. The riots had destroyed everything. There was literally nowhere for kids in the ghetto to find entertainment or to spend the quarters and dollars they got working their little jobs. That meant there was a lot of money on the street nobody was claiming.

I was all about creating a safe environment for the kids to have a good time so they wouldn't have to hang out on the corners, getting in trouble. We called it the Pac Jam II. We didn't serve anything harder than Coca-Colas and 7-Up. We did our own security to keep it safe. I paid off-duty cops to work the parking lot to make sure the kids were safe and there was no dope or alcohol on the premises. The kids knew it was a safe space, as safe as we could make it in a place like Liberty City. Parents knew that, too. We had a lot of support from the community. Weekends, that place was *packed*. It was a place for all the Liberty City groups to play their music, and the little jitterbugs were a great audience to try out new stuff. It was the perfect place for me to break records. Everything was in place for me to take off.

By the time we opened the Pac Jam II, around early '84, hip-hop was blowing up out of New York. Kool Herc and Grandmaster Flash and Afrika Bambaataa, those guys had started laying the groundwork in the 1970s, turning rap into a cultural movement, the voice of the ghetto. Then in '79, the Sugarhill Gang came out with "Rapper's Delight" and it was a huge hit all over the world. I still remember the first time I heard it. I sat there listening to it and I thought, This shit is *hot*. This is for the young people. We already had DJs rapping over songs, closing out their shows on the radio by doing little raps and shit. So it wasn't entirely new. But it was just that moment where you could feel something was coming together. I knew it was going to take off.

After "Rapper's Delight" came out of nowhere and made all that money, lots of people were out there looking for the next hit. Afrika Bambaataa got a deal, put out a few singles. Kurtis Blow signed with Mercury, had the next big mainstream hits with "The Breaks" and "Christmas Rappin'." Grandmaster Flash and the Furious Five signed with Enjoy, a small black-owned label out of Harlem, and put out "Superappin'." Kool Moe Dee and the Treacherous Three signed with Enjoy, too.

Then you had Fab Five Freddy. He came along and he started taking hip-hop downtown and introducing it to the white artists in SoHo and the punk-rock scene in the East Village. All these white folks downtown were just loving it. New York was still a very segregated place, and hip-hop started smashing through that. Everybody was embracing this music. Afrika Bambaataa's "Planet Rock" came out in '82. It cost $800 to make, and it sold 650,000 copies. Run-D.M.C.'s "It's Like That"/"Sucker M.C.s" single came right after. That sold 250,000 copies. At the Pac Jam, we played those records right when they started coming out. People loved it.

Everybody played the big hits, but I was always looking for the newer shit, the more obscure shit. Part of being a DJ is you join a record pool. I was in the Jerry Jarvis record pool. I would pay a monthly fee, go to the record pool meetings every Saturday, and in my mailbox I'd have some thirty, fifty records. It was mostly dance albums, R&B, but every week I was seeing more and more rap singles when I made my pickup. They were mostly out of New York, but every now and then I had a couple from the West Coast. I would take all these songs and go home and listen to them. I didn't pay much attention to the major labels, the shit from RCA, Atlantic, or Warner Bros. I'd play that stuff because it was popular, but I also knew the radio stations were already all over that. Everybody was playing "Rapper's Delight." Everybody was playing the Furious Five and the Treacherous Three. I was looking for records I could break. I would pay more attention to the singles from the independent labels. I'd sit there and listen to every one. I always found the different stuff. I was always looking for the next guy. If I heard something and thought it was hot, I would stand behind it and break it.

I remember one of the first records I picked out was Divine Sounds' "What People Do for Money." They were this obscure group out of Bed-Stuy. Nobody in Miami had ever heard of them. I took their album and I started playing it and I really hyped it. I was up there yelling, "This is the shit, people!" Friday nights I'd be DJing a dance at Allapattah Middle School, in the gymnasium or cafeteria, playing for about a thousand people. Saturdays I'd be at the high school doing it for two thousand people. Sundays I'd be at the Pac Jam II with another two thousand people. Collectively, I was DJing for five thousand people the whole weekend in different pockets all over the city. They were all going out, calling up the radio station to make requests, going into record stores asking for the single.

All of a sudden you had this indie label putting out this no-name group that nobody's heard of, and the guys at the label were looking at their orders and scratching their heads because they were selling thousands of singles way the fuck down in Miami. They'd call up their local contacts, the music directors at the local radio stations, the regional distributors, and ask how this was happening. The word they got back was, "That's Luther Campbell and the Ghetto Style DJs. They're making your shit hot all over town."

That's how I became a real DJ. That's how I separated myself from everybody else. People who came to my shows, they knew they were gonna hear new music. I became respected as the guy who's gonna break the hot shit. Word started to get out: if you want to break a record in Miami, get it to Luther Campbell. Pretty soon I had record reps standing outside the fucking door of the Pac Jam before I even got there. They'd be hanging around outside with copies of their singles, like, "Yo, you need my song. Break my song, man. Break my song."

I was breaking this shit and the club was doing great, but I was already thinking, How do I take this to the next level? Let me be smarter than this. I started calling these artists up, these guys in New York. I'd call them up and I'd say: "I like your shit. Your stuff is hot in Miami. Let me make you a deal. I'll bring you down here, cover your expenses, but you're going to do a free show for me, a promotional gig. You'll do your thing in front of the people and then I'll keep pushing your record and later on, four or five months down the line, I'll bring you back and I'll give you a paid gig. Or I'll bring you down and you can book some other gigs in Florida while you're here." I started cutting deals like that. I'd get these guys just before they were about to blow up.

The first act I brought down was this duo, Dr. Jeckyll & Mr. Hyde, Andre Harrell and Alonzo Brown. Harrell would go on to found Uptown Records and take over as CEO of Motown, but back then he and Alonzo were just a couple of kids from Harlem who'd won a few rapping contests around the city. I called up their managers, brought them down. They had a great time, sold a lot of records.

Pretty soon I was getting everybody. Mantronix, T La Rock and Jazzy Jay, Divine Sounds, Schoolly D, Run-D.M.C., EPMD, Jazzy Jeff and the Fresh Prince, Biz Markie. They all came down. MC Hammer slept on my couch.

Back then, nobody was booking hip-hop acts outside of New York. I know I was one of the first because a lot of those guys, before they got down here, they'd never left the city before. Shit, some of these guys had never been outside Harlem or the South Bronx before. When I flew them down here, they'd all tell me the exact same story: One, they'd never been on a plane in their life. Two, their record company was fucking them. "All these records I'm selling, and I ain't seen no money from my deal." That was the same for every single one. And three—and this happened all the fucking time—they knew nothing about cars. Cars were completely foreign to them. One day I was out with Jazzy Jay and somebody needed a jump. I said, "Jazzy Jay, we gotta fucking jump this car. You put the cables on and I'm gonna get in the car and jump it."

He was like, "Huh? Cables? Batteries? I don't know what the fuck you're talking about. We don't drive cars in New York. We ride the train."

I said, "Oh my God, y'all fucked up in New York."

Just getting those guys down here was a crazy story sometimes. There was this one group, Ultimate 3 MC's. They had one song, "What Are We Gonna Do," and never really did anything else. I brought them down on People Express Airlines. The thing with that airline back then was there were no tickets. You'd get on the plane and you'd pay on the plane. You'd take your seat, and the lady would come down the aisle with the cart and you'd pay her cash money on the spot. It was like the Greyhound of the skies. I didn't want to Western Union them the money because I was afraid they would end up spending it on something else and not get on the plane, that those motherfuckers would just take the money.

They got on the plane and the stewardess came down the aisle with her little cart and she said, "Where's your money?"

"Oh, we don't have no money," they said. "Our man Luke's gonna pay you when we land."

Back when you could just walk up to the gate, I was at the airport waiting. Of course there was a swarm of cops there. The pilot had radioed ahead to say there's these fucking black guys on the plane who ain't got no money to pay for their ticket, and somebody was going to jail. Those guys walked off the plane and the cops were going to arrest them and I had to go running over yelling, "Hey! No, no, no! I got the money! They're all right! Here's the money! They good!"

That ended up working out. But it was a crazy time. Hip-hop was just taking off. There were no tours, no regular venues that booked these guys. We were just making the shit up as we went along. For these rappers, coming down to Miami was a big chance to party. I'd put them in a hotel by the beach or some shit and they loved it because they'd never been to the beach before. But I wasn't partying. I was working. My days were busy, busy, busy. I'd have one group down and I'd be on the phone to New York working on the next group. I'd be out promoting the gig, putting out fliers, booking radio promotions. When Run-D.M.C. or whoever it was came in, they'd do the party that night and leave the next morning. I'd pick them up from the airport, bring them into the hotel, get them situated, get somebody to get them some food and all that. Then I'd be back to the venue making sure everything was in place there, doing sound checks and all that. Then right before the show I would give them their money, get their ass onstage, come backstage after the show, make sure they get back to the hotel, and then get them back to the airport the next day. Next week, different group, same thing.

The shows were great, but the crowds were tough. Crowds in Miami are like the legendary Apollo Theater crowds. These guys would come down and go back to New York with horror stories about it. It was funny, because in New York, fans might know their whole album, but down here we only promoted the single. Back then it was the single days anyway. Guys would come to the Pac Jam and get up there and start singing all this other shit nobody'd heard of. Those motherfuckers in the club would be sitting up there looking at the acts like, "Can you hurry the fuck up? Get to the shit we want to hear." If you didn't fucking perform, the people in the Pac Jam would look at you like you were fucking stupid. These guys would get off the stage, saying, "Man, that was the fucking toughest crowd I ever played. That bitch is hard. Them mother-fuckers are crazy."

These acts were selling gold and platinum singles, but almost all of those sales were made in the New York City area. Hip-hop hadn't broken out nationwide yet. It was mostly still a local phenomenon in New York and a tiny scene in LA. I was really one of the first promoters calling and offering these guys gigs outside of New York. Even though it was a tough crowd, they kept coming because I treated them well. They were all used to getting ripped off; promoters would book them with some big promise and then not pay. I couldn't pay much, but I always paid what I said I would. Wherever these guys got together back in New York, they'd tell the other groups, "Luke's down, man. Go to Miami. He'll take care of you." That's how I was able to get all these guys down in Miami practically for nothing.

I realized all that was about to change with Run-D.M.C. I booked them maybe three times. This was before they were on MTV with Aerosmith or any of that. The first time I paid them

$700. The second time I paid them $1,500. The third time I paid them about $2,000. I remember very clearly one night we were sitting at the Howard Johnson hotel and they said to me, "Luke, you ain't gonna be able to book us no more, man. We gonna be big-time."

"The fuck you mean, 'big-time'?"

"You gonna have to pay us a lot of money. We gonna be doing major concerts and all that. We gonna go out on big tours around the country. We gonna be blowed up."

And they were right. After that night I never booked them again.

The East Coast hip-hop scene was on its way. Run-D.M.C., LL Cool J, the Beastie Boys, all those guys. Everybody was signing deals with these start-up labels like Def Jam and Profile Records. Meanwhile, the West Coast scene was just getting started. The groups out there weren't coming out on a real label at all. There was this vinyl pressing plant out there called Macola, run by this Canadian guy Don MacMillan. Most pressing plants produced in bulk for the major labels. Macola was a small vanity-press type deal. You'd go to Macola, pay this guy a few hundred dollars, and he'd press you however many albums you paid for and then you could go and hustle your records on your own, at the clubs, flea markets, swap meets, wherever.

Macola had opened its doors just as hip-hop was coming up, and a lot of these aspiring rappers were going to him because the major labels in LA hadn't taken any interest in hip-hop at all. Pretty soon this MacMillan guy, he was seeing the numbers that these rappers were selling, thousands of records, just out there hustling on their own. He saw the angle. He saw that he could make a lot more than just this little pressing fee he was charging, and he started acting more like a label. He was offering to print up extra inventory for free. He was offering to help with distribution. Of course, once he started doing this, he started taking a cut. The whole thing seemed a little shady, but this MacMillan guy was literally the only game in town. Ice-T, N.W.A, all those West Coast guys got their start through this one place.

The second act Macola ever signed was this group called 2 Live Crew. The thing about 2 Live Crew is that they weren't really a part of the whole West Coast thing. They weren't wannabe gangsters coming up on the streets of South Central. They were all in the air force. They were three guys stationed at the March air base in Riverside, California: David Hobbs, Chris Wong Won, and Yuri Vielot. Back in 1982, after "Planet Rock" was this big success, some promoter put together a deal for Afrika Bambaataa and a few of the other New York guys to go over and tour in Europe. Hobbs was stationed in England at that time and he was into music in a big way. "Planet Rock" blew his mind with the possibilities of where hip-hop could go. He got a chance to see and talk to Bambaataa on this European tour and he asked him what kind of equipment he used to make those kinds of sounds. Bambaataa told him about the TR-808 drum machine. Cut to a year later and Hobbs was stationed back in Riverside, DJing parties in the barracks at the air base with some turntables and this brand-new 808 drum machine he's picked up for himself.

Hobbs started calling himself Mr. Mixx onstage, and some of the other soldiers started getting up and rapping and MCing at these parties. Yuri, who named himself the Amazing V, and Chris, who named himself Fresh Kid Ice, they got with Hobbs and started performing together as a group on the base. Mixx reached out to Macola, and they agreed to produce the group's first single, "The Revelation."

A lot of people don't know this, but 2 Live Crew started out as conscious music. They were one of the first socially conscious groups. That was the direction Yuri Vielot wanted to take it. The lyrics to "The Revelation" were trying to be like "The Message" by Grandmaster Flash, rapping about life in the hood and brothers struggling against oppression: "You go down to the unemployment line, but the man throws you out on your behind." Shit like that.

It didn't work. It was flat. But the B-side to that single was this joint called "2 Live (Beat Box)." You could tell from that record that Mr. Mixx knew how to lay down a fucking track. I listened to it, and I was like, "Oh, *shit*. This is it right here." "Beat Box" was a dance song. It was party music. You could speed it up and it would still hold its own. To hear the bass on this song, the way Mixx used the 808, you'd have thought that shit came out of Miami. It really fit the kind of music people were doing around here. It also had one line I really liked: "Like Luke Skywalker, I got the Force. Wherever I rhyme, I am the boss." Since Luke Skyywalker was the name I'd started using as a DJ, that single was great for me to play at shows. I started spinning "Beat Box" at the Pac Jam, and people loved it. I decided to reach out and bring those guys down to do a gig. Same as everybody else, every time those guys came down, damn near the first thing out of their mouths was, "Our label is fucking us."

In the recording industry, a deal with a major label is the closest thing to modern slavery there is. You sign on the line and they own your ass. But at least with a standard recording contract they spell out in black and white how they're going to fuck you. The label owns all the masters and they're going to hold all these marketing and promotion costs against your advance and you're never going to see a dime on the back end. And you sign it anyway, knowing that they're going to fuck you, because you want to make a record and be a big star.

This MacMillan guy out in California, he wasn't running a real label, so these guys didn't even know where their money was going.

Since Macola ran its own production plant, they could be pressing extra inventory and selling it out the back and you'd never even know. It was small-time, off-the-books kind of shit. These guys in 2 Live Crew, if it's true they were getting fucked, they didn't even know *how* they were getting fucked. All they knew was they were selling records but they weren't seeing any money. Since I'd been bringing all these acts through Miami, listening to all their problems with the business side of things, I'd learned more about the industry than these guys had. So they came to me and said, "Hey, look, can you find us a record label?"

The music industry has always had a strong presence in Miami. It's a regional hub. All the music of the Caribbean gets produced and distributed here. A lot of the reggae and calypso labels from the islands, they produce their records in Miami because there's better infrastructure here. All the major American labels that want to sell their music in the Caribbean and in South and Central America—since records retail for less in those countries, those records have to be pressed at a lower cost per unit. There are so many pressing and distribution companies here that produce records more cheaply than they do it in other regional hubs, like Philadelphia or Chicago.

I was confident I could get the 2 Live Crew guys a deal. I really liked them, especially Mr. Mixx. The two MCs, Fresh Kid Ice and the Amazing V, they were just okay, in my opinion. But Mixx, I knew he could crank out singles like "Beat Box" that would get people out on the dance floor. I told the guys straight up: I'll help you get a record deal, but first thing you do, you've got to ditch this conscious stuff and focus on the dance music. I'm all about Black Power and building up the community and fighting the Man, but I just didn't think the conscious thing would sell. Folks in the ghetto live that struggle every day. They come to the club to forget about that shit.

Bringing all these acts through Miami had educated me on what the people liked about the music. I learned how to spot a hit. I was a DJ, but I was also breaking records, so I was really working more like an A&R guy, a music director. These A&R guys from the major labels, when they're picking songs, they'll go through a thousand demos and find one and say, "This is the next guy. He's hot." I was always working with that mentality. I learned that the groups that took off in the South had a lot of bass and were real up-tempo. That's what worked down here. Most of the New York stuff was about sixty beats per minute. A lot of the LA records were slow records: "Boyz-n-the-Hood" and all that. It's a car culture out there, and that music was cruising-around-in-your car kind of music. We'd speed all that up down in Miami. We'd crank songs up to 120 beats per minute and the crowds would dance to it all night. Schoolly D, he was the first guy I knew who cussed on a record. I saw that the crowds loved that, too.

I recognized that performance was the key. Putting on a show, giving people a spectacle. That was a big deal. You had to have great music, but most importantly your shows needed to pop. You had to get the crowd going. Every group I brought through had a different style, but the good ones were the ones who were really competitive about putting on the best performance. It's part of the reason I didn't think the conscious music was the way to go. We needed to make party music, music to give people a good time. Mixx and Fresh Kid Ice, they liked the idea. Yuri Vielot didn't want to go in that direction, so he left the group. Mixx reached out to a friend of his from Riverside, another MC named Mark Ross, Brother Marquis. Marquis was down for it. Those guys did one more single for Macola, this song called "What I Like," and then they were done with that mess.

Around this same time, Mixx and Ice were getting out of the service. They'd been coming down to Miami on their weekend leave, doing gigs, and going right back. When you get out of the service it's like getting out of college, not knowing what direction to take. But I was there making them this offer and they figured, Okay, let's move down to Miami and put this record out and see what happens. I got them an apartment and we started looking to make something happen. Without any planning on my part, my career as a music entrepreneur was about to take off.

There was no rap in Miami when I set out to do this. There was no rap group in the South before 2 Live Crew, period. We were the first. I was trying to do something that had never been done. I first took 2 Live Crew to this company called Music Specialist, run by a guy from the Party Down DJs. I thought we could do a deal with him, but he wasn't interested. He didn't want to do rap, just dance music. I went to some other people at the radio station; they weren't interested, either. People weren't interested in rap. People kept telling me the music sucked. I kept saying, "No, this music is hot!" Everywhere I went with these guys, doors kept closing.

At that time I wasn't in the group, and I wasn't even considering being a part of it. I didn't want to be a rapper. I didn't want to be in a rap group. After starting off being a DJ, I'd realized that my real talent was not just spinning records but in putting these shows together. What I wanted was to be a concert promoter. I wanted to be like Bill Graham. I wanted to be the greatest concert promoter in the world. That's what I was grooming myself to be. I didn't want to get into the music business as far as owning a record company, either. But I did it anyway because I was really upset that nobody would give these guys a shot. That was just my stubborn, bullheaded personality, the same part of me that started a riot by telling the cops in the park to go fuck themselves. I said, "Okay, fuck all these small-time labels. I'll put the record out and do it myself." I told the guys, "Look, I don't know nothing about the record business, but I believe in this, so let's go make some music."

I started my own label: Luke Records. Suddenly, I really was an A&R guy. Now I just had to find the right single for these guys. One of the things I did with the Ghetto Style DJs was make up dances, really get the crowd whipped up. I'd mess with the tempo of the record, speed it up or slow it down and get everybody on the dance floor moving together, doing the same call-and-response. It was always a lot of fun and everybody knew it as one of my signature moves. We had one dance called Ghetto Jump. I'd play the opening to the theme from the TV show *The Wild Wild West* and then say, "Jump! Jump! Everybody Ghetto Jump!" The whole place would jump, just like that, everybody jumping up in the air.

I figured since these dances were popular, I could make some extra money selling singles to feed local dance crazes. This was right before I met the guys from 2 Live Crew. I went to this local group, these two guys, and said, "Hey, I wanna make a song called 'Ghetto Jump.' I'll give you the idea. You write it, you record it, we'll break it, the song will get hot, and you can give me a free show to promote and we'll sell the fuck out of some records."

They did the song and brought it to me. At the time, I didn't know nothing about being a producer, publishing rights, credits, none of that. I just put it out there. The shit got hot and I went to those guys and said, "Okay, let's do this free show." The guys did not want to do a show. They didn't hold up their end.

I was pissed off. By that time I was talking to the guys from 2 Live Crew and they were coming down here and they were getting screwed by their label and so I was like, fuck these other dudes. The Ghetto Style DJs, we had lots of dances. Me, I was making that shit up every day. I created that one, I'll create another one. One of the other popular dances we did was called Throw the D. It was a funny dance that all the kids would do. So I said, "I'll just do that with these California guys and that'll be their next single. I'll use that to start Luke Records and I'll make a hit out of that."

So I went to Mixx and the other guys and I said, "I'm gonna lay this shit out for you. I want y'all to do a song. We do this dance down here called Throw the D. That's gonna be your next single."

They said, "How's the dance go?"

I said, "Just come to the club and check it out."

So Fresh Kid Ice, he came in and checked it out and went home and wrote it up and we laid it down in the studio: *There's a brand-new dance and it's coming your way, it was started in Miami by the Ghetto Style DJs!*

I was like, "Okay, shit's hot. We got us a damn song. Let's break this motherfucker."

I went to those guys who did "Ghetto Jump" for me and I told them to go fuck themselves. Then I took "Throw the D" and I blew it out all over Miami. And that's when the shit just took off.

2 LIVE

When I signed 2 Live Crew and started Luke Records and put out "Throw the D," I had no idea how the record industry worked. None. It was all on-the-job learning. I jumped in with both feet and told myself I was smart enough to figure it out as I went along.

When I started, I was literally putting copies of "Throw the D" in the trunk of my old Honda and driving them to the local record stores and flea markets. I did that for months. After a while, I realized it was too slow. I was not working smart. I had to learn how the professionals did it. I talked to record-store owners and asked how they got their records.

"I get them from a distributor."

"What's a distributor?" I asked.

He said, "Talk to Fred Hill. He can help you."

I called up Fred, a local distributor. I went to meet him in person. He explained it to me. "You sell your record to a distributor in bulk at wholesale, and then we turn around and sell it directly to the store. We take our cut and pay the rest back to you."

That made sense. Immediately I started selling to Fred. Quickly I noticed that I was only in certain stores in certain regions. I discovered that different distributors had different accounts and worked in different regions. I wanted to be in the big chain stores, so I went and made another deal with the guy who had those accounts.

"Are there other people like you around the country?" I asked Fred.

He introduced me to the distributors who handled the Southeast and California and New York. I started making deals with them.

That's how it went the whole time, me asking questions, learning on the fly. I had to learn fast because "Throw the D" was blowing up. It was all word of mouth. No advertising, no radio play. The shit just started spreading. For six months after that song came out, in south Florida you couldn't walk into a club or a house party or a college dorm without hearing it. The word kept going north, into Georgia and Alabama. We sold a *lot* of records.

Since I was moving all this product, I went in to my distributors and asked for my money.

They told me I couldn't have my money. They said, "Oh! You don't know? You don't get paid for that record until you do another record. You gotta make another record."

That's the industry. In order to get paid for the last record, artists had to give them another one. Distributors held back earnings until they received more product to sell. All the distributors operate this way. What the fuck? I have to make another record?

Back then, rappers always did response records. One of the biggest came after UTFO released "Roxanne, Roxanne." There were something like two dozen response records: "The Real Roxanne," "Roxanne's Mother," "Roxanne's Revenge," which was done by this thirteen-year-old girl Roxanne Shanté. It gave me the idea for the next album. For the response record to "Throw the D" we'd do "Throw the P." I went to my cousin who'd just finished high school and some of her girlfriends and asked them to do "Throw the P."

We wrote it up, laid out the music, and took them to the studio. They had no idea what the hell they were doing, had never rapped before. We made them into a female rap group called Anquette, put out the song, and it was another hit.

At that point I started getting my money out of the distributors. I think the first check I got was for something like $20,000. After that, more checks kept coming. A lot of these distributors were pretty creative with their accounting. They'd take inventory off the books and pay in cash. I'd go into places with some boxes of records and come out with five, ten thousand dollars in cash on me. Fuck, it's Christmas! I liked it. It beat the hell out of taking five dollars at the door to put on a dance. I realized I could keep doing dances to break records, but I could also put records out and make the real money there. That's when I decided to build Luke Records into a real company.

Those early years were crazy. Everything was moving all at once. "Throw the D" came out of nowhere and became a hit so fast that I was just working to keep up, driving my little Honda all over south Florida, hitting up record stores and radio stations, going from the pressing plant to the distributor and back again the next day. Plus I was still DJing and bringing down these New York guys on the weekends. It was nonstop.

I don't know exactly how many copies "Throw the D" sold. I was doing these cash deals with distributors on the side, hustling it myself at gigs and flea markets. I know it sold enough to be certified a gold record. I didn't even know what a gold record *was* at that time.

I didn't know the industry very well when I started, but the one thing I did have was common sense. Everything I did was about what made sense. If it don't make sense, it don't make dollars.

I decided that 2 Live Crew needed to do an album. That may seem obvious now, but back then it wasn't. At first hip-hop was about selling singles. "Rapper's Delight," "The Breaks," "The Message," those were all singles. By the end of '85, Run-D.M.C. and Whodini had put out their debut albums, and LL Cool J had just dropped *Radio*, but there weren't many. A lot of people in the industry didn't think interest in hip-hop was big enough to carry a whole album and get people in stores to buy them.

Fuck that. I planned to do an album and then cut the singles off. My thinking was if the song was hot enough, people would buy the album when they couldn't get the single anymore. I could do the math. I may have struggled in school, but I'd been a business-man since I was ten years old. I could do money and numbers in my head on the fly. I could look at anything and see it on a balance sheet: the cost per unit, the up-front capital I'd need, projected revenues and expenses. It came natural. It was instinctual. I started out doing it with mowing lawns and selling weed and putting a Pac-Man machine in my mamma's wash house to get kids to come over and buy lemonade at an 80 percent markup. Selling records was no different.

As soon as I started moving product, I could see that the cost of pressing and shipping an album versus the cost of pressing and shipping a single is marginal, but I could charge four times as much for the album as a single. You can make more money selling a hundred thousand albums than you can selling a quarter million singles. If the album really took off, you could quadruple your money.

My industry contacts all said, "Don't do it. You're never going to be able to make it work." We put out our first album in July of 1986, *The 2 Live Crew Is What We Are*. I pulled the single of "Throw the D" out of stores. I was selling a shitload of singles, and I just cut it off. It was no longer available for purchase. It forced people to buy the album, and we made more money.

I decided to get serious and educate myself about how the business worked from top to bottom. I researched manufacturers and learned about manufacturing hubs around the country: in New York and Philadelphia, who made product for the Northeast; others in California for the West Coast; a few in the Midwest. I learned how manufacturers in Miami pressed for lower fees because they had to sell records for cheaper in the Bahamas and Jamaica and the Dominican Republic. I located these guys and made some deals. Since they were already making their money on their Caribbean accounts, the work I brought in was gravy, so they sold their services to me dirt cheap. I was getting my records manufactured for less than any of the New York or LA guys. Out the gate I was making more per album.

There was one manufacturer down here who was so small that I basically took over his whole operation. I became his only client, but he still couldn't keep up as I got bigger. He couldn't handle the fulfillment. That's when I learned about shipping. You can make a record for seventy cents, but then you have to ship the thing, and the shipping ends up costing you three times manufacturing costs. Shipping is always what kills you. So again, I was looking at the math and using common sense. Word of mouth was spreading and we were selling records everywhere, so it started making sense for me to use a pressing plant in California to service the West Coast, one in New Jersey for the Northeast, and one in Detroit for the Midwest. I paid more for pressing the albums, but my cost per unit went down on the shipping.

My focus completely shifted away from wanting to be a DJ or a concert promoter. Now it was more about being a great record guy. After putting the album out, I was thinking, I *like* this shit. I'm making money. I began going to all the industry conventions. I went to the New Music Seminar in New York. I went to Jack the Rapper in Atlanta. I went to these things and sat in on any kind of panel I could learn something from. I listened to all these people talk about the business: radio DJs, program directors, industry execs. I would go to these different panels and listen to people talk about how records are sold, how to promote a record, what you were expected to do in the industry.

I'd grab some of the older guys outside these panels and ask them a million questions, getting their advice, especially at Jack the Rapper. It's the black music convention started by Jack Gibson, who'd been an early DJ at the first-ever black-owned radio station in Atlanta, WERD, back when it opened in 1949. The old-school DJs and program directors at Jack the Rapper, the black guys who'd spent the last thirty years in the business shut out of the mainstream, fighting to establish themselves, getting paid half what guys at white radio stations were making, watching Elvis Presley and the Beatles come along and steal their shit right out from under them—I'd sit and listen to those guys talk for hours, the way I used to sit and listen to my uncle Ricky, learning everything I could about the history of black folks getting fucked and how we fought back.

This one old guy at Jack the Rapper, he was one of the first black music promoters in the business, and he taught me the importance of marketing and promotion. You can have the best record in the world, but you got nothing if you can't promote it. He told me, "All these people running around this convention, they couldn't sell a fucking dog. Most of em, ninety percent of em, they got records but they can't sell shit. And you ain't in this business unless you're *selling* records. When a window of opportunity opens up, you better go and take advantage of it."

Talking with guys like him, I realized that marketing and promotion was where I really needed to concentrate my efforts. I became all about marketing. Common sense was: okay, what makes a hit in Miami? I had to get to the mobile DJs on the street, the DJs breaking records in the clubs. Where do guys like me find new records? In the record pools. I reached out to find all the guys like me around the country. I was in the Jerry Jarvis record pool. I asked him, "What are the other record pools around the country?" He broke it down for me: there's always a pool director in every city. I'd call that guy up and say, "Hey, man, what's up? This is Luke. I got this record that's hot down here in Miami. Check it out for me." I printed up extra promotional copies and sent them to record pools.

Marketing was a real challenge. All that promotional space you used to see in the front of record stores, the racks by the registers and the tables by the window? All that space is bought up by the major labels. They pay to get their albums up there. I didn't have that kind of money. I didn't have $60,000 to work a region. I had to find new ways of doing things. I noticed how political figures ran their campaigns with the fliers and the yard signs and all that. It would be an inexpensive way for me to promote a song. I made fliers and yard signs. It was cheap advertising.

One of the other things I did was I still had my old van, the van we used to haul our DJ equipment. I took the van, put a sound system in it, painted it with our logos and girls and shit, and we traveled around the state. We would go to record stores in Jacksonville and Gainesville, all the way up to Georgia. We'd park the van out front, fire up, and play the music. It was our real live in-store promotion. We created this whole club atmosphere outside of a record store. People heard us and went into the store to check out our album. We generated sales that way. Back then, people didn't have these massive, state-of-the-art sound systems in cars. So anytime we would leave south Florida, people thought our van was fascinating. I was one of the first rappers to do that kind of guerrilla street marketing to promote a record.

I created my own rulebook, just working on a shoestring budget and using my community. We created a street-team mentality, what they call guerrilla or viral marketing today.

The record pools were a great way to spread word of mouth. The promotional guys have the local relationships and physically take the record to radio stations and clubs to get them in the rotation. I did that for myself in Miami, but I couldn't do it in Atlanta, in Charlotte, in Houston. You could hire an independent promoter, but back then independent promoters got paid something like sixty to a hundred thousand dollars a year. I couldn't afford that, didn't have a budget for that. I decided to use colleges.

One of the things that made "Throw the D" such a hit was spring break in Fort Lauderdale and Daytona and Miami. There are ten cities in the country that are considered breakout markets. Miami has always been considered one of them. Any kind of tourist destination is a breakout market. People go there, party, and then go back home and say, "Man, I heard this shit in Miami. Shit is dope." College kids from all over the country came for spring break, heard the new single, and took it home with them.

Young people were getting turned on to rap quicker than the established radio stations and clubs anyway. I called up the DJs at the college radio stations. I sent them promotional records, and they played them. Next thing I'd do is say, "Hey, college DJ. You got somebody there wants a job? I need a promotion guy to take my record to the club. I'll send him a couple of dollars and some free albums to keep and give away."

As an extra incentive, I came up with the idea for Luke Gear:

T-shirts, jackets, bandannas, all branded with my logo. I got all these college kids working for me, and I'd send them a Luke Records jacket to make them look official. I'd tell them that with this jacket they could go around getting in the clubs for free as a representative of the label. They thought that was pretty cool. So I would send two jackets to every college radio station in every college town in the Southeast, and those would be my independent promoters. They would take the albums and bring them into the dorms, the frat parties, and the clubs where all the college students hang.

We were growing so fast and getting so many orders that I could barely keep up. For the first year or two, I had no corporation or anything, didn't know what a corporation was or how to form one. I just had cash coming in, checks being written to me personally. Suddenly I was bringing in tens of thousands of dollars a month and had to learn how to manage it. I got myself incorporated. I started adding all of these people to my business. I had some real smart, brilliant brothers working for me. I knew people could lose money through tax evasion, and I didn't want to get caught up like that. I found an accountant.

For a long time I was picking the inventory up from the pressing plant in my old Honda. Now I couldn't even fit all the records in my car. I had to start using a truck to deliver to the distributors. We started out storing the excess inventory in the apartments I'd rented for the other guys in the group. Then we were pressing so many records that the boxes took over the damn apartments. There were walls of boxes about to fall over. Dudes were sitting on boxes in the living room like it was fucking furniture. They were like, "Man, you got to get these records out our apartments. We got our girlfriends over."

The thing about 2 Live Crew was we weren't like a lot of these other groups, like Run-D.M.C. We weren't a couple of kids from the neighborhood who came up together and started a rap group because we were pals. I joined the group because they needed me to get them a deal. Marquis came on to replace this Yuri Vielot guy who'd left. We liked each other, but it was always more of a business arrangement. Me and Mixx were friends outside of work, even from the beginning. We were probably the closest. We pretty much did all the business and everything together. Mixx was the one I always talked to when things came up. Chris was actually very shy, much more reserved, laid-back, and quiet. Marquis was the wild guy of the group. He had the drugs and the girls and the booze, a real rock and roller. He was the only one who really came close to the public image we put out there in the music. Me, I never did drugs or partied as much, so I was never that close with him.

I wore a lot of hats in the group. I owned the label. I was the manager. I helped write a lot of the songs. During shows, Mark and David did most of the MCing while I was more of the hype man. I had to get out there because onstage those guys had the personalities of fucking turnips, no idea how to work a crowd. I brought in this persona I'd created with the Ghetto Style DJs, this wild man: Luke Skyywalker. I'd get the crowd going, start the call-and-response. Basically, I would be in between all those guys and I just did whatever the hell I wanted to do.

Originally, the business side was supposed to be all of us together as partners. But the guys started distancing themselves from that part of things. They were like, "Nah, man, we're artists. We don't talk to record distributors and shit like that." They didn't want to be businessmen. They wanted to be rock stars. They wanted to live that life. They wanted to get money, go hang out with the girls. They wanted to smoke dope. They wanted to snort dope, all that wild shit. Not Mixx so much. Mixx just wanted to stay in the studio. Since they just wanted to be the talent, I handled the business aspect.

I removed the records from their apartments, rented an office for myself in a high-rise on Biscayne Boulevard, and moved all the inventory to the wash house out behind my mother's house, the shack where I used to hook up the Pac-Man machine in high school. I had boxes of records packed into that place and a ten-foot fence with razor wire put up around it to keep the neighborhood punks from stealing my shit. Next thing you know I had eighteen-wheelers backing into my mom's backyard to get the product and take it to the distributors to get it out across the country.

The 2 Live Crew Is What We Are went gold, and I owned a big piece of it. As soon as I started making money I bought my parents a house, a real nice ranch in Miami Lakes with a pool and a big yard and safe streets where kids can play. That was the whole goal. Grow up, make some money, buy your mom a house. My mamma didn't want to leave. She kept saying, "I've got all my friends here." But Liberty City had changed and wasn't safe anymore, and I just wanted her to be safe.

I got myself a nice car, some big jewelry. Of course, the cops assumed I was selling drugs and started hassling me more than ever. Jerry Rushin, the manager of the radio station where I interned, called for a sit-down with the head of the local precinct and we showed him something like a million dollars' worth of record-sale receipts. The same cop motherfuckers who set off a riot when they kicked me out of African Square Park for playing my music too loud, and now they couldn't fucking touch me.

ALL IN

Down in Miami, I was rolling in more money than I'd ever imagined possible, but that wasn't true anywhere else. All these rappers in New York and LA were throwing off gold records, and they were fucking broke. They were all getting fucked by the industry.

At the time, there were six major players in the record business, the "Big Six": Warner, Polygram, CBS, EMI, RCA, and MCA. Those were the corporate labels, and all of them had subsidiaries that dealt with specific genres of music, like Atlantic Records, owned by Warner, which did a lot of big album rock and a lot of classic R&B. In the early years, the only rapper to land a deal with a major label was Kurtis Blow, who signed with Mercury to do "Christmas Rappin'" and "The Breaks."

"Christmas Rappin'" sold four hundred thousand singles. "The Breaks" went gold, selling over five hundred thousand. But the major labels still wanted nothing to do with rap. The white executives didn't get us, or just didn't want us. But it was really the black executives, the ones who'd been brought up to run the R&B imprints, who tried to kill hip-hop at the start. To them, rap was too black, too ghetto. It reminded them of life in the streets, the world they'd spent their whole lives running away from. They were caught up playing that respectability politics game for these white-owned companies. They wanted to make R&B into upscale, sophisticated music, show how far blacks had come, show how we were becoming high class. It was the same in the black media. Black radio stations didn't call themselves black anymore. They were "Urban Contemporary." They barely gave rap any airplay at all, or if they did it was only in special shows on the weekends. *Ebony* didn't put a hip-hop artist on its cover until 1991, twelve years after "Rapper's Delight" sold eight million copies. The white folks over at *Rolling Stone* had Run-D.M.C. on their cover in 1986, five years ahead of *Ebony*.

Since the major labels and black execs didn't want us, most of the early rap singles were put out by these little mom-and-pop labels, like Enjoy and Sugarhill Records, or by little shoestring vanity labels. They'd pay these New York guys a couple hundred dollars to do a single. It looked like a lot of money to a couple kids from the ghetto, but it was actually a total rip-off. They'd rush out some single, sell fifty, sixty, maybe a couple hundred thousand copies, mostly around New York, and that would be it. The artist would never see a penny of it. These little vanity labels, they weren't interested in building up these guys' long-term careers or in seeing hip-hop take off as serious music. They were just trying to cash in on what they felt was a fad.

The only real A&R guys who took hip-hop seriously were the white and Jewish guys who ran some of the independent labels. A lot of these guys had a couple of big hits with disco, and ever since that died out they were looking around for the next big thing.

These guys had their ear to the streets. They were going up to the clubs they'd heard about in the Bronx, to rap battles they'd heard about in Harlem. They were usually the only white guys in the room, but they got it.

A real A&R man knows a hit when he hears it, and these guys heard it. They saw the potential. Unlike all the black A&R guys, they didn't have any resistance to the rawness of it. They *liked* the rawness. There was Tom Silverman, who started Tommy Boy Records and signed Afrika Bambaataa to put out "Planet Rock." You had Clive Calder at Jive Records. He signed Whodini. You had Cory Robbins and Steve Plotnicki, who started Profile Records and picked up Dr. Jeckyll and Mr. Hyde as their very first act.

Even though these guys genuinely believed in hip-hop, they still ran their labels like old-school record companies. They paid the artists shit and kept all the ownership for themselves. They were offering these rappers terrible deals. The first single that Dr. Jeckyll and Mr. Hyde put out for Profile, "Genius Rap," sold 150,000 copies. After that came out, Profile offered to sign Andre Harrell and Alonzo Brown to a long-term deal, giving them $2,000 for the publishing rights to everything they recorded under contract. Two lousy fucking thousand dollars to give up every penny on the intellectual property of everything they did. But they took it. They didn't know any better. Shitty deals like that were everywhere. All those guys were being taken advantage of. They didn't have any choice—or at least they thought they didn't.

At that time Russell Simmons was the guy at the center of New York hip-hop, as a promoter, as a manager. He had a hand in just about every major artist coming up, from Kurtis Blow to Whodini to his own brother's group, Run-D.M.C. With Russell as their manager, Run-D.M.C. signed with Profile Records in

1983, and they got a $2,000 advance for their first single "It's Like That"/"Sucker M.C.s." The single sold 250,000 copies. The next year, their first album, *Run-D.M.C.*, went gold. But they still weren't making any real money.

Even before the video with Aerosmith for "Walk This Way" made them a crossover hit and *Raising Hell* went platinum, Run-D.M.C. were already a big success. Their deal with Profile only paid a 10 percent royalty, which was shit. They were making maybe seventy cents an album. And Profile could hold back those royalty payments for all kinds of reasons, which they did, basically keeping Run-D.M.C. on a short leash. The label wants you to put out a new album but you don't have an album you want to put out? They can stop payment on the royalties from your last album—the money you've already earned—until you deliver what they want. They own you.

Russell was starting to realize what a bullshit deal his guys had with Profile. He was looking to find something better. That's when he hooked up with Rick Rubin, this Jewish kid who was running his own label, Def Jam, with his parents' money out of a dorm room at NYU. He'd put out "It's Yours" by T La Rock and Jazzy Jay, had put out the first Beastie Boys single, and had just signed LL Cool J. Russell and Rick Rubin teamed up to make Def Jam into a serious player.

LL Cool J's first single, "I Need a Beat," was a huge hit. Hip-hop was looking more and more like a business the major labels wanted to be in. Columbia Records made Def Jam an offer. Now Russell and Rubin had to make a choice. They could have taken what's called a production deal, which would essentially make Def Jam a front for the bigger label. Columbia would put up the advance money to sign new artists, pay the production, distribution, and marketing costs, and split the revenues with Def Jam. That would offer Def Jam cash up front, but it also meant less long-term profit and less ownership. Columbia would own the masters.

Or Def Jam could have taken a pressing and distribution deal. In that deal, Def Jam would have remained more of its own business, with Columbia just acting as a partner giving the albums a bigger push, lower production costs, and wider distribution. Def Jam would have had to use its own cash in signing artists and would have had more exposure for any acts that flopped, but Russell and Rubin would have owned their own masters and kept a much bigger share of the back end. Bigger risk, better reward.

The mid-eighties was a big turning point in the history of rap. The old-school guys like Kool Herc and Grandmaster Flash, their time was done. There were many guys coming up to replace them, guys like Run-D.M.C., Schoolly D, Too $hort, Doug E. Fresh. There was also Hollywood trying to cash in, treating hip-hop like a teenage fad, putting out these ridiculous, blaxploitation-style rap movies like *Breakin'* and *Beat Street*. They were selling "break-dancing mats" at toy stores at the mall. Hip-hop had to decide what it was going to be. Was rap some fad that was going to disappear, like disco? Or was it a musical revolution that was going to change the whole culture of America? Everybody in the entertainment business was deciding where to place their bets.

Me, I went all in. Nobody was offering me the chance to sell myself out, but it wouldn't have mattered if they did. I believed in black ownership. I'd seen what happened in Overtown when they put the expressway through and we didn't own our own land to protect what was ours. I'd seen what happened after the riots, when all the white-owned businesses took their insurance money and bailed on us because they didn't care about investing in the community. I'd learned a lot from all of these guys coming through doing shows at the Pac Jam II, who had fucked-up contracts and were starving. I put all my chips on 2 Live Crew and Luke Records and into building the biggest black-owned hip-hop label in the South.

In October 1985, Def Jam took the production deal from Columbia. They got $2 million in operating capital, including a $600,000 advance for Russell and Rubin. Low risk, low reward. Nobody believed in hip-hop more than Russell, but he underestimated himself. He underestimated what black artists and entrepreneurs were capable of. Just a couple months after Def Jam signed with Columbia, the label put out its first full album, LL Cool J's *Radio*. LL Cool J was hip-hop's first teen idol, the first rapper to go on Dick Clark's *American Bandstand*—the perfect crossover. *Radio* blew up. It went gold in less than six months, eventually selling over a million copies. That $600,000 advance that Def Jam got, Columbia made it all back just from the sales of *Radio* alone.

All the money that came from gold- and platinum-selling Def Jam artists flowed up to the boardroom at Columbia Records instead of out to the streets to the people who actually created the music. Def Jam could have set the standard. Hip-hop could have been owned by black entrepreneurs alongside white and Jewish allies who were sincere about forming a partnership, not just exploiting us. If Russell Simmons had done with Def Jam what I did with Luke Records, today he'd be a billionaire. But Russell Simmons hedged his bet.

Luke Records started with nothing, came from nothing, just a twenty-five-year-old DJ a few months out of cooking in a hospital kitchen, out hustling gigs in one of the most fucked-up, riot-torn ghettos in America. I always had to do everything on my own because I was an outsider. Being from Miami I was considered a nobody, an outcast by the music industry. I didn't have Tommy Mottola or Jimmy Iovine to be my mentor. There was no road map for a rapper to build his own record company. Nobody in New York was doing it. Nobody in LA was doing it.

I sold over 750,000 records in my first year. I had a beeper and all of a sudden I was returning calls from Europe on pay phones. European distributors wanted the album. I carried a sack of quarters on me for all the long-distance phone calls. But I was expanding and adding other artists, too. I signed the first rapper out of Atlanta. In the late eighties in Atlanta, hip-hop barely even existed. On the radio, all they were playing was New York singles. There was no hip-hop scene in Atlanta at all in terms of labels and record companies and industry. It was all underground, small-time.

We were doing shows up there at this club, Sharon Showcase, and this guy Peter Jones, MC Shy D, would always open up for us. He was a hot kid around the area and already had a following in Atlanta, so it was a no-brainer. He also brought the Miami Bass sound with him. The first rapper out of ATL was on Luke Records. That's how the whole Atlanta scene started: I started it. It was a satellite of Miami.

At the same time, because of what 2 Live Crew was doing, more Miami rappers were stepping up, creating different kinds of bass music. It never bothered me that other rappers were copying our sound. I looked at it as more like we were starting a movement, a whole new genre of music. The bigger Miami got, the better for me. Plus I never got the point of all those bullshit rap feuds anyway. LL Cool J and Kool Moe Dee going at it, dissing each other. I didn't beef with other Miami artists. I signed the motherfuckers and I kept making money.

I was still promoting most of my own concerts, too, putting 2 Live Crew and MC Shy D on with whoever I had down from New York. In one night I was getting paid to perform, had a piece of the door, *and* was moving records and merchandise for half of the acts on the bill. I was making serious money, but people thought it was a joke. They didn't know. All the New York guys, they were out there selling gold and platinum records, they were the ones getting the videos on MTV, who had everyone telling them they were gonna be famous rock stars. To them, they were the big shit and I was just this clown, this small-time guy in Miami. There was a couple of times I remember I was on tour with Kool Moe Dee, and Fresh Prince and Jazzy Jeff. They'd laugh at me and say, "What label you on? Luke Records? The fuck is that?"

I'd sit there and I would hold court with them. I'd tell these guys, "Luke Records is *my* label. I get *all* the money."

"What?"

"Look, your money gets split up ten different ways, all these people taking a cut, holding their expenses against your royalties. I'm getting back two dollars a record and you're probably getting back two cents, and that's if you get anything back at all. So who's the joker on that?"

They also saw me selling my own merchandise. Most labels would get a third-party vendor like Winterland to make and sell the shirts, and then the artist would get a fee. Luke Gear was mine. I owned it. I designed it, manufactured it, distributed it, and I was getting all the money from it. We would roll up to a venue, and there'd be a table out front selling all the T-shirts and shit, theirs and mine. Only after the show they'd see me in the back counting out stacks. They'd say, "What you doing?"

"I'm counting my money, motherfuckers. I made about thirty grand in merchandise tonight."

They'd be like, "What the *fuck*?!"

I'd be like, "Yeah, man. You see, Winterland pays you a flat fee, about twenty-five hundred dollars, to sell your shit at these concerts. But that shirt they're selling for fifteen dollars really costs about two. Me, if I put up ten thousand dollars for merchandise, it retails for about one hundred thousand, and I'm selling the shit out of it."

I would do commercials on local TV for Luke Gear. I was getting mail orders even when we weren't on the road. College kids loved it. We had University of Miami football players wearing our scarves on the sidelines at games. Derrick Thomas of the Kansas City Chiefs, he was wearing the shit. I started sending out free promotional gear to professional athletes, doing cross-marketing with sports ten years before anyone else in hip-hop. This was all before Rocawear, before Wu Wear, before Sean John or any of that shit.

Owning my own label, owning my own masters, my own merchandise, I was doing all that years before anyone else in the business. I paid retail for every ad I ran. I paid retail for every piece of equipment I owned. The only break I got came from the U-Haul place. When the Ghetto Style DJs were starting out we'd built up enough equipment that we needed a second van. When we rented the truck for the weekend, the guy from the U-Haul place would let us keep it during the week to store the gear; he only called it in if he needed it for another customer. That was great. Nobody did shit for Luther Campbell except the U-Haul guy. I fought for everything else.

What I did down in Miami basically changed the whole face of hip-hop. At that time, everybody was just happy to be on Atlantic Records or CBS or Warner Bros. They didn't aspire to have their own record label like I did. Most of these guys, coming fresh out of the projects, they didn't know something like that was even possible. But after I'd hold court with them and show them what I was doing, how much money I was making, they'd get pissed. These dudes would go back to their labels and say, "Hey, we want to do our own stuff. We want our own merchandise. We want better royalties. We want ownership. *We want to be like Luke!*"

These artists now wanted to be entrepreneurs. They'd heard

the horror stories of what had happened to all the old-school guys getting exploited. Artists became a little more educated about the business. This led to Bad Boy Records and Cash Money Records. The music business had to change. Tupac, Biggie, Jay Z, that whole next generation, the corporate labels had to go back and change their contracts and give them more, give them better royalties, give them ownership. Lots of rappers are doing it now, but I did it first. In the 1980s, I had the only artist-owned, black-owned hip-hop label in the country. After Berry Gordy sold Motown to MCA in 1988, I had the biggest independent black-owned label in America, period.

MOVE SOMETHIN'

Luke Records took off as a business because I was relentless and smart, always making up for what I didn't know by learning on the job and using common sense. On the musical side of things, the reason 2 Live Crew got hot was because of two things we did. We used funny, everyday ghetto language to talk about an interesting subject that everybody enjoys and hears about all the time, and we had a bass beat that you could dance to. It's that simple.

Because 2 Live Crew became so notorious for its lyrics, Mixx never gets the credit he deserves. He never gets mentioned with Jam Master Jay and Eric B. as one of the great influential DJs, but he should be. How many songs can you point to that launched a whole genre of music? Little Richard's "Tutti Frutti" and rock and roll. Nirvana's "Smells Like Teen Spirit" and grunge. Ice-T's "6 in the Mornin'" and LA gangsta rap. "Throw the D" belongs on that list. It launched the whole Miami Bass sound, which inspired crunk music in Atlanta and bounce music in New Orleans. You're talking about millions and millions of records sold, and all that started with David Hobbs.

Mixx was like a mad scientist. Didn't party, didn't do drugs. Lived in the studio, poring over old records for samples, looping beats together for new songs. I was the executive, and he was the producer. I would come up with ideas, like, "Hey, let's do a parody of 'Do Wah Diddy.'" I would tell Mixx and he would disappear and run with it and call me a few days later to hear what he'd cooked up. Every time I went in there to listen to a song with Mixx, I'd get excited. It was like going home when your mom tells you she baked a cake.

The other half of our success—using everyday language to talk about a subject that everyone enjoys and participates in—well, that got a little more complicated. Given our reputation, people are usually surprised to learn that Uncle Luke and 2 Live Crew started out in a teen club. We performed fun, innocent party music for them. The teen clubs we played were even endorsed as wholesome, safe entertainment by a conservative watchdog group called Informed Families of Dade. Even when we did "Throw the D," that song was more suggestive than explicit. It was PG-13, not XXX. We even got asked to be talent-show judges at some of the local high schools.

When we started recording albums, I told the rest of the group that we had to do something different. New York already had its style. The major record labels, they already had big stars and the big budgets to promote them. If we were just another bunch of guys wearing gold ropes and yelling, "Throw your hands in the air," nobody was going to know who we were. Fresh Kid Ice and Brother Marquis, they obviously couldn't flow like Big Daddy

Kane, so we needed to jazz them up. We needed to stand out. We needed a signature style to go with this new bass sound Mr. Mixx was cooking up in his laboratory.

"Let's be different. Let's be funny. Let's be explicit." They were all down for it. Back then everyone was sampling James Brown and old-school R&B artists. My idea was that we would sample music, but on top of it we would use movie quotes from Dolemite and stand-up bits from Redd Foxx and Richard Pryor. We'd sample bits from Cheech and Chong, from Eddie Murphy. We started adding in things that New York rappers would never do.

On *The 2 Live Crew Is What We Are*, a lot of the songs aren't explicit at all. But the dirty ones were the ones that everybody liked, songs like "We Want Some Pussy" and "Get It, Girl." When we put out our second album, *Move Somethin'*, in 1988, we did more of it. We made it raunchier, dirtier. That was the first album we put out with a girl on the cover. It was the four of us in the hot tub with the woman standing over us in the bathing suit, her legs and ass facing the camera. We did things like that to get noticed. I didn't have a marketing budget, but you put that record on the shelf, guys are going to pick it up, buy it, and take it home and put the album up on their wall.

By the time we came out with *Move Somethin'*, we'd created our own image and our own style: we were party music. We had fun and made people laugh, singing "Me So Horny" or "Pop That Pussy." At first, people bought the records and danced and laughed along at our shows. The numbers speak for themselves. *What We Are* hit No. 24 on the *Billboard* R&B chart and No. 128 on the *Billboard* 200 chart. *Move Somethin'* went to No. 20 on R&B and No. 68 on the *Billboard* 200. Both were RIAA-certified gold records, and that was all word of mouth and college radio and us driving around in our van marketing ourselves. No major label or commercial radio promotion at all. People liked the music. People *loved* the music, with one exception: rappers from New York.

At that time, there wasn't no such thing as southern hip-hop, and as we traveled throughout the country we started getting friction from the New York artists. They thought we weren't real hip-hop, the same way they felt about LA. Those New York guys liked me fine when I was a promoter in Miami, booking their shows and selling the fuck out of their records. Once 2 Live Crew came out and started competing with them, it was like all hell broke loose. They hated us. It was like every single one of those New York guys hated us with a passion. They'd be on BET talking bad about us. We were totally discriminated against. They'd never let us share the stage with them. It was like they were the white people and we were the niggers.

We would go and perform and we would have to literally fight with these dudes. What was happening was that as hip-hop started to blow up outside New York, all these big New York acts were getting booked on these tours throughout the South: Atlanta, Birmingham, a bunch of these college towns. On a lot of tours, the opening act is chosen by the local promoter, and these local guys all knew how popular we were. "Hey, these 2 Live Crew motherfuckers are the hottest guys down here. I'll add them to the bill and sell some fucking tickets."

The promoters would put us on the show. They were using our name to sell tickets, but then, when it came time to do the concert, the road manager of the headliner, he controlled the house. He controlled how many lights you got, how much sound you got, how much stage time you got, everything. We were booked for a show with Run-D.M.C. in Biloxi, Mississippi, and I had to fight with their manager. Before the show, this guy was bitching to the promoter, "We don't like these motherfuckers. They're not hip-hop. They're not from New York. Fuck them. We're not going on after them." The promoter tried to compromise. He had a contract with us, so he had to let us do something. He came to me and said, "Look, y'all guys can go on, but you only have three minutes."

"Three minutes? We got to do 'We Want Some Pussy,' 'Throw the D,' and all these other songs! How we gonna do that in three fucking minutes?"

"Well, man, I'm sorry, but that's the best I can do."

"Fuck that. They only want one song? I'll give em one song," I responded.

"Peter Piper" was Run-D.M.C.'s big single at the time, so I went to Mixx and said, "Hey Mixx, we're gonna go right up there and we're gonna do 'Peter Piper.'"

We got up onstage and I said, "Look here, ladies and gentlemen of Biloxi, Mississippi. Run-D.M.C. says we ain't got but three minutes to perform. We can't sing 'We Want Some Pussy.' We can't sing 'Throw the D.' We can't do all the shit that you came to hear in three fucking minutes. What we're gonna do is have Mr. Mixx cut 'Peter Piper.'"

The crowd started yelling, "'Peter Piper,' 'Peter Piper,' 'Peter Piper'!" Mixx got on the turntables cutting the song. All those guys, Run-D.M.C. and their manager and their security, they all rushed the stage, ready to fight. "Hey motherfucker, what the fuck y'all doing? Come on! Let's go! We can do this right here on the fucking stage!"

We went at it. The fans went crazy, cheering the fight. Security came. Cops came and separated us.

"Fuck this! We out!" And we left.

It was the same bullshit whenever we shared a bill with any of those guys. I kept my pistol on me, because I knew what was coming. Memphis, Tennessee: we did a show with Eric B. and Rakim. Drove all the way to Memphis from Miami, had all our equipment on the front of the fucking stage, and same thing. Their people said, "Y'all got one song. Three minutes."

I went out and I took the mic and for three solid minutes I yelled, "Fuck Eric B. and Rakim! All these motherfuckers, they don't like us. We from the South and these motherfuckers got a problem with that. They think they're better than the South. They won't let us perform." Shit hit the fan. Started a fucking riot. People were throwing shit, yelling, "Give us our money back!"

Then it was Savannah, Georgia, and Public Enemy. Here we go again. I was getting ready to go up onstage and the road manager, this white guy, he came to me in the kitchen in the back of this club and started talking shit to me, started telling me what we could and couldn't do. "Yo, y'all motherfuckers can't put y'all shit onstage. Y'all can't do this, y'all can't do that."

I told him, "Look, motherfucker. You can't tell me what to do." He started getting up in my face and I started getting up in his and I don't remember who took the first swing but I ended up beating his white ass all up and down that damn kitchen. Cops came and it was a whole thing. We ended up not being able to do that show.

If you ain't from New York, you ain't shit. That was the attitude. Every time. It wasn't just us. The Philadelphia guys, Schoolly D and all them. They would be alienated, too, kicked out. Same with N.W.A and the guys on the West Coast. We weren't getting on the Fresh Festival concerts. We weren't getting on the big corporate tours. We could get on college radio, but New York had control of the commercial radio. We couldn't get played, even the clean versions of our songs. That's why we had to work the chitlin circuit as long as we did, because they had control of local commerical radio. We ended up hooking up with N.W.A and Ice Cube and doing shows with them, because we were all outcasts. We started sharing stories about how the New York artists were disenfranchising us and not letting us on the major tours. We'd sit there and share these stories and get fucking pissed off.

The wild part about it was that these New York guys were on this trip that their shit was better, but I was my own executive, so I knew what my sales figures were. In all my history and all my career, my number-one-selling market was New York. The fans in New York loved 2 Live Crew. They loved bass music. I sold more records in New York than I sold anywhere else. Which shows you that all that macho East Coast–West Coast posturing, all that Tupac and Biggie shit, it was all bullshit, pointless.

People liked *all* the music, every kind of rap: dance rap, kiddie rap, gangsta rap, conscious music, bass music, New Jack Swing. The variety is what kept hip-hop alive and made it grow the way it did. If the sound had never changed from what it was in the South Bronx, hip-hop would have died in 1983. It would have been a fad. But here we were, beefing with each other over what was "real" hip-hop. We were tearing each other apart when we should have been united. There was something bigger out there for all of us. White kids were starting to buy our albums. They were popping up at our shows. Hip-hop was taking its first steps across the color line, which indicated that shit was about to blow up.

After we put out *The 2 Live Crew Is What We Are*, I got some letters from a PTA group in Birmingham, Alabama, saying that children were getting hold of our songs and that they were inappropriate and what could I do about it? I was totally sympathetic to their concerns. Once we started doing more adult material at the Pac Jam II, I drew a clear line between kids' shows and adult shows. We'd do an early show, serve nothing but soft drinks, and all the kids could come in and have a good time.

Later we'd clear the club and let all the grown-ups line up for the late show. We IDed everyone to make sure everyone was over eighteen, and then do an explicit show for the adults.

With the albums, I turned to my old friend common sense and decided to do something similar. I did what the movies did. They had a ratings system, PG and R and so on. That worked and everyone agreed to it. Music didn't have anything like that, but I figured it should. I put parental-advisory stickers on my records. I called retailers and told them, "Hey, if you see a sticker on our album, do not sell it to kids under eighteen." A lot of stores kept it behind the counter, the same way they'd do with *Playboy* and *Penthouse*, so that people had to ask for it and show ID. That parental-advisory sticker was my idea, not the recording industry's.

Where I first ran into trouble was that some leftover, unstickered copies of the explicit version of *The 2 Live Crew Is What We Are* were still out in stores. In April of 1987, in Callaway, Forida, some little town out in the Panhandle, a store clerk sold a copy to a fourteen-year-old girl. The clerk got arrested for the "sale of harmful material to a person under the age of 18," a third-degree felony. A lot of stores around the area started pulling the album.

That first arrest in the Panhandle, I thought it was unfortunate, but I didn't see it as the start of a pattern of legal censorship. I didn't want that to happen again, so with *Move Somethin'* I was even more careful. We started doing clean versions of the songs alongside the explicit versions. We made a clean album for minors and an explicit one for adults, and on the explicit one I put a parental-advisory sticker and gave specific instructions to every retailer that it was not to be sold to minors. We put age restrictions on alcohol, cigarettes, R-rated movies, porno mags—there was no reason we couldn't do it with music.

Or so I thought.

The legal war against hip-hop started on June 29, 1988, in

Alexander City, Alabama, this little backwater town on I-280 about forty-five minutes north of Auburn. The record store there, called Take Home the Hits, was run by a guy named Tommy Hammond. He knew he was working in a conservative, rural community, so he kept all the rap and explicit albums behind the counter and out of sight. Customers had to ask for them. One day a cop came in and asked for a copy of *Move Somethin'*, and Tommy sold it to him. Nobody was underage. This was a grown man selling recorded material to another grown man. In America.

The cop left and came back a half hour later with a detective and uniformed officers in tow and they arrested Hammond for selling pornography. It was the first time in the history of the country that a record-store owner was held liable for "obscene" music. The cops, apparently, had been getting complaints from Christian fundamentalist groups about the sale of offensive and vulgar material, and the Alexander City sheriff Ben Royal was, I suppose, a real God-fearing, Bible-thumping, easily offended type of guy.

At first I wasn't even mad. I was genuinely confused. Dolemite and Skillet & Leroy and all these comedy records we were sampling, those had been around for years. They were filthy as hell, *real* nasty, and nobody had ever tried to censor them. Andrew Dice Clay was doing his stand-up act and putting out his albums at the same time we were, and his routines were just as raunchy as what we were doing. Nobody was getting arrested for selling his albums. What was going on? My father and my uncle Ricky taught me a lot about racism and how it works, but I was about to learn a lot more. I was about to feel the full weight of American racism come down on my head. I'd unleashed something incredibly angry, and incredibly powerful.

Dice is white, you see, so he could say whatever he wanted. Parents might protest him, and they did, but he was a white man making a lot of money for a white-owned corporation; nobody

was going to take away his right to free speech. All those old chitlin circuit albums we sampled, they were dirty, but white people
never listened to them. They didn't cross the color line, so nobody
in power really cared. It was the same with the first 2 Live Crew
records. We'd sold hundreds of thousands of records to black
people at black record stores, and no cop or judge ever said shit
about it. Nobody cared if we were corrupting young black minds
with our evil jungle music. But the day some white teenager got
caught with a 2 Live Crew album, that's what started the whole
shitstorm right fucking there. There were black record stores in
Alexander City that sold our music and went on selling our music
during this whole controversy, and not one cop ever darkened
their door. But Tommy Hammond's record store was the record
store serving the white side of town. 2 Live Crew had done the
one thing you're never supposed to do. We were black men coming across the color line talking about sex. We were black men in
the company of whites, and we'd forgotten to lower our heads and
shuffle away.

Back when I was doing the Pac Jam Teen Disco at the skating
rink, the owner of the rink, who was white, told me I had to have
security. I thought, Okay, let me get some security this white guy
will feel good about. I brought in these two huge white dudes,
Damien and his brother Rocco. Fucking huge guys. Big fucking
necks and shit. I got them and a couple of off-duty white cops to
make everyone in this suburban strip mall feel okay with us having all these black kids out here. Damien and Rocco always used
to hang out at this strip club down the way from the skating rink,
this place called Tootsie's. One night after we closed up they said,
"Hey, let us take you over to Tootsie's."

I said, "*Fuck* no. I ain't going to no white strip club."

"Why not?"

"Look, you and me, we friends. We cool. But I can't go in there, a black man looking at a bunch of naked white women. Those rednecks in there will fucking kill me."

Growing up, I was never scared of anything. I bused over to Miami Beach for school, hung with all the rich white folks out there, no problem. I stood up to the corrupt white cops hassling us every night on Twelfth Avenue and got my ass thrown in jail. I was a bullheaded, stubborn motherfucker who always spoke his mind and went and did as he pleased, but even I knew where the line was—and the line was at the door of that strip club. Slavery, Jim Crow, the whole history of black oppression in this country was built on the fear of the oversexed black man threatening the purity of the white race by coming after innocent little white women. For a hundred years down here in Florida, black bodies had turned up shot by the railroad tracks or drowned in the swamp, and nine times out of ten it was some guy accused of raping a white woman, or just looking at her the wrong way.

"Nobody's gonna do shit to you if you're with us."

Naked women were everywhere. It was the first time Uncle Luke ever set foot in a strip club—a historic moment in the history of hip-hop, and a lot of inspiration for future 2 Live Crew concerts. But I never would have done it without those two big white dudes having my back.

When we started making the music raunchier and dirtier, it was all black folks buying the records and coming to the shows. This music was part of our culture. *We* got the joke. My mom always used to say our music was hilarious, but we were the only ones who knew it was supposed to be funny. Since we started out making black music for a black audience, I never really thought much about how it would be perceived when white people started listening. Even when the records took off and it was clear that white

THE BOOK OF LUKE | 115

people were buying them, I didn't see it in the same way as me going to that strip club. In that club, those rednecks might see me as a physical threat and jump me. That I understood. But these were just some funny raunchy songs. I honestly didn't see that people would react the same way.

Not only was I breaking the single biggest racial taboo in the country, I was breaking the rules of how business worked, too. Up until that time, black-owned businesses were allowed to thrive in America as long as they stayed in their place. Black-owned beauty-care companies were allowed to sell beauty products, but only to blacks. A black man could own a hotel that served blacks, but only in Overtown or Harlem. John H. Johnson could print *Ebony* and *Jet* for black readers. But black companies didn't serve whites and they didn't take business away from whites; that wasn't allowed, especially in the music industry. The first man to do it was Berry Gordy with Motown, and he did it by making Motown and its acts as squeaky-clean and respectable as possible, by being safe for white people, safe for *The Ed Sullivan Show*. When they put the Jackson 5 out there, Gordy deliberately shaved two years off the ages of each kid in the group so white families would be sure to see them as black boys and not black men. They were teenagers singing about schoolyard crushes, not grown men singing about love and sex.

When the hip-hop generation came along, we refused to play that game. We didn't apologize for our blackness. We bragged about it. We told the truth about life in the ghettos and we were selling a ton of records to white kids. Rap was doing what school busing and affirmative action and these other things failed to do: it was integrating the culture. Busing and affirmative action put blacks and whites in the same building, like when I was back at Beach High, but we still didn't share any culture in common. Hip-hop changed all of that. It tore right through all those barriers.

The Alexander City case was the signal to me that white kids getting into our music was the source of the problem. That's when Focus on the Family started putting out their pamphlets and leaflets and we became their menace. My staff would talk to record-store owners on a weekly basis, so we knew what was going on. They'd call us and say, "The cops were just in here and threatened to put us in jail for selling your record." I got a call from a record-store owner in Fort Lauderdale who told me that. Some people didn't think it was worth the trouble and didn't sell the product, but others were like, "Fine, take me to jail. You can't do this. This is America."

All these older, conservative white folks, they were upset by all hip-hop, but what was unique about Luke Records was that I owned it. It was *mine*. Viacom could control the videos that Run-D.M.C. and LL Cool J put on MTV. Time Warner could control what songs they wanted Ice-T to put out on his albums. Nobody could tell me shit. Nobody could put a muzzle on me. *I* owned the megaphone; they didn't. And unlike the generation of black businessmen who came before me, I didn't stay on my side of the color line. I wasn't safe and respectable. I took ownership and control away from them. White people didn't like the explicit language of what we were saying, but what really scared them was that they had no way to stop me from saying it. They couldn't boycott me. They couldn't call up and threaten the shareholders. They couldn't send Jesse Jackson and Al Sharpton down to guilt me and hustle me. They couldn't do shit. That's why, in Callaway and Alexander City, they were coming after me with the only thing they had left: using the cops and the courts to try and take away my First Amendment right to free speech.

Part of the reason those New York groups looked down on us was just that attitude of being New York: "We created hip-hop, so all that West Coast and southern shit ain't hip-hop." But part of it was just they didn't like our image. They were "serious" hip-hop, and we were just a bunch of rowdy, unsophisticated niggers from down South, making them look bad. Maybe 2 Live Crew wasn't socially conscious rap, maybe the lyrics were silly and raunchy and juvenile, but doing what we did, taking ownership of our music and breaking those sexual taboos, was more dangerous, more political, than anything coming out of New York. Chuck D used to say that hip-hop was black America's CNN. He's right except for one thing: White people own CNN. White people own Fox News and ABC and NBC and Facebook and Google. They can set the agenda. They can say whatever they want. Black people didn't own hip-hop back in the eighties.

Out on stage, Public Enemy was doing all their "Black Power" and "Fight the Power" and all this, but it was all for show. Behind the scenes, Public Enemy didn't have any power, no real economic power. Chuck D didn't own shit. He was on Columbia Records. White corporate money controlled his voice. His white road manager was backstage in Savannah, telling us, his own brothers, that we couldn't have any stage time, couldn't have a voice, because they thought they were better than us, more important than us. But they weren't. When you're black and you're from a place like Liberty City, just showing the world that you're having a good time is a political act. It's a statement: you can't get us down, you can't break our spirit, we're still gonna dance and fuck and have a good time. Bass music and 2 Live Crew gave black people in Miami and all over the South something we could brag about, something that *we* owned and *we* controlled. And that scared the hell out of these stale white bitches who tried to take us down.

HANDSOME HARRY

Those early years of getting Luke Records and 2 Live Crew off the ground, it was nonstop work, work, work, one day rolling into the next, making deals, driving that van from college town to college town, doing shows, knocking down groupies back at the hotel, trying to keep track of all my money and what to do with it.

By the time we opened the Pac Jam II, Liberty City had gone crazy. It'd become a psycho ward. The whole city had been taken over by cocaine smugglers and Cuban refugees. It was the time of the cocaine cowboys: Cuban and Colombian cartels shooting up the streets like it was the Wild Fucking West. Mass shootings and gangland executions were on the five o'clock news every goddamn night. Miami had the highest murder rate in the country, by a wide margin, for years. There were so many bodies in the Miami morgue that the coroner had to line up refrigerated trucks to hold the overflow.

In the year after the Mariel boatlift, gun sales in Dade County went up by 50 percent: everybody was either about to kill somebody or worried about getting killed themselves. The white folks in Miami, most of them just left. They moved to the suburbs out in Broward. The only ones that stayed were holed up in gated communities on Miami Beach or in Coral Gables. But the blacks in Overtown and Liberty City, they were stuck. They couldn't afford to get out of the cross fire.

When I was growing up, Liberty City was a working-class neighborhood. Parents came home at six o'clock. The kids played in the park. No wild shit. No shooting. No ambulances coming in to pick up a body every single night. But even before the riots tore us up, you had all these cheap drugs flooding into the neighborhood. It started in the early seventies, under Nixon, really. By the 1980s, it was an epidemic. You had more drugs, cheaper drugs, and no real jobs to keep kids from doing shit other than selling drugs.

The community changed. On every other corner, somebody was out trapping. Every block had a drug house. Marijuana, cocaine, crack, heroin, everything. Walking down West Ninth Street, instead of kids out in their yards playing football, they were standing outside their house waiting on a car to pull up. A lot of the customers came from outside of the neighborhood. Cars would roll by slow with the window down and guys on the corner would yell, "Yo, yo, yo, yo! I got it right here!"

It was a goddamn open-air drug market, everywhere. Every night at ten o'clock, the shootings would start. *Boom, boom, boom, boom!* Somebody's house was getting shot up. Somebody was trying to take somebody else's turf. Somebody was short-stopping somebody else's drug spot. Short-stopping is if I have a hot trap, and you come and stand on the corner right up the street and you stop people before they come around the corner, you're stealing my customers. Now I've got to pull out my gun and shoot up the block.

These little pockets of gangs formed, and the tougher the gangs got, the more wild shit they had to do to each other to maintain control of their territory. Then, on top of that, you had the cops. Now they're empowered by Reagan and Bush and the DEA to go after drug dealers like terrorists. They had SWAT teams, riot gear, automatic weapons—all this shit to go after some nineteen-year-old kids peddling dope on the corners. Everything just escalated.

After I'd gone to DC to visit my brother Stanley, I'd been trying to keep my head right, stay out of the bullshit. But I still had some thug in me that I had to deal with. Back in the day with Ghetto Style, we all carried that thug attitude, and sometimes our DJ battles broke out into fights, but back then you were talking about fistfights. Just guys going at it. Macho bullshit. The worst you got was a black eye or a busted lip or some shit like that. As the years went on, DJ fights turned into gunfights. Gunfights turned into drive-bys and straight-up executions and revenge killing. That's how I lost my best friend, and almost lost everything I'd worked for.

Handsome Harry was one of the Ghetto Style DJs, and he was also one of my best friends, my right-hand guy when I launched the Pac Jam II and Luke Records. His real name was Daryl Williams, but I gave him the nickname Handsome Harry. Handsome Harry wasn't handsome at all. All his front teeth were rotten. But girls would gravitate to him anyway because he was such a kind and generous guy.

One night at the Pac Jam, around the time when 2 Live Crew and the label were just getting going, some kid was walking through the club and Harry accidentally stepped on his sneaker, scuffing it up. It wasn't even a nice pair of shoes. It wasn't Air Jordans or anything like that, just some cheap, department-store sneakers. Kid was fourteen years old, but already he had an attitude. Kid turned on Harry, a grown man, and yelled, "Hey, watch it! You scratched my shoe!"

Harry had shit to do. The club was busy. He didn't have time for this punk, so he yelled back, "Well, if you don't want em scratched, take em off and put em in your pocket."

With that, Harry was done, but this kid kept trying to start something. Harry grabbed him, dragged him to the front door, and tossed him out, same as we'd done with dozens of trouble-makers before. It's how we kept the club safe; we had zero toler-ance for guys like that. But this kid, he was one of these mini wannabe thugs that had started infesting the neighborhood. He decided he'd been disrespected or some shit. He went home and got a .22-caliber Uzi. A fourteen-year-old with his hands on a fucking Uzi. When I was a kid we played with marbles and G.I. Joes and shit. Now they had automatic weapons. This kid, he got this gun and he came back and hid in the shadows outside the club and waited for Harry to come out.

Around eleven o'clock, the club closed and Harry was walk-ing this young woman home when all of a sudden this kid and his friend jumped out of the bushes, put the gun in Harry's side, and pulled the trigger. Harry was armed—we all were, you had to be for self-defense—but this shot put him down before he could get a shot off to defend himself. He fell to the sidewalk and blood poured into his perforated lungs, choking and drowning him in minutes. One of the best guys I'd ever known, shot dead by some fourteen-year-old punk over some bullshit about some cheap shoes. We'd heard the shots at the club; this all went down a couple blocks away. But on a Friday night in Liberty City, gunshots are as com-mon as car horns, so nobody paid it much attention. We didn't even know Harry had left to walk this girl home.

The girl, she was too scared to testify. There's no witness protection program for young black girls in the ghetto. Without her testimony, the cops had no case, and they had to let the little murdering tykes walk. No justice for Handsome Harry. Now the whole neighborhood was on edge. This kid's friends and family, they were expecting retaliation from the Ghetto Style DJs. And the Ghetto Style DJs, we were out on the street, looking for these punks. Me, I was just lost, in shock. Harry was one of my right-hand guys, like a brother. I went and bought a damn machine gun, a Colt AR-15, and I was out looking for these guys, too.

One day I was in my office at the club working when this kid's brother and a couple of his guys came to see me. They parked their car right in front for a quick getaway. They wanted to call some kind of truce. I was not in a forgiving mood. I wasn't intending for any shit to go down. I left the gun locked up in my office while I went out to talk to them. I told them to leave. They got hot, and pretty soon the verbal shit was flying. They were flashing the guns in their waistbands, saying they knew how to use them. I was unarmed, and most of the DJs were off doing other shit.

Fortunately, one of my guys showed up, saw what was happening, went around the side, broke into my office, and grabbed my AR-15. He ran out, tossed it to me. These guys took one look at my weapon with its thirty-round clip and they ran for their fucking lives. They got to their car, but by the time they started fumbling with their keys I'd already aimed the barrel dead at the car's windshield. They ditched the car and took off on foot.

At that point they were gone. I could have just turned around and gone back to work. I know that's what I should have done. But instead I just saw red. I was filled with rage for my dead brother. I emptied the whole clip into that fucking car, sprayed it with high-powered military steel jackets the same way I'd water my lawn. Window glass was spraying. Blue water was spewing from the radiator out of the front grille. The whole car sank to the pavement as the tires went flat.

Cops heard the gunfire, called it in, and patrol cars came swarming the club. Next thing I knew, I was in cuffs, bent over the hood of some police vehicle. They dragged me down to the station and locked me up. At the end of the day, no charges were filed. The gun was legal and registered, and I was defending myself after being threatened on my own property.

It was stupid. Stupid, stupid thug bullshit. Shooting up that car and getting thrown in jail wasn't going to bring justice for Harry. Here I was, building a successful business, well on my way to my first million dollars, and I nearly threw it all away over some stupid beef with a couple of punks.

That was a major turning point for me. I had to figure out what I wanted to do with my life, what direction I was going to go. I couldn't be doing all that wild shit. It was a decision that the whole hip-hop community had to face. Right around the same time, in September of '86, at a Run-D.M.C. concert in Long Beach, California, rap's first-ever major arena tour, a bunch of LA gang members broke out in a riot with knives and snapped-off legs from the stadium chairs, put dozens of people in the emergency room with stab wounds. Same thing would happen to 2 Live Crew a couple years later, doing a show in West Palm Beach in '88. It was a Luke Records show with us, MC Shy D, and a few other acts, and these two rival gangs went after each other in the audience. It would have turned into a riot if the cops hadn't come in and broken it up.

These rival gangs in West Palm Beach chose our concert to start that shit because they wanted to use our fame to get attention for themselves. Shit had nothing to do with us. Of course the way the white media twisted it, they got it all wrong. They said that hip-hop had a culture of violence, that we were promoting violence. That was never true. Hip-hop started as a way to get away from violence, a way to channel all the pent-up energy of these black youths into something positive. Afrika Bambaataa used his music and his concerts in the South Bronx to bring rival gangs together and stop warring against each other. We started the Pac Jam II to keep kids off the corners and give them a safe place to go at night. But the violence follows you. It's all around you. It's inside your own head, because you were raised with that mentality. If you grow up in Beirut, you're going to act like you're from fucking Beirut. That's how I found myself cuffed in the backseat of a patrol car, next to some shot-up piece-of-shit car, wondering if I'd just fucked up my whole life.

I was lucky that time. Nobody got hurt. But I knew that was the day I had to leave all that thug shit behind me. I couldn't let my future get dragged down by all the bullshit from the past. I turned that part of my life around, and I knew from that day forward my life and my career would have to be about more than just making money for the sake of being successful. I need to use my name and my money and my influence not just to save guys like Handsome Harry, but to save the kid who felt he had to pick up an automatic weapon to solve his problems. If somebody had helped that kid early enough, my friend would still be alive today.

THE HURRICANES

I was always a Miami Hurricanes fan. They were my team. On the cover of *The 2 Live Crew Is What We Are*, me and Brother Marquis and Fresh Kid Ice were in a Jeep wearing Hurricanes jackets and Hurricanes drawers. Part of that was marketing, to let everyone know that we were from Miami, to get the attention of people in south Florida. But it was also because I was just such a huge fan.

My whole time growing up, Miami was terrible, just the worst team you could imagine. There were several years the administration thought about shutting the program down, it was such an embarrassment. Then they hired Howard Schnellenberger. He'd been offensive coordinator under Bear Bryant at Alabama and was doing the same for Don Shula and the Dolphins when the University of Miami hired him to be head coach in 1979. Schnellenberger came in and he turned everything around, not just the program but the whole damn city.

Florida A&M, the historically black college up in Tallahassee, had always been my second college team, after Miami. When one of my brothers was at FAMU, every year at homecoming we would drive up to Tallahassee to watch the games. At that time, FAMU was beating the dogshit out of everybody. People were saying they were so good they should go into Division I and play against the white schools. During one of Schnellenberger's first years, Miami played FAMU, and FAMU just destroyed them—the privileged, middle-class white kids at Miami were scared of all the tough black kids at FAMU.

Schnellenberger saw this and he said to his players, "Y'all scared of these black guys? Okay, I'm gonna bring in the toughest and the hardest black guys I can find. They're going to rough you up real bad. Toughen you up." He went and found some semipro teams with these hardcore black players to come in and scrimmage with Miami. I remember going to one of those scrimmages. It was a big deal. That was probably the first time blacks ever started going down to Coral Gables. At that point, Schnellenberger realized that he needed to recruit some black kids. He got out a map and said he was going to build a fence around south Florida and make it his own. He started looking at every black high school in every black neighborhood in and around Miami. He wasn't just looking for players for the team. He was building a fan base of loyal families to support the team. It wasn't just good coaching, it was brilliant marketing.

Today they call a top high school prospect a five-star player. Back then they were called blue chippers. Those were the players all the recruiters would fight over. These black kids, they weren't blue chippers. Their stats weren't always that impressive because their schools didn't have competitive schedules. Lou Holtz and Joe Paterno, those coaches and those programs weren't even looking at these kids. They were out looking for the blue chippers: the next

Joe Namath, the next Johnny Unitas, white-bread, All-American-type motherfuckers. But Schnellenberger and his scouts, they recruit from black schools and find kids who were hungry, who had real talent, who came out of tough environments and played real football like it was life or death because it was all they had in the world. They came into Liberty City and recruited all the best guys, including Melvin Bratton, who I knew from the neighborhood. He'd gone to Northwestern, one of the best running backs ever to come out of Dade County. Same with Brett Perriman, a wide receiver from Northwestern.

Schnellenberger did three things. One, he built himself a ruthless, powerhouse team that would go on to be one of the biggest dynasties in college football history. Two, he was giving all these black kids from the worst neighborhoods and the worst high schools a chance to get an education at one of the top private colleges in the region. And three, he married the University of Miami to the inner city. He took this institution from the richest, whitest part of the city, and he made it something that black and brown people could take pride in, too. After four years of rebuilding like that, in 1984 Miami won the national championship against Nebraska right here in the Orange Bowl.

It was insane. That moment right there, winning the championship, that was the moment Miami started to come back. As bad as the riots were, it was like that in reverse, everyone celebrating. I mean, you're talking about a city where, at that period of time, it was like a fucking civil war. It was whites against blacks. It was kill or be killed. People in Liberty City just hated white people—white or anything that looked white, white Cuban or whatever. Because as far as the judicial system was concerned, it was legal to kill black people in Florida. For every Arthur McDuffie there were dozens of young black men every year who barely made a mention on the obituary page of the *Miami Herald*, and their killers were getting off scot-free. Even though the cops were doing the killing, the white juries were the ones letting the cops off. Every white person walking down the street could be one of those people on those all-white juries. So when black Miamians looked at white Miamians, they looked at them with the idea that all white people were responsible for the constant injustice.

And at the time, black people couldn't even go to parts of Miami Beach. There were certain places you just couldn't go, because you'd be profiled, dragged from your car, arrested, and possibly killed. So when Schnellenberger finally said, "Fuck it, I'm a take some of these black kids and bring them to Coral Gables," he not only changed the course of football in Miami, he changed the whole city. He said, "I'm not just gonna bring these guys to play. I'm going to bring some black people over to a barbecue at my house in the neighborhood. I don't care who likes it or not." And when you have somebody in Schnellenberger's position doing that, white folks just have to accept it—and black folks, we have to learn how to adapt to it, too. We couldn't just hole up in Liberty City and hate white people. We needed to be inclusive of everyone so we could win a championship and do it together. We had to look at this lily-white university and understand that it could belong to us, too, that we could be a part of it. That was hard.

Schnellenberger left the team in '83, and Jimmy Johnson took over. But the change was already underway, and Jimmy was committed to the same methods of recruiting and coaching the team. I credit Schnellenberger with turning this whole place around. I look at him as more than just a football coach, because he brought people together who were never together before and who never cared to be together before. What he did with that school was one of the greatest things to happen in the history of the city of Miami. It was revolutionary. But just like every other form of racial progress in this country, that change brought with it a whole new set of problems—problems that would draw me closer to the team and change the relationship of sports and hip-hop forever.

A lot of the local black kids who played for Miami in the eighties, they'd started out coming to the Pac Jam II as teens. Now they were in college and they were coming to Strawberries Too, a new club I'd just opened in Hialeah, and they were bringing a lot of the players from the team. Strawberries became the place to go for after-game parties. Through Melvin Bratton and some of the other guys I knew from coming up, I was meeting all of these players and getting to know them. I started hearing a lot of stories. They were having these issues on campus with guys selling drugs and carrying guns. They were also putting on ski masks and going out and boosting stereos from the cars of all these rich white folks in Coral Gables. Every week there was something.

They committed these crimes because they needed the money. These kids were coming from the poorest communities in Florida and going to this rich private university. They were scoring the big touchdowns and winning these games, but then they'd come off the field and be like, "Oh, fuck. I'm broke!" They'd go home and everybody in the dorm would be screaming and hollering and celebrating, and they'd be back in their rooms, hungry, couldn't even buy a pizza. They needed money for clothes, for food. Some of these guys already had families; they'd knocked some girl up in high school and needed to buy diapers. It was great that Miami was giving these guys scholarships, but scholarship money doesn't buy diapers.

It wasn't just the money. It was also the culture change. You're talking about the toughest kids from the toughest neighborhoods in Tampa, Orlando, Jacksonville. Those guys were coming into one of the wealthiest, whitest communities in all of Miami. Whenever black people first go into that type of situation, there's always tension. These players didn't have any positive experiences with white people, and that's if they had any experiences with white people at all. A lot of them were angry, resentful. These players weren't looking at the white kids like, "Hey, you're all right. You're good guys. You and me are classmates." No. They were looking at them like, "Motherfucker, your police shot my uncle." They still had that anger, that thug mentality that stayed with them from the streets. They had to learn how to let go of it, just like I had to learn how to let go of it.

This wasn't every black student at Miami. A lot of the black kids over there came from middle-class families who grew up in better neighborhoods. Or, like me, they'd been bused to a place like Miami Beach where they'd been around white people and worked a lot of that anger out. This wasn't even a majority of the players I'm talking about. It was maybe about 10 percent of the players. But it only takes one. It only takes one to screw up, and everybody's fucked.

But at the same time, it only takes one to be a leader, to set the example for the hard cases to follow. When I started hearing the stories of the trouble these guys were in, I realized they could make us all look bad. I knew this was bigger than football. I felt like I had to take it upon myself to do something. I wasn't alumni. I wasn't a booster. I just knew a lot of them frequented the club and looked up to me. Let me just go down there and have a conversation with them.

I reached out to Melvin Bratton and asked him to bring some of these dudes by the house. I explained to the players that they had a huge opportunity to get an education and they were about to fuck that up.

I spoke to them from a larger, historical standpoint, not just about the team. I'd say, "Do you know these people never wanted blacks in Coral Gables from the beginning? That they put clauses in the deeds to the houses over there that made it illegal to sell houses to black folks because they think we're animals? They *want* us to look bad. Here you got a guy like Schnellenberger opening up opportunities to bring y'all down there and y'all doing wild shit? There's a lot of people on that side of town saying, 'Don't bring them niggers down here. Why you brought them niggers down here?' And if y'all fuck this up, then they going to say, 'Yeah, they are fucking animals. Those are some fucked-up people.'"

I schooled them, "You have to think about the black kids coming up after you, because when you fuck this up, another black kid after you won't be able to have the opportunity to get an education. And on top of that, you're going to get your ass thrown in jail and any chance of you going to the NFL is going to be done. Y'all need to get your shit together. Y'all need to think about this as an opportunity to better yourself, get your education, and be able to move on to the next level."

I would deal with the toughest of the toughest on the team. Jerome Brown was a tough guy, Winston Moss was a tough guy. Warren Sapp was a tough guy. I would keep tabs on them. I'd mentor them. The nice guys didn't need any help. The tough ones? I was looking out for them. Every year, the freshmen were coming in and I'd ask, "Who's the gangsta? Who's the hard case? Tell him to come see me. Bring that crazy motherfucker over here. Let me make sure his head is screwed on right." I'd bring him to the club, show him a good time, try and keep his mind on the positive.

The hardest of the hard cases was Mark Caesar, who played defensive tackle. Mark was a good kid, but crazy. Lots of bad ideas in his head, a lot of anger. He didn't hate every individual white person—he had white friends on the team—but he hated the Man, the establishment. He was always wound up about it.

I could see it getting worse the longer he was out in Coral

Gables, full of anger and resentment, surrounded by all these rich white people.

Tough situation, tough kid. I knew he was a fuse waiting to blow. I knew I needed to keep him close by me, keep him occupied, keep his mind right. Any downtime he got, I told him to bring his ass by my office, to come to the club, to stay out on my boat for a night or two. At that time I'd just bought my yacht. After *As Nasty as They Wanna Be* sold a million copies, I bought a fifty-foot yacht and named it *Scandalous*. I put "Liberty City" on the back, so when the police saw all these black people on a boat they'd know that we didn't steal it. I'd send Mark Caesar to go spend the night out there because I knew staying in the dorm, being in that kind of rich, white environment, it just wasn't comfortable for him. He spent most of his college life not necessarily living in the dorm but staying out on the boat because he needed that space. I would take him out there and make sure he was all right.

Mark Caesar and Warren Sapp, those were the main guys I was working with. I had to keep an eye on those two. They couldn't have any downtime or they'd end up in some kind of trouble. I had to make their life comfortable, even brought them on the road with me. Those fuckers would play on Saturday, leave after the game, and get on the jet with 2 Live Crew. If I was in Dallas, they would be in Dallas. If I was in Detroit, they were in Detroit. We'd fly out Saturday and they'd be back Sunday night for school the next day. They were playing football at the University of Miami and living the life of a rock star on the side.

None of this was authorized by the school, of course. It wasn't anything associated with the athletic program, the NCAA, the alumni, or the boosters. It was just me taking it upon myself to talk to these kids. From what I could see, they didn't have anybody at the school to talk to, because nobody at that school came from where they came from. I felt like they needed help, and I helped them. I helped a lot of those kids get their heads right, but unfortunately all the mentoring in the world wasn't going to make a dent in the biggest problem they faced: money.

The NCAA regulations on student athletes are inhumane. It might be going too far to compare it to slavery, but it's an immoral system no matter how you try and justify it. The NCAA makes billions off of these kids, and they get paid nothing. My first thought was, Shit, I'll give you a job, hire you on at the warehouse. But then I learned more about all the regulations and found out I couldn't. They are not allowed to get jobs while they play. People don't want alumni or boosters using fake jobs to funnel money to these kids. They can't work, can't accept a free burger or a sandwich, can't even take five dollars for autographing a jersey for another student. They can't accept money or benefits of any kind from anyone other than their parents or legal guardians, but these inner-city kids, their parents didn't have shit to give them. They were all poor. Some of the athletes had families of their own. I had guys coming to me, saying, "I can't feed my family. This shit ain't feeding me, man. I got a daughter. My mamma and them crying. I got a thousand goddamn family members at home. Everybody think we made it, but I don't got nothing. I gotta get money."

It reminded me of my uncle Ricky and those invisible chains. These kids were working, but they didn't own their own labor. They didn't have the freedom to earn a living, on or off the field. It made me think back to when I was bused over to Miami Beach High, how they got me over there with the promise of education, making me feel like I was part of the club, but really they were just passing me along and using me to play ball. It was the same thing with the kids at Miami. On the one hand, they had a great opportunity. On the other hand, they were being used and exploited.

The University of Miami has a billion-dollar impact on the economy of south Florida. After Schnellenberger took over and the team started winning, applications to the school went up every year for years after that, all driven by the popularity of the team. You're talking about millions of tuition dollars to pay for new teachers, new programs. Damn near every time the team went to a bowl game, the administration put up some new building on campus, but the kids responsible for it weren't getting shit. And we know damn well they weren't in there getting the same level of education. They were like me, coming out of school and reading on a fifth-grade level, and if they didn't make it in the NFL, they were done.

I knew these kids were being forced into a situation where some of them were going to do some bad shit, make some big mistakes. So I'd tell them, "Guys, if you're having problems, come talk to me. If you're about to go into somebody's house and rob some kids, whatever you do, don't do that. Before you go do any kind of stupid shit, come see me. If you need to feed your family, I'll get you some money to feed your family."

I didn't know how I was going to do it. I couldn't even hire them off the books. That was too high profile, and people could find out. Going back to my roots and how my parents raised me, I wasn't about giving handouts. You want something, you work for it. You want to go to the high school dance, get your ass out there and clean the windows. I didn't want these guys demeaning themselves, coming around and begging, asking me for a couple hundred bucks here and there. It's degrading for anybody to have to do that. Back to common sense: how can I do this to where I can help these kids help themselves in this situation?

I decided to pay them to be the best at the work they're already doing. If the school won't pay them a fair wage for their labor, I would. I told the guys, "If you get a tackle, come by the club and I'll give you twenty-five dollars. If you get a sack, I'm gonna give you fifty dollars. An interception, one hundred dollars." It was comparable to what my parents did when we received good grades as kids. It was always that way with youth football, too. You went out to the park, you got a touchdown, Uncle Joe gave you five dollars. That was customary shit in the neighborhood.

I wasn't paying for dirty hits, or for knocking opponents out of the game or anything like that. It was just for clean tackles, completed passes, for doing their job well. I wasn't some booster, bribing these kids just because I wanted to see my team in the playoffs. Hell, I wasn't even an alum. My focus was 100 percent on the kids.

After I started paying them, these kids worked their asses off even more than before, because that's how they were gonna take care of their family.

The players developed that same work ethic I always had. They were increasing the value of their stock. You accumulate sacks and become one of the dominant players in college football. Every NFL team wants you. A million sacks will get you drafted in the first round, or a million receptions will get you drafted in the first round. I gave them the incentive to help them out of a fucked-up situation. Together, me and those guys started to change the game of football forever.

I was having the time of my life. I was helping these kids but also, as a fan, I was more involved with the game. There weren't any security checks, and the players started inviting me down to the sideline. I became a part of that crew every week. If I was in Miami and there was a home game, I was there watching from the sidelines. It was fucking incredible. Every year, from the Schnellenberger era through Jimmy Johnson and Dennis Erickson, these kids from Liberty City and the poor black neighborhoods of south Florida were building one of the greatest dynasties in college football. There were more national championships in '87 and '89 and '91. They put together the longest home-game winning streak in NCAA history. These players were coming out as top NFL draft picks year after year: Warren Sapp, Michael Irvin, Alonzo Highsmith, and dozens more.

The Hurricanes were dominating the game, but the sports media hated them. They were too black, had too much attitude. The sports media has a story they want to tell, same as the regular media does, and the story they wanted to tell about college football was that old bullshit about Knute Rockne and the Fighting Irish, Lou Holtz and Joe Paterno molding the fine, All-American white boys of the Midwest with a few respectable negroes thrown in, some Jackie Robinsons, to show how far everything had come.

The black guys at Miami didn't fit that story, so the media started writing a different one. There were sportswriters in New York claiming that the University of Miami is a bunch of thugs. It came from everywhere. The 1988 game between Notre Dame and Miami, they named it "Catholics vs. Convicts." *Sports Illustrated* named Miami "Thug U." In one issue, instead of the players' game stats, they printed the players' criminal records. These were kids that came from neighborhoods where life was tough, where you didn't always make good choices and where the cops would arrest you for any kind of bullshit. They were playing at Miami because they were good kids who wanted like hell to get out of that life. The media had already made up their minds on it: these kids are no good.

The Miami Hurricanes and 2 Live Crew, we had a lot in common. We were both outcasts. We were both winning teams that got no respect for our success. They were living the same life I was living. We'd sit in my living room talking about what to do about it.

They wound up taking on a lot of ideas from my life because our situations were similar. The way I responded to all my censors and critics, they decided to do the same: If you think we're too loud, we're gonna be louder. If you think we're too black, we're gonna be blacker. Because we can. Because this is *our* game. Because we're better than you, and we can prove it on the field. We don't have to back down and lower our heads for you anymore.

Those guys became the Muhammad Alis of college football, not just dominating the sport but boasting and talking shit about it. It became known that there was a certain type of guy who played on this team, a Miami guy, a guy who played the game with a chip on his shoulder. Miami became known for that swagger, that flashy attitude. Those guys used to sit up in my house during the week, Wednesday or Thursday, and talk about the shit that they were gonna do at the games. "Yeah, I'm gonna take my helmet off and we gonna dance!" "Yeah!" The end-zone dances, the finger wagging, the high-stepping across the goal line, doing backflips, dancing over the guy you just tackled. We all concocted that shit. It was our way of venting our frustration with the way we were treated. It was our way of saying: "Fuck everybody."

That changed the game forever right there. These guys weren't just numbered jerseys anymore. They had personalities. They were superstars. Eventually, the NCAA tried to censor the team the same way it was being done to me in the music arena. After the 1991 Cotton Bowl against Texas, when Randal Hill ran a forty-eight-yard touchdown straight through the end zone and then up the stadium tunnel, pretending to shoot the Texas players with imaginary pistols, the NCAA passed new regulations against excessive celebration on the field. People called it the Miami Rule. The video they put together to show teams how not to behave was pretty much just a Hurricanes highlight reel.

For a long time, nobody knew I had anything to do with the team. I was just another black guy on the sidelines. Covering the sport were old white sportswriters from the *Miami Herald*, guys like Edwin Polk, who didn't know anything about 2 Live Crew, didn't know anything about the hood. I wasn't immediately recognizable to them like a Mick Jagger. These old guys didn't know who the fuck I was. Then came this young journalist, Dan Le Batard, who went to Miami before going to work at the *Herald*. He knew what was going on. He was aware of the hip-hop influence. The writer questioned what the fuck is a rapper doing down on the sidelines? Maybe he's a bad influence on these kids?

One part of my thing was that I had these Luke Records scarves that I wore during my performances. It was part of my persona. Offstage I was Luther Campbell, playing golf and taking meetings with my lawyers and accountants. Onstage, I'd put that scarf on and turn into Luke, Uncle Luke, Luke Skyywalker, up there yelling, "Fuck everybody! Fuck you! We want some pussy!" It was my thing, to put that scarf on and transform. Before I knew it, all the black guys at Miami were going, "We want the scarf." They were wearing the scarf on the sidelines. And when they put that scarf on, it had the same impact as it did on me. "Fuck it. Fuck everybody." They were talking shit, walking all over people, dancing on top of folks, getting in everybody's face.

The president of the university, Tad Foote, and the athletic director, Sam Jankovich, didn't like the street attitude these guys were bringing, and they didn't want to be associated with some rapper. Jankovich did an editorial in the paper saying the scarf had to go and they were going to have this big meeting to put a stop to it.

At the big meeting: "Anybody wearing the scarf, you're going to be suspended." At that time, it was just the black kids wearing the scarf, and for them it was really a black pride, Black Power kind of thing. What happened was surprising. The day the administration had this meeting was the day the white players asked the black kids to bring them to my warehouse to get scarves. They all wore them at practice that day. The white kids and the black kids, scarfed up. *That's* what integration was supposed to be. Integration didn't have to just be blacks submitting to white folks' rules. Integration was supposed to be young blacks and whites together, making a new set of rules.

The scarf, by extension, meant Luke Records wasn't just a black thing anymore. It was a Miami thing. It became a totem. Now if a kid didn't go to the University of Miami, even if he went to another college, he called for the scarf. Ben Hanks, this kid from Overtown who went to the University of Florida, called for a scarf. Derrick Thomas wore one. He came from Miami and went to Alabama and then on to become the all-time sack leader for the Kansas City Chiefs.

I had successfully blended sports with hip-hop. It all started at the University of Miami with Luther Campbell and 2 Live Crew. We had players in Luke Gear out on the field. We had girls in Miami gear dancing in our videos. We were bringing the hip-hop culture together with the culture of college sports and, later on, with the culture of professional sports.

A few years later, Snoop Dogg was out on the sidelines at USC games, head to toe in Trojans gear. There was Ice Cube hanging with the Oakland Raiders, the fucking tough guys. Big-name rappers started wearing the jerseys of the tough guys, the players we felt were hip-hop oriented. I had read about Allen Iverson. He was a tough kid who grew up in a tough neighborhood. He was a hip-hop kid. He made it out of the ghetto, similar to what we did. I related to him. So I got me an Allen Iverson Georgetown jersey and I started wearing that onstage.

On the other side you had the pro ballplayers acting like the University of Miami guys. They started bringing that swagger to the NFL, to the NBA, wearing the cornrows and shit. They all wanted to be rappers. You had Shaquille O'Neal putting out platinum rap albums, Kobe Bryant putting out singles. A few years later, it all came together at the highest possible level: Jay Z bringing the Nets to Brooklyn, owning a piece of the team, designing the gear with an all-black hip-hop style to it.

The marriage of hip-hop and sports was an important cultural moment. Same as we did with the music, we used the power of sports to tell the rest of America, "Hey, we're coming in. This color line y'all tried to put up, get ready, because we're coming over and we're bringing all of our blackness with us."

I taught those kids who came down to my club, not knowing how to feed their families. I taught them how to walk that line that every black man from the hood has got to walk. I taught them to leave that thug shit behind. No breaking the law and doing wild shit. But you also don't ever apologize for who you are or where you come from. You don't ever apologize for being black. You obey the law, you play by the rules, but that doesn't mean for a second that you conform to what other people want you to be. You be yourself. Be as loud and as flashy and as nasty as you wanna be, and don't ever apologize for it.

NASTY

The arrest of the store clerk in the Panhandle, the trial in Alexander City, the harassment I was getting from the administration at the University of Miami—I knew I was doing something right. If the morality police hadn't come after 2 Live Crew, I probably would have gotten tired of the dirty rap and just moved on to the next thing. But that's not what happened.

By 1988, around election time—any kind of election, from Congress to district judge to county commissioner—2 Live Crew became a target. To get some instant press, politicians would make a speech about the dirty nigger music corrupting the youth of your Podunk Alabama town, then they'd send the cops to arrest some store clerk and make a lot of noise about how we needed to be locked up, too. We had sheriffs coming after us, city councils coming after us. We had judges, lawyers, the PTA. We even had Vice President Dan Quayle making statements about us. It's when

I became more aware of all these hypocritical right wingers with nothing better to do.

For whatever reason, censorship became the white establishment's big crusade that year. All these local two-bit sheriffs and district attorneys weren't just spontaneously deciding to come after us: the morality police had put us in their sights, as well as every major Christian and family organization in America—Tipper Gore and the rest of the Washington housewives of the PMRC, the American Family Association, the Moral Majority, Focus on the Family, the 700 Club, the PTL Club. Every two-bit pro-family anti-obscenity group you can name, they all came out of the woodwork to attack us. All you needed was a fax machine or a TV camera and you could join the crusade to save little white kids from the evil of four-letter words. At first it was moms and church groups going after heavy-metal bands with bullshit accusations of satanism and devil worship. Later it was Jesse Helms and Congress going after the National Endowment for the Arts and artists like Robert Mapplethorpe for using tax dollars to create "homosexual pornography." Following came the biggest villain of all: hip-hop. The dirty, horny, violent, angry, oversexed black man. Pretty soon all the attention was on groups like N.W.A, Public Enemy, and 2 Live Crew. We put the black in the blacklist.

When *Move Somethin'* went gold and we had the problems in the Panhandle and Alexander City and I felt the controversy starting, again I wasn't afraid. These family groups were usually good for business. They got us instant notoriety. Most of the white people buying our records were hearing about our music for the first time when somebody tried to ban us. But at the same time, it pissed me off. It was the same as when we played the concerts in African Square Park back in the Ghetto Style days and the cops tried to break us up. I wasn't doing anything wrong and people were messing with me for their own political ends. I was young. I was stubborn. I was part of a generation of young black folks who weren't going to do what we were told anymore. We were going to stay true to who we are and what our fans liked about us.

It was my introduction to how the media worked, how politics worked. It's not about telling the truth. It's not about giving people the facts. It's about telling a story, making the facts fit an exciting narrative, either to get ratings or to get elected or to get people to give you money. Every story has to have a good guy and a bad guy, and the way this story was being told, I was the bad guy. This was an old-time western, the Gunfight at the O.K. Corral, and I was the guy in the black hat. I realized that no matter how many stickers I put on the records or how many times I called record stores to say please do not sell this to kids, no matter what I did, I would always be the guy with the black hat. I embraced it. If I'm the bad guy, I'll be the bad guy; if that's the role they want me to play, I'll play it to the hilt. If white folks were scared of the big, bad, oversexed black man, I'd be the biggest, baddest, nastiest, dirtiest oversexed black man they could possibly imagine—just to prove that I could be. Just to prove that I had a right to be that if I wanted to. When we went into the studio for our next album, I was angry. This shit was personal. The result of that was our biggest album ever and one of the biggest rap albums of all time: *As Nasty as They Wanna Be.*

Our goal with *Nasty* was to take the concept of a 2 Live Crew album to the absolute limit, to make it as insane and explicit and raunchy as we could while still keeping it funny. It was all there in the title. It was a provocation, a dare to the morality police: This is who we are. You want us, come and get us. It worked. *Move Somethin'* sold nearly a million copies. *Nasty* would double that. When we released it in the summer of 1989, it shipped with five hundred thousand preorders, certified gold before it even left the warehouse. The radio-safe version, *As Clean as They Wanna Be,* came out at the same time, and that sold less but it still did well.

We took everything that made our first albums a success and took it even further. It was some wild shit. The songs were raunchier: "Dick Almighty," "The Fuck Shop," "Put Her in the Buck." People loved it. And not just because it was dirty. It was me and Mixx and the other guys firing on all cylinders and coming up with great shit.

I'll never forget the night I was sitting up late watching TV. I love war movies, and Stanley Kubrick's *Full Metal Jacket* was on HBO and that scene with Matthew Modine and the Vietnamese prostitute came on and she's going, "Oh, me so horny. Me so *horny*. Me love you *long* time." I couldn't stop laughing. I was like, *bam*, that's a song right there. That's the hook. The next morning I went to the guys, gave them the idea, and they ran with it. Ice and Marquis wrote up the lyrics, and my man Mixx was all over it. He always had a crate of R&B, soul, rock, and funk records that he had ready to cut and sample. He pulled out "Firecracker" by Mass Production and had the basic track done the next day. The whole album was like that.

Everything we did got harder. The music got harder. The album covers got more graphic. The shows went off the deep end. In the beginning it was just us onstage, me being the hype man and Mixx on the turntables with Marquis and Fresh Kid Ice out front. We added dancers, male and female. I knew the girls liked the music and they would come to the shows; the guys were there for the girls, and the girls were there for the guys.

The music was getting more sexually driven and shocking, and the shows began to reflect that. We got rid of the guy dancers and started bringing on the girls with the big asses, girls like Cindy and Mona and Annette. We kept putting women on our album covers, and I didn't want no skinny-ass models. Down in Miami, it's all about a full-figured woman. Girls with curves. Somebody who can shake that ass. They were real women who could dance and they was fine as hell. People loved them.

During the shows, sometimes the girls in the audience would jump onstage and pull off their shirts and dance around topless, just because they wanted to. It was crazy. I started thinking about Tootsie's, the strip club my bodyguards Damien and Rocco used to take me to back in the Pac Jam days. I said, "Fuck it. I'm just going to bring strippers onstage." We started replacing the dancers with strippers. They were coming out with G-strings and wet T-shirts and pasties. It was like a strip club onstage. I brought on other elements to the show, like a big-ass fucking Jacuzzi coming down out the ceiling with some naked girls in it. Shit was wild. Whatever I thought of, I did. These were rock shows. I was living the life of a rock and roller, because that's what I wanted. I always considered myself a rock and roller. I listened to that more than R&B. That's why you hear the Kinks and Manfred Mann and Van Halen and Bruce Springsteen on our records. I wanted to bring to rap the visual element and lifestyle that you saw at rock shows and rock videos but in a way that had a black sensibility and showed black taste.

It was the same with our videos. If you look at the rap videos from those days, there were no girls in the videos. There was no sex in the videos. It would just be a couple of rappers on a soundstage with a boombox and some breakdancers and a little fake graffiti to make it look ghetto. Total bullshit, and that was the only thing happening. The video vixens and the real black women, nobody else had done that yet. This was years before Sir Mix-a-Lot and "Baby Got Back." There were no rap videos set in the club or out on the beach with girls in bikinis. We changed all that.

Like everything else I did, I usually had to do it on my own and use common sense to figure it out. The videos were no different. There was no such thing as the film commission down in Miami to do these videos, no unions and crews and shit like that. I got these college guys from the University of Miami film school. They came down to my house in Miami Lakes to shoot the videos for us. They got credit as interns for their class. Around the same time, a black strip club called Rolex opened up in Miami. From there I was getting more exotic dancers for the videos. I would shoot the pretty girls' faces and then I'd shoot the ass of a curvy woman. So when you saw it, you'd be like, "Man, they got these fine girls with curves!"

I would tell the girls, "Make love to the camera like you making a guy spend more money." They would get into the camera and they would be fucking dancing in a seductive way. In these videos we're all in the pool, dancers shaking their asses, it's all some wild and crazy party. Once our videos started airing, Miami strip clubs started blowing up because everyone was coming down wanting to see these girls in the 2 Live Crew videos. More and better-looking girls started coming down to work and make that money.

The first video we shot was "Move Somethin'." We took it even further for "Me So Horny." Initially they wouldn't even let us on MTV or BET. But there was this channel called Video Jukebox. With Video Jukebox, you could call up, pay a fee through your telephone, and they would show the video. Our songs would come on and you had these videos of half-naked women and people in the pool partying. When that shit hit the TV it fucking blew up. Instant hit. We stayed on all day. All around the country, people were calling in to pay to see it. Now we had a visual vehicle. We weren't being played on the radio, but motherfuckers were locked into Video Jukebox, and they were buying our videos religiously. Eventually, MTV2 had to buy Video Jukebox because it was taking so many of their viewers, which we all thought was great.

Nasty was selling tens of thousands of copies a week, plus I had all the sales of our earlier albums and the other acts I was signing. As I told Will Smith and all those guys back in the day: I was getting *all* the money. They say that the total net worth of your assets is ten times the amount of cash in the bank. The most I ever had in the bank was ten million, over half of that from *Nasty* alone, so I'd have to guess the most I was ever worth was $100 million—and I was only twenty-eight years old.

I can't really say for sure how much there was. To be honest, I wasn't counting the money. I was too busy making it. And I never cared about the money. I really didn't. None of that was promised to me. I was supposed to be in a prison cell or in a coffin alongside my man Handsome Harry. Everything I got on top of that was gravy, as far as I was concerned. For me, what I was doing with Luke Records, it was more about the fight, the struggle, proving I could do something that society had told me I couldn't do. Aside from buying my parents a new house, I spent some of the money on myself, bought a house on a golf course in Miami Lakes and a waterfront condo downtown. I bought a yacht, some cars. But almost all the money I made up to that point I reinvested in my businesses. I put it toward creating jobs in Liberty City. That's what was important to me.

As the 1990s took off, I was on fire. Everything I touched turned to gold. Most of the major hip-hop acts of that time were busy complaining about getting fucked by their labels. I was the manager and face of one of the hottest rap groups in the country. I had twelve acts signed to my own label, the largest independent black-owned record label in America. I had seventeen employees working under me at my plush office on Biscayne Boulevard. I had an old guy named Joe Coalsky, a legend in the music business, doing the distribution and the collecting. I had another guy, Slack Johnson, who had worked at major record companies, doing marketing and promotion.

Just two years after selling records out the back of my old beat-up Honda, I'd moved to this plush office suite on Biscayne Boulevard. Now I'd even outgrown that. The offices weren't big enough. My warehouse wasn't big enough, either. I moved into a bigger space, one massive, all-in-one complex right in the heart of Liberty City. It was probably the single biggest commercial investment in Liberty City since the riots. We took over this building, cleaned it out, and made it into a warehouse, a studio, an office with conference rooms, and a teen disco that could hold a thousand kids every Friday and Saturday night. All under one roof. We even had a retail shop where people could come in and buy records and merchandise right from the source. The records were moving so fast I hired a couple dozen more guys from the neighborhood to handle the inventory.

My empire was growing one piece at a time. I started diversifying. The club scene was blowing up in Miami, and I'm the kind of guy who'd rather own the club than spend money in someone else's. If I'm throwing the party, I also want to be the one selling the booze. I decided it was time to break into adult nightclubs. That's when I bought Strawberries in Hialeah. The club was already popping when I bought it. My brother Brannard, the executive chef, I brought him in to run it. I was making all this adult music, and now I had a place to test that, too. After Strawberries took off I opened another club, Miami's, in Pensacola.

All of my businesses were operating in the black: the clubs, the record label. I was making shitloads of money. I was producing more albums, signing new artists, expanding my operations. Everything I did with my money was to make more money. Like when I bought a company jet. With 2 Live Crew, we were on the road constantly, but I always needed to be back in Miami during the week to run the businesses. It was a waste of time to fly commercial; I needed to fly when I needed to fly. I wanted to do two shows in one night and then get back home for the next morning. When I saw how much it cost to rent a private jet, I was like, Why pay that money to someone else?

I bought a plane, and instead of having the promoter pay the travel expenses to the private jet company, I had them pay me to provide my own transportation. You hear about rap stars buying private jets and you think it's some crazy rock-star bullshit. Not the way I did it. My jet paid for itself and then some. Fifteen years later, Jay Z was rapping, "I'm not a businessman. I'm a business, man." Guess who he learned that from?

The wealthier I got, and the higher I climbed, the more racism and hypocrisy I saw. I'd take a bunch of guys out on my yacht for Miami's Columbus Day regatta, and we'd go from boat to boat, partying. The shit I saw rich white people doing was way raunchier than anything we ever put in a 2 Live Crew song. I saw white executives, politicians, lawyers, all having this huge drug-fueled orgy out on the water. They were all respectable, upstanding citizens, and I was the bad guy. The only real difference was they were hiding their sins while I rapped about it and put it on TV. Oh, and I was black.

Once *Nasty* came out, the controversy surrounding it showed the racism and hypocrisy of America for what it really was. With that album we were spoiling for a fight, and we got it, thanks to one batshit homophobic Bible-thumping clown named Jack Thompson. Every crusade starts with a true believer. Most of the people who came after us ended up being self-serving hypocrites who wanted to score political points; they didn't actually care about obscenity. But Jack Thompson really and truly believed that 2 Live Crew was the single greatest threat facing the future of America's youth. Jack Thompson is—and I can't emphasize this enough—crazier than a shithouse rat. He actually was made to meet with a psychiatrist to prove his sanity because everything he did and said was insane. He used to attach pictures of Batman to his letters and faxes to identify himself. That's how convinced he was of his own importance as a crusader for decency and morality.

Thompson's first real headlines came when he went after the popular Miami radio DJ Neil Rogers. Rogers was gay and out of the closet, and Thompson didn't believe homosexuals should be allowed to poison the airwaves with their filth. Thompson was obsessed. He harassed Rogers so much that he ended up getting barred from ever saying Rogers's name in public. Thompson then decided to run against Janet Reno, Bill Clinton's future attorney general, when she ran for state's attorney for Miami-Dade County. The black community loved Janet Reno, black women especially, because she had a reputation for putting deadbeat dads in jail for not paying their child support. You'd go to the Martin Luther King parade and Janet Reno would be the only white person there—period. So I thought, Man, we gotta do a fucking Janet Reno song. I called my cousin Anquette and we recorded a track called "Janet Reno" supporting her candidacy. *"Janet Reno come to town, riding on a pony, dah, dah, dah. . . ."*

It was just something we did as a fun little joke, but the song blew up all over local radio, big fucking song. Everybody was talking about it on TV. Thompson got pissed. He started calling the radio stations, saying they had to take the song off during the election because you have to have equal time for each candidate. I did a radio interview about the whole thing. It was a Christian radio show, and Jack Thompson was on the segment. Thompson just lost it, going off and telling everyone that Janet Reno was a dyke, 2 Live Crew was evil, and all this wild shit. That was my first encounter with somebody telling me to my face that my music was devil music. I was like, "What the fuck you talking about? Y'all crazy."

I thought this guy was just a crackpot. I didn't give him one moment's thought after that. He ended up losing the election by a lot, but he felt like *I* made him lose it, and then he went on this mad crusade. He tried to get Janet Reno to prosecute me, but Janet

Reno wouldn't fucking touch me. Then Thompson led an antigay protest in front of her house, and I launched a protest in front of his house. I took everyone from Liberty City and sent them all to his neighborhood, sent all these black people out to lily-white Coral Gables. I rented buses, vans, and shit and loaded all the people with protest signs and went and stood out in front of his house. I fucked with him hard.

Thompson started a fax and letter-writing campaign. He wrote to every politician, judge, media outlet, and law-enforcement official in Florida, sending them lyrics from *Nasty* and telling them that my music was obscene and a dangerous threat to innocent children across the state. Thompson was just an ex–golf pro with a law degree. I always knew he was a joke, but some people thought he was credible just because he was a lawyer; they thought he was writing as someone representing the law and the Constitution, not as a nut job chasing his own personal obsession. Plus it was a juicy story for the media. So he kept picking up more and more steam and people started interviewing him. He was getting his fifteen minutes of fame.

Almost every sane Florida politician that got harassed by Thompson ignored him. Every one except the big one: Bob Martinez, the governor. He fell for it hook, line, and sinker. Martinez, being Hispanic, was always looking for issues to play to his conservative white Republican base, and he thought this would be a big win: he'd silence the foul-mouthed nigras debasing the image of the fine state of Florida. After getting Thompson's letter, Martinez turned around and sent out a letter of his own to the state attorney, Peter Antonacci, calling us "vulgar" and "disgusting," and even suggesting that Luke Records could be prosecuted under Florida's RICO act—that's the anti-racketeering statute they use to go after organized crime and the mob. Antonacci thought it was bullshit and basically kicked it down to county-level law enforcement to pursue if they wanted. Pretty much all of them took the letters and tossed them in the garbage. In Dade County, Janet Reno went on record saying she had real crimes to worry about.

Only one guy took the bait. Sheriff Nick Navarro of Broward County, the asshole from *Cops* who was busy making himself a reality-TV celebrity by hounding drunk rednecks at the beach and throwing young black dudes down on the hoods of cars. Navarro never met a camera he didn't like, and when he saw a chance to go after this obscene rap group in his own backyard with the blessing of the governor, it was the role he was born to play. He sent one of his deputies out to buy the album. They typed up the dirty lyrics and an affidavit and took it to a judge, Mel Grossman, to get a determination of probable cause saying that the material was likely to be found obscene, had no artistic merit, and could therefore be banned. Grossman, who apparently didn't care for our sense of humor, gave them the order for probable cause.

At that point, there hadn't been any hearing or jury trial to establish that the album was obscene by the standards of the law. But that didn't stop Navarro. He and his deputies went around Broward letting record stores know that anyone who sold the album could be arrested, even before the album had been legally deemed obscene during an adversary hearing. In other words, they were engaging in prior restraint. They were violating my First Amendment right to free speech.

Up until that point I hadn't been taking any of this seriously. I thought it was all a bunch of posturing for the cameras. But now my albums were disappearing from stores. My constitutional rights were being taken away. This was what my father and my uncle Ricky had prepared me for when they taught me the history of what black folks in this country had been through. I'd seen this fucking movie before, and I was ready to fight.

At the time I had an entertainment lawyer, Allen Jacobi, but he

felt like I would need more legal help than he could offer and rec-
ommended me to Bruce Rogow, a former professor of his at Nova
University in Fort Lauderdale. He was like, "Let's hire the best.
This guy Bruce Rogow."

Rogow had no idea who 2 Live Crew was, didn't even know
much about rap, but he was the perfect guy for the job. His track
record made him look like the Perry Mason of lawyers. He didn't
fucking lose. Not only was he a First Amendment expert, he'd been
a lawyer with the civil rights movement in Mississippi back in '64
and '65. He had spent a lot of time in Africa, and his house was
full of African artwork. He was this older white dude in a double-
breasted suit and a bow tie, and he seemed to know more about
black and African people than I did.

"Do you think I can win?"

"Yeah, I think you can win. And even if you lose, you win."

"What kinda jive white-man talk is that?" I asked.

"If the courts don't find the album obscene, you're off the hook.
If the courts do find it obscene, you'll sell a ton of records and make
a lot of money." After he told me that I was like, Okay, I like this
dude. He would defend anyone's right to free speech. Even mine.
During the trial, we went to lunch one day and he even picked up
the check. It was the only time in my life I'd ever seen an attorney
pick up a check. After that, I liked him even more.

Rogow felt that the best defense was a good offense. He immediately wanted to make a preemptive strike against Navarro by accusing him of prior restraint. Nineteen days had already passed since
Navarro had started harassing record-store owners. Yet all they had
was the order declaring there was probable cause for obscenity; there
was still no official ruling on the subject. None of what Navarro was
doing was legal. It was pure intimidation. We had to force the issue
and make them prove the album was obscene. On March 16, 1990,
we sued the sheriff of Broward County.

The case that Rogow put together rested on the Supreme Court's *Miller v. California* test on obscenity. There's three parts to the test. First, does the material, taken as a whole, appeal solely to the prurient interest? In other words: does it turn you on? Second, does it violate the standards of decency in the local community? Third, and most importantly, you have to prove that "the material in question, when taken as a whole, has no serious literary, artistic, political, or scientific value." Usually, if something has any value, artistic or otherwise, it cannot be banned. The question was: is *As Nasty as They Wanna Be* art? The federal district judge in the case was Jose Gonzalez, a Hispanic liberal who had been appointed by Jimmy Carter. Rogow thought he would be a strong First Amendment defender. Also, in the Alexander City trial, the jury had judged our last album not obscene—and that was in Alabama. This was a slam dunk. There was no fucking way we could lose.

The hearing started on May 14. The first thing we had to prove was that Navarro had engaged in prior restraint. That was easy. It was clear that he'd overstepped his authority by intimidating store owners without bothering to get a ruling on the album. Next we came to the *Miller v. California* test. Here Rogow was brilliant. To prove that the album didn't solely appeal to the prurient interest, he called a clinical psychologist. She testified to what we knew was true: the album didn't make you want to have sex, like pornography does. It made you laugh. People are far more turned on by visual stimulation than audio. She said she'd never had one patient who ever complained about getting a hard-on by listening to rap.

Then, to prove that the album didn't violate existing community standards of decency, all Rogow had to do was go shopping. Across the street from the sheriff's office in Broward County— literally right across the motherfucking street—was one of the largest adult bookstores in south Florida. Rogow went in there and bought a whole bunch of shit. I'm talking nasty, freaky shit, videos and magazines, S&M, bondage, people having sex with animals. It was wild.

Rogow brought all this back into the courtroom and he put it all on display in great detail. One of the exhibits he submitted to the court was this lesbian movie with two women masturbating together. There was no jury in this trial, only the judge. Rogow played this for Gonzalez, who was all alone up there. He had to sit there and watch as Rogow played him this tape. Rogow played *the whole scene*, beginning to end, nothing but two chicks fingering themselves. It went on for like ten minutes. Gonzalez was so fucking uncomfortable up there. It was fucking brilliant.

Proving the album had artistic merit was the other leg of the case. Rogow knocked that out of the park, too. He brought in Greg Baker, a music critic for the *Miami New Times*, who knew all about us and the history of Miami Bass. He brought in John Leland, a music critic from New York who was one of the most knowledgeable critics on the subject of hip-hop at the time. Baker and Leland laid it all out for Gonzalez: the history of call-and-response in black music, how Latin and Caribbean sounds evolved into Miami Bass, the whole history of scratching and sampling that started with Kool Herc and Grandmaster Flash in the Bronx, how this was a groundbreaking, innovative form of music.

It was now time for the defense to present their case. Only they didn't have one. The lawyers for Sheriff Navarro didn't call one expert witness for their side. They thought all they had to do was show the judge transcriptions of our lyrics and the rest would be self-evident: it's a bunch of black guys rapping about pussy in front of white people. Guilty. Case closed. It's also important to point out that this whole trial revolved around violating community standards for decency, and how many citizen complaints had Navarro received? Not one. Literally not a single citizen of Broward County, black or white, had actually called or written his office to complain about our music. In fact, it was just the opposite: people were buying thousands of copies a month. All this had been stirred up by one religious zealot and some publicity-seeking politicians. The whole thing was unbelievable.

We were sure we had it in the bag. At the end of Rogow's closing arguments, I was all smiles. Besides, no album in the history of recorded music had ever been found obscene. But there has to be a first time for everything. When we gathered back in court to hear Gonzalez's ruling, he started out by slamming Navarro for engaging in prior restraint. Navarro, he said, was guilty on that count. But then Gonzalez dropped a bomb. He declared that *Nasty* was, in fact, obscene. We couldn't believe it. I don't think Navarro and his lawyers believed it, either. It turned out that Gonzalez, though politically liberal, was actually very culturally conservative. He only listened to classical music and opera, and no matter what the experts told him, he thought our music was a bunch of noisy filth.

I was shocked, angry, dumbfounded. I walked out of the courthouse into the wall of cameras and microphones. Bruce was cool as a cucumber. He hadn't expected the verdict, either, but he was confident we'd win on appeal. He'd told me at the beginning that even if I lost I'd win. I tried to keep that mind. When they asked me what I thought about the decision, I said it was worth less than toilet paper. And it was. I wouldn't have wiped my ass with it.

I thought I'd leave them with one last sound bite before I rolled out. Jack Thompson, the man whose delusions of grandeur had started all this shit, was a few feet away, preening for some reporters. I turned to Jack and I yelled, "Hey Jack, you need to get some pussy!"

OBSCENE

Gonzalez handed down his ruling on June 6. The blowback was quick. Everything started to spiral out of control. *Nasty* started disappearing from record-store shelves all over south Florida. One Broward County record-store owner named Charles Freeman refused to comply. Freeman, who's black, made a public announcement that he would keep selling the album until the Supreme Court said he couldn't. The day after the ruling came down, an undercover cop went to Freeman's store, EC Records, and bought a cassette of *Nasty* for $8.49. Then he turned around, told Freeman he was under arrest, and put the handcuffs on him. Five other deputies swarmed the store, like Freeman was some kind of violent criminal or something. They made Freeman sit there in cuffs for forty-five minutes. The television news crew was running late and Navarro was waiting until the cameras showed up to film him walking in and making the arrest in person.

Store owners were scared to conduct legal business. All across the state, prosecutors were convening grand juries to try and have our album banned. It escalated quickly. *Nasty* was found obscene in seven different Florida counties: Sarasota, DeSoto, Manatee, Putnam, Volusia, Flagler, and St. Johns. Cops in Vero Beach started acting like Navarro, warning store owners that they'd be charged with a felony for selling the album. The bannings spread; a judge in Indiana ruled the album obscene. We were banned in San Antonio, and prosecutors in Dallas fined two record stores for selling the album.

For every sheriff or district attorney who went after us, there were plenty of officials who said, as Janet Reno did, that this wasn't worth their time. One sheriff in Georgia said he really enjoyed our show. But the crackdown was severe enough that it started to have a chilling effect on the industry. People were starting to watch what they said, who they did business with. Geffen Records had no problem putting out explicit records by Andrew Dice Clay and Guns N' Roses, but they backed out of a deal to distribute the Geto Boys, who were just starting to establish the rap scene in Houston.

Meanwhile, I was under attack on a completely different front. Back when I'd been an intern at the radio station, *Star Wars* was the big movie, and guys had started calling me Luke, which naturally led to Skywalker. I'd changed the spelling to Skyywalker, and used that as my DJ name and then in the name of my label. As my profile increased, I'd figured this might be a problem. When I started my label, my lawyers asked me if I'd gotten permission to use the name. I hadn't. So I got a release. I actually had a release signed by George Lucas. It said as long as we didn't use the name for movies or anything related to the actual character, we were okay.

Apparently, the lawyer I had back then didn't know shit. I was later told the letter release was no good because it was never executed. So now Focus on the Family and all these Christian groups started calling Lucasfilm in California. They put pressure on George Lucas, and he came back after me. I ended up having to write George Lucas a check for $500,000 and recalled tens of thousands of dollars of merchandise with Luke Skyywalker on it that had already been printed. Whatever. It was just money. I paid it and moved on. I didn't need the name. My real name was famous enough on its own at that point.

The Skyywalker thing was a dumb, expensive mistake. I was twenty-eight years old, a black kid from Liberty City who didn't go to college and barely graduated from high school. I was making all this up as I went, figuring things out on the fly. I didn't have powerful mentors showing me the way. All I had was my own God-given common sense and the character and the backbone my parents had raised in me.

Once the Gonzalez decision blew everything wide open, I really had to step outside myself and look at the whole situation and think. I knew that, deep down, no matter what anyone said, it was really about race. What the politicians and the media were doing was so obvious. Some days the newspapers ran our story next to the coverage of the Central Park jogger case, where five black kids from Harlem were on trial for assaulting and raping a white woman in the park. Guilt by association. Look at the dirty jungle music driving young black men out to rape white women. The five guys in the Central Park jogger case were innocent, too, by the way.

Censorship and free speech were this thing that had the whole country in a frenzy. It was affecting everyone, from heavy-metal bands to painters and photographers trying to get their work in museums. But we were getting it worse. Andrew Dice Clay was putting out his dirty albums at the same time. He was talking more wild shit than I ever did, and they invited him to host *Saturday*

Night Live. When Skid Row's lead singer, Sebastian Bach, used profanity onstage in Philadelphia, he was arrested, but they let him off with a fine. Madonna was probably the biggest name facing problems. She was drawing a lot of controversy with her provocative Like a Prayer tour. In Toronto, cops told her to tone down the show. She told them if they tried to make her she'd cancel the whole thing and they could deal with the thirty thousand angry fans. The cops backed down.

All of those people were white, and at worst they were just being hassled and inconvenienced. We were the only group in the country that was having its First Amendment rights curtailed in a court of law. We were even getting it worse than the other hip-hop acts, and when I understood the reasons for that, that's when I really realized exactly what was going on.

White America was getting itself all worked up about every hip-hop act that came along, not just 2 Live Crew. N.W.A, Slick Rick, Too $hort, all those guys got flack. But there were three specific artists around that time whose work became legal flash points in terms of talks of boycotts and censorship and pulling records out of stores. One was Ice-T's song "Cop Killer," which had every police union in the country calling for the song to be banned. The second was Professor Griff of Public Enemy, who made some ignorant anti-Semitic comments about Israel in an interview, kicking up a shitstorm in the media about blacks and the Nation of Islam and Israel. And the third one was some black guys in Miami talking about sex.

Which of these three did America consider the most dangerous? It was the black guys talking about sex. In America, that was the single biggest taboo you could be breaking, the fear of miscegenation, the terror that kept four hundred years of slavery and Jim Crow in place. And not only did we break that taboo, we smashed it, stomped on it, and danced on it. People were more upset about us than they were about talk of killing policemen and Jews. Think about that.

That was the reason the 2 Live Crew controversy blew up so big, but the reason it kept going so long was because I had the balls, and the means, to fight back. And that's what really pissed these white conservatives off: my freedom, my power to tell them no. Ice-T was on Time Warner. When the police unions threatened boycotts over "Cop Killer," the label pressured him to back off, and he did. He took the song off his album. Public Enemy was on Def Jam/Columbia. When the Anti-Defamation League folks went after Public Enemy, Columbia pressured them to throw Griff under the bus, and they did. They kicked him out of the group. But nobody could pressure me. I was black-owned, independent, and making tons of money. I was my own man—a free black man. Nobody owned me. That, I realized, was the thing that really drove them so crazy.

And because I had the only black-owned label, I was the only one who *could* fight this fight. If I didn't stand up, corporate America would keep trying to censor all of us. That's how I saw it. Unfortunately, nobody else in hip-hop saw it that way. Not at the time. The major-label artists, instead of backing me, they distanced themselves. Groups like Salt-N-Pepa and Kid 'N Play, they wanted to stay acceptable to middle America and sell records. They went on BET and publicly slammed us. Other groups just didn't say anything. No major rappers came out in our defense. *Not one.* Even guys like Russell Simmons, who as an executive I thought would understand the dangers of censorship, I never heard him say a word. No comment. No commitment.

Mainstream artists wanted to play that respectability-politics card. They wanted to throw 2 Live Crew under the bus and show white people that hip-hop could be well behaved. But you only deserve free speech in this country if you're well behaved. In fact, the people who need free speech the most are the ones breaking taboos and challenging the status quo. Respectability politics weren't going to save hip-hop from censorship at the hands of corporate America. We had to save ourselves. We had to fight.

Me, there was never a time I wasn't thinking about fighting. I was *born* to have this fight. As far as this country was concerned, I was already supposed to be dead or in jail. So I had nothing to lose. The millions I had in the bank—I didn't care about that. They could take it all. My father never apologized for being who he was, and neither would I. This was my music and I was going to fight for my right to make it. Not because I particularly cared about being a dirty rapper, that wasn't really what the fight was about. The question was whether or not the laws of the land applied to a black man the same as a white man. That's what was driving me. If Andrew Dice Clay and Hugh Hefner have the right to do it, then I have the right to do it. I believed that a black man deserved to have his day in court and see justice served.

After Gonzalez handed down his verdict, Rogow and I hadn't even left the courtroom when we were already plotting the next steps: Rogow would appeal Gonzalez's ruling to the Eleventh Circuit Court of Appeals in Atlanta, where we knew we'd find people with some sense to judge this case, but that would take months to play out. I couldn't have my career on hold for that long, so I decided I'd challenge the law directly by doing the show at this run-down little place in Broward called Club Futura.

On June 9, 1990, Mr. Mixx, Fresh Kid Ice, Brother Marquis, and I rolled up to the club in our white limousine. There were at least thirty police cruisers parked outside. We went in and got ready backstage. I put on my 2 BLACK, 2 STRONG, 2 LIVE CREW shirt. I normally didn't wear that to perform, but that's how I was going out that night. As soon as I got onstage I was looking in the crowd. I could see all these out-of-place people: undercover cops. They were easy to spot because they were old as hell and dressed like they'd just run through K Mart grabbing shit off the racks with the lights out. They kept making eye contact with each other, nodding at each other, talking into their earpieces.

Rogow had told me that if I sang about elected officials, our performance could be defended as a political rally. So we got the crowd going with chants: *"Fuck! Martinez! Fuck! Fuck! Martinez! Fuck Navarro! Fuck! Fuck! Navarro!"* Fans were wearing T-shirts that read LET LUKE PLAY. A lot of them had shirts that said: I USED TO LIVE IN AMERICA, NOW I LIVE IN BROWARD COUNTY. It turned out it was a political rally after all.

The cops in the front row all had those mini-cassette recorders sticking out of their front shirt pockets, and you could see the red lights flicking on and off in the dark. I didn't want to make things difficult for them, so I leaned down and sang my dirty lyrics right into their little microphones. They must have had over a dozen officers in the club that night. Two would have been plenty. I was there to get arrested. I was there to take a stand for the First Amendment—to take a stand for hip-hop, for my community, for everyone who's ever been bullied into silence by a man wearing a badge.

After the show we left the club, climbed into our limo, and rolled out of the parking lot. We were followed by a dozen cruisers. They tailed us for a few miles before they hit the lights and pulled us over. All these cars were passing by, fresh out of the show, honking their support for us. I liked that. I stepped out of the limo and some deputy threw me down on the hood and started patting me down. Then they threw us in the back of the police van. And, of course, Navarro had orchestrated the whole event with the media so the television camera crews were conveniently waiting right where they pulled us over—just like an episode of *Cops.*

The whole ride down to the precinct, I kept telling them, "I'm not staying in this motherfucker over two hours, bitch! As soon as you get me downtown. I'm bonding out. The bondsman is waiting with the money." They booked me around three in the morning. It was a total clown show. The deputies in the station were all smiling and high-fiving each other and slapping each other on the back. Because catching a white limousine going thirty-five miles an hour is really something to be proud of, I guess. Then they threw me in a cell and left me there until the sun came up. All night the cops kept coming back and poking their heads in the window just to look at me, like I was the first black man in handcuffs they'd ever seen. Later, I walked out of there with a big smile and a show lined up that same night in Phoenix. Life goes on. See you assholes in court. The next day, somebody hacked the Broward County police-radio band and played "Me So Horny" on it, over and over again, which was hilarious.

Before I had to face a jury, I had to face the nation on daytime TV and the nightly news. The media shitstorm over *Nasty* had been simmering for a while. Now it erupted. Our arrest for performing at Club Futura was the moment the shit really hit the fan. When I walked out of that jail, I was public enemy number one. Luther Campbell, the hip-hop pornographer. The man in the black hat. The next day, 2 Live Crew was the lead story on *Nightline*, with Bruce Rogow debating the First Amendment with the barking lunatic Jack Thompson. I went on MTV, Geraldo, Donahue. *USA Today*, the *New York Times*, *Newsweek*, *Time* magazine—all of them put us on the front page. We were even front-page news in Norway.

As an artist and as a record-label owner, I knew you couldn't buy publicity like this. For every store that pulled *Nasty* from its shelves, another store doubled its orders. I was printing money with the albums we already had, but I knew we needed to put out a new release to capitalize on and capture the moment. Our current situation called for an anthem.

Every song I hear, I automatically change it around in my head. That's how I listen to music. I'll remix it in my head, break it into pieces, looking for the break or a good bit to sample. I'll think up a good parody. I was listening to a rock and roll station that summer and Springsteen's "Born in the U.S.A." came on. Given the situation I was in at the time, in my mind I heard it as "Banned in the U.S.A." It was obvious.

I needed to get the song cleared. At that period of time, everybody was getting sued. Hip-hop had built itself on sampling other records, which was fine at a block party, but then people went out and started making commercial recordings with it before standards were ever set for fair use. I had to be careful. I didn't need any more legal problems. I called up Springsteen's manager, who called up Springsteen and got him on the phone. I talked to him for maybe five minutes. He said, "It's no problem, man. I understand the struggle. You can use the song." Basically, I used it with his blessing for free.

After getting so much opposition from all sides, including from my fellow rappers, it felt good to get sympathy and support from a fellow artist, especially somebody as big as Springsteen. We wrote the song, quickly cut it in my studio in Liberty City, shot a video in a fake courtroom, and rush-released it for the Fourth of July. It was a challenge getting it to the radio stations on time, and we wanted every radio station to play it at the same time on the Fourth. If we found a new way to get it out there.

"Banned in the U.S.A." was actually the first single ever digitally distributed to radio stations. We beamed it to everyone via satellite. MP3s and Napster and iTunes and all that was still a decade away. I was actually the first person ever to use digital-distribution technology for music, only four years after selling albums out of the trunk of my old Honda. Every station in the country played "Banned" on the Fourth of July. That was amazing to me because all of my success to date had largely come without mainstream radio or TV attention. Now we were too hot to ignore. *As Nasty as They Wanna Be* had shipped gold. *Banned in the U.S.A.* shipped platinum.

That summer we went on tour to support the new album, and that was the craziest three months of my life. I was the most dangerous black man in America. Hands down. After Broward and all the media, law enforcement had this huge hard-on for 2 Live Crew. "Lock these motherfuckers up" was the mission. Every two-bit Nick Navarro wannabe from Jacksonville to Baton Rouge was lining up to be the next guy to bust Luther Campbell. The cops never wanted Brother Marquis or Fresh Kid Ice, the guys who sang most of the lyrics. Nobody wanted to lock them up. They wanted me. I was the leader. I was the guy on the Phil Donahue show talking shit. I was the big prize. Before each show, these cops would be like, "Hey, you sing that shit and we'll lock your ass up." I'd just smile and act all innocent and say, "Oh, you're going to lock me up? What you gonna lock me up for?"

To lock me up they'd have to arrest me first. In order for them to say I was evading arrest, they'd have to tell me, "You're under arrest!" I didn't even give them the opportunity to say that. After every show, I escaped. I was like fucking Houdini onstage. There was a thing we used to do back when I had the original Pac Jam disco. We were famous for "dropping the bomb." I would take a bunch of gunpowder, put it in a pipe, take two electrical wires, twist em together, put one end in the powder and the other end in a socket and *Boom!* It'd blow up. They were Jamaican pipe bombs, basically. Big explosion and a bright, bright light that would blind you for a second. It was a big flash but it was over real quick. Used to scare the shit out of everybody.

Detroit was where I first started dropping the bomb. The cops were all over the place at that show, and just as we went on somebody told me the cops were waiting outside by my limo as well. It was all planned. "We're gonna get this guy." The Detroit show was crazy. It happened right in the wake of Broward, and that was when we really started amping things up. We brought guys onstage to get lap dances from the girls and some of the guys would eat the girls out. Sometimes the girls would do backflips and give the guys head onstage. We got this one girl from Chicago, she, like, sucked dick backward. Like, she'd flip over and be sucking the guy's dick onstage. It was some acrobatic shit. It was like a fucking freak show. All those naked women onstage, and the cops were glaring at me, just watching and waiting for their chance to nab me.

I was like a symphony conductor up there, a ringmaster, whipping the crowd and all these people onstage up into a frenzy. Then, right at the climax, right at the end of the last song, I'd grab the mic and yell, "Yeah! I want all these police, the mayor, the governor, and everybody to know one thing: they can suck my motherfucking dick and kiss my ass! Yo! Thank you! We are 2 motherfucking Live in yo *ass*, and we don't give a fuck about no fucking cops!"

They cut the house lights. Pitch-black. Now drop the motherfucking bomb. *Boom!* Bright flash. Everybody blinded. Next I hopped down into the crowd and took my shit off. I always had two shirts on. Ditch the Luke Gear, just a plain T-shirt on, hoodie up, and I was out the door. Gone. Lost in the crowd. No security, no nothing. Just another young black dude in a hoodie. Cops never bother to tell the difference between us anyway.

I made my way outside, flagged down this random group of chicks in a car, going, "Yo, yo, I need a ride, I need a ride." They saw who I was and were like, "Oh my God! Oh my God!" They were all excited and shit. I hopped in the back of their Toyota, ducked down, and sped away. I watched all the fucking cops standing around my limo, looking for my ass. We cruised back by my hotel, and cops were looking for me there, too. So we just drove past, went to this other hotel I knew on the riverfront, checked in, and I spent the rest of the evening laughing my ass off at all those cops wasting their fucking time.

I did that shit probably twenty, thirty times. Some cities were worse than others. Cincinnati was wild. Those people were scared to fucking death. The police chief actually came and met us at the airport and gave us the usual warning. "Don't play those songs. Don't do fucking nothing in my town." Blah, blah, blah. It was always the same shit.

Outside the club it was like the cops were waiting for a full-blown riot, like this was going to turn into Watts or Newark or something. They had the whole street cordoned off. Rows of cops on horseback. Batons. Tear-gas cannons. Helicopters flying over-head. Snipers on the roof. Motherfuckers had that shit surrounded. The police presence intimidated a lot of the people who'd come to see us. They stayed away. The show was sold-out, but by the time we were about to go on, the place was only about half full. There wasn't enough of a crowd to do my Houdini act; I couldn't disap-pear if there weren't enough people.

I was still ready to go ahead. Fuck it. Arrest me. I'll beat this one, too. But the other guys wanted to back off. There had been a divide growing between me and them since the early days, when they just wanted to be rap stars and didn't want to be part of the business. With the trial and the controversy, that divide was becoming a rift. A lot of people were confused when *Banned in the U.S.A.* came out and it was subtitled *The Luke LP, featuring 2 Live Crew.* But that was just a reflection of where the group was at that time.

That trial was all my initiative. Those guys just didn't want to fight, period. With Mr. Mixx, because the trial was all about the explicit lyrics, he was never really implicated in it the way the rest of us were. It wasn't really his fight. Brother Marquis and Fresh

Kid Ice, for the Gonzalez trial, they did what they had to do. They showed up in court and testified on the days they were called to testify, but that was about it. Beyond that, they didn't want to have anything to do with it. They felt like I was dragging them into it. They just wanted to be rap stars and live that lifestyle.

They didn't see what we were going through as part of an important struggle. They weren't putting any money into the trial. They weren't footing any of Rogow's billable hours or the cost for the expert witnesses, even though it was their asses on the line, too. I paid for the lawsuits and the trial, everything. Also, I kept paying their royalties while this was going on. I could have held the royalties against legal expenses—but I never did. To me, this wasn't about the money. It was about the principle.

When we were on tour, whenever a promoter or police chief got in our face, half the time the group wanted to back down. Whenever the police started knocking down our door, I was the one that had to step forth as the spokesman. I had to step out front and take all the heat and answer all the questions and make all the public comments. So when we were facing arrest in Cincinnati that summer, they were like, "Yo man, we don't want to go to jail." They said, "We should take a vote." They voted me down. They wanted to do a clean show. We performed the clean versions, like we were doing a kids' show.

The audience was pissed. I was pissed, too. At that point, I knew that when people came to our shows they weren't just coming to see a show. They were coming to be a part of the spectacle, part of this movement, a part of saying "fuck you" to the establishment. We let them down. I regretted that we backed down. That was really the beginning of the end of 2 Live Crew.

A few weeks later we did a show in Texas, and by that point I was like, "Fuck *everybody*. I'm doing this shit my way." This promoter booked us to do a show at the Longhorn Ballroom in Dallas, and the local authorities came down on him, said they would sanction and fine the club if we were allowed to do an explicit show. We were backstage in the dressing room, and the promoter said he wasn't going to pay us if we did an explicit show. We'd only get our money for a clean show. Place was sold-out. Promoter already had the money, our money, but he was telling us we wouldn't get paid if we did the thing he brought us out there to do. I told him, "You're going to pay us, and then I'll decide what kind of show I want to do." He said no. We kept going back and forth like that. Hours passed.

In the meantime, the crowd showed up. They filled in the seats and were just sitting out there, waiting and waiting and getting drunk and pissed off. Me, I'm always thinking on the spot. I'm always improvising, making adjustments. "Okay, okay. We're gonna perform. We'll do it clean. Give me the mic and let's do this."

Promoter gave me the cordless mic. We were still in the dressing room. I turned that shit on, and my voice was booming to the audience out front. I said, "Hey, look here. Y'all paid money to see 2 Live Crew. The way it goes is you pay the promoter, the promoter pays us. But this promoter ain't paid us our fucking money. So we out. Y'all can tear this motherfucker the fuck up and get y'all money back the best way y'all can!"

Promoter's jaw hit the floor. We grabbed our gear and before we were even in the car, that shit was blowing up. We watched the whole thing on the local news that night at the hotel: "The Longhorn Ballroom is on fire!" Those motherfuckers had a riot! They tore that place up, smashed tables, smashed chairs. We were laughing our asses off. Apparently, the crowd inflicted $100,000 in damages. Promoter should have just shut up and paid us.

That whole summer was madness from start to finish. It was the same thing wherever we played: sold-out shows, armies of cops in the streets, crazed fans, groupies. We were surfing this incredibly powerful wave. The Gonzalez ruling and our arrest in Broward had fired up the conservative Christian morality police. They thought they were winning, and that's how the media was spinning it, too. So everything I did had to be bolder and brasher.

In public, I played the man in the black hat, played it to the hilt, always had a big smile and the right quip for reporters, whipping the crowds into a frenzy every night. But behind the scenes it was incredibly stressful. Here I was, going all over the South and the Midwest with a target on my back. I had all kinds of angry letters and death threats, thousands of them, pouring into my office. "We'll kill you if you come to our town." "You're a nigger." "You're an un-American piece of shit." We were only twenty years out from the time when I'd have been lynched for doing what we were doing. On one of the talk shows I did, they had guys from the Ku Klux Klan sitting right next to me, spouting off about how my degenerate nigger music was destroying the country. I had to have security guards surrounding me 24/7. I never would have admitted it then, but looking back I can say there were times I was actually afraid of what I'd unleashed.

Still, despite those moments of fear, I never wavered from my goal: to have my day in court. Our first trial back in May, in federal court, had been a civil trial. No jury, just Judge Gonzalez. The trial for our arrest at Club Futura would be a criminal one, which meant facing a jury. The same was true for Charles Freeman, the Broward record-store owner arrested for selling *Nasty*. He went on trial before we did. I'd told him back in June, "Look, man, you don't need to do this. It's not gonna help anything." But he did it anyway. He basically had the same attitude as me. He said, "I sell everything from N.W.A to Dice Clay, you name it. All these different types of records, and y'all going to single this man out? Fuck that." I respected him for standing up, and told him I'd do anything I could to help. I paid Bruce Rogow to handle his defense. Freeman was facing a thousand-dollar fine *and* jail time for selling a dirty record. Despite Rogow's best efforts, Freeman was up against an all-white, suburban jury, six wealthy white women all over the age of forty, women who didn't understand anything about our music and who, like Gonzalez, couldn't see past their own prejudices about our music to fairly apply the *Miller v. California* test. Freeman didn't stand a chance. He lost.

I got worried. The weird thing about obscenity is this: every other crime, you know it's a crime when it's committed. You break a window, you steal a car, you put a gun at somebody's head. Those are criminal actions. With obscenity, you don't know if an actual crime has been committed until the jury comes back and tells you, yes, that was obscene. Which means the whole thing comes down to what the jury thinks, and in the American justice system, as you may have noticed recently, blacks and juries haven't traditionally done well together.

In Florida, the all-white jury had been condemning innocent black men and absolving guilty white men for decades. When we went to trial, it had been exactly ten years since an all-white jury had acquitted the men who murdered Arthur McDuffie, and the city of Miami burned. After the riots, the state had actually tried to improve the jury selection process, had made it harder to purge black jurors through peremptory challenge, but in Broward it almost didn't matter. Most of the black folks in Miami lived in Dade County. Broward was built by white flight; its black population was small to begin with, and the percentage of blacks on its voting rolls, which is where jury pools are drawn from, is even smaller. We'd be looking at at least a majority white jury no matter what we did. If they agreed with Gonzalez, my ass was going to jail.

Given the nature of an obscenity trial, the most important part of the trial wasn't going to be the trial itself but the jury selection, voir dire. Who do you choose to sit in judgment of you? Your money, your career, your freedom, and maybe your life hangs in the balance. It's a nerve-racking process. You need to know a lot about people to pick a jury. Fortunately, that's exactly how I built my business and worked my way up from the ghetto, by using common sense and reading people and building relationships, with black folks and with whites.

There were times when Bruce and I disagreed. One potential juror was this little old white lady. She was a principal at an integrated school. Bruce was hell-bent to get her out. He was like, "No, this lady is gone." And I was like, "Nah, she's a schoolteacher! She meets and deals with people of all different nationalities, all different races of people. She'll see through all this racial nonsense." We picked her. There was also an older white guy who was a plumber. Bruce thought he was too old and too conservative. I said, "That man works in shit. He works in shit all day. None of this will faze him." Another one of the jurors was an older white woman who had taught sociology years before at Howard University. The two prosecutors had no idea what Howard is, that it's the most important historically black college in the country. But I knew. I told Bruce, "This lady knows what's going on."

I went with my gut on every choice. If I was gonna be judged, I didn't want to have any regrets. Some of the selections went our way, some didn't. There was another guy in the jury pool, a biker, like a Hell's Angels type of guy. Dude was ugly, had a wife-beater on, tattoos up both arms. Bruce wanted to keep him. He said, "This guy doesn't like authority. He's a biker, and bikers are not sympathetic to the police. I think he'd be good." But I didn't like him. He looked like the kind of redneck asshole who'd go around fucking with black folks, wearing Confederate-flag T-shirts and shit. I said, "Nah. He's a nigger hater. I want him out." Bruce used one of our peremptory challenges and struck the biker down.

Then, when the dude came down from the jury box, he walked by my table and reached out and high-fived me and said, "Go get em, brother!"

My mistake.

We only had a few blacks in the jury pool to choose from, and unfortunately several of them disqualified themselves up front by saying flat out that they didn't think we were guilty. It was nice to hear, but it kept them from being considered. With a jury of six, we ended up with only one black person, this old grandmother. But we had at least a couple of white people I felt would be sympathetic to my position. Given the pool of jurors we had to work from, it was probably the best we were going to do.

The prosecutors were doing their best to manage with the racial aspects of the trial, too. The lead prosecutor was this white lady, Leslie Robson. She was the worst possible person to try a case like this. She had this shrill, monotonous voice, and even when she smiled she looked like she was smelling something unpleasant. They brought on this black guy, Pedro Dijols, to serve as her co-counsel, to try and make it look like this wasn't a racist prosecution. But Dijols wasn't an African-American. He may have looked black to the jury, but that motherfucker was Puerto Rican. He tried to act like he wasn't just there to look black for the jury, but prior to our trial the only thing he'd ever prosecuted was DUI cases. Robson didn't let him talk much. If you ask me, the dude was just there to be window dressing.

I actually ran into Dijols in the bathroom during the trial, and he said to me, "Man, I like your music. We was just jamming to your shit in the office the other day. I don't know what the fuck they got us doing this here trial for. This is just my job, you know? I gotta do it." He wanted to have it both ways, play the respectable token for his white bosses out in the courtroom and then turn around and try and act like he was down with me in private. It made me think even less of him, but it made me realize the prosecution didn't have much of a case if half of them were dancing to our music in the office.

This trial was the reverse of the Gonzalez hearing. This time we were the defendants and it was up to the prosecution to make its case first. They couldn't use the lyrics from the album as proof of obscenity; the thing on trial was our performance of those lyrics, which meant their only evidence was the recording of the show at Club Futura made by Navarro's deputies, who didn't know shit about recording music in a club. They'd all used those little mini-cassette recorders, and they'd been standing five feet away from the huge, blaring speakers. The tapes were nothing but garbled, distorted noise. No one could understand what was on them. Listening intently the best you got was blown-out distortion with the occasional *shit* or *bitch* or *ass* coming through.

The prosecution played clips from tapes for hours, just blaring loud, unintelligible noise at the jury. Since the tapes were so bad, their whole case came down to Navarro's deputies testifying about what they heard and explaining what was on the tape. What you had was a bunch of stiff, wooden cops on the stand stumbling through lyrics like "Put your lips on my dick and suck my asshole, too." They were worse than porn stars reciting dialogue. It was fucking hilarious. They thought reciting the lyrics was going to indict me, but they ended up making themselves look ridiculous. The whole thing was a farce.

On his cross-examination, Bruce was brilliant. He made the cops go back and repeat the lyrics over and over again, being very specific. By doing that, he drained all the shock value out of the words. While the deputies were cursing up a storm of *dick* and *ass* and *pussy*, Bruce never uttered a single word of profanity. He would always say "anal sex" or "intercourse" or "Are you referring to the lyrics about the man's penis entering the woman's vagina?"

He sounded like a doctor discussing normal, basic human bodily functions. Bruce managed to make sex so boring that at one point a juror fell asleep. The psychological effect it had was brilliant. We came off as normal, sane people while the cops sounded like a bunch of dirty perverts obsessed with dick and ass and pussy.

This went on for days. One of the sheriff's deputies who testified was this petite young lady with this tiny little voice like Mickey Mouse, and she was up there reciting lyrics like "Lick my asshole up and down / Lick it till your tongue turns doo-doo brown." Everybody in the courtroom was cracking up, including the jury. They were putting their heads down and turning beet red trying not to bust out laughing. They were doing their best to play this impartial, respectful role, but it was impossible with these witnesses up there making clowns out of themselves. Eventually the foreman of the jury passed the judge a note, and she announced to the courtroom, "The jurors have made an unusual request. They want to know if they are allowed to laugh."

The second she read that note, I was like, "Oh, shit, we won this motherfucker." The intent of the music was always to make people laugh. When given a fair hearing, and in the right context, the jury liked the music and were entertained instead of offended. The judge told the jury they could respond to the testimony however they liked. For the rest of the week, it was like a comedy show up in that courtroom.

Then it was time for our defense. All we had to do was prove to the jury that our music was comedy, that it was art, same as we had in the first trial. Bruce called as our star witness Dr. Henry Louis Gates. Today Gates is famous as the Harvard professor who got arrested by some white cop for trying to open the door to his own house and ended up having beers with Obama on the White House lawn. Back then he was a professor of English literature at Duke

University. Rhodes Scholar, degree from Oxford University, brilliant guy. Bruce had called him because of an op-ed he'd written for the *New York Times* called "Decoding 2 Live Crew." Gates's testimony was the highlight of the trial.

Gates's expert opinion was basically what I'd been saying all along, that our music was a joke, a comedy routine set to music, only he was able to speak on it from a historical perspective that gave everyone, including me, a deeper understanding of what we'd been doing. On direct examination from Bruce, Gates compared the profanity in our music to Chaucer and Shakespeare, which had always used raunchy language and wordplay about sex to get laughs from the people, but most importantly he put our music in the broader context of the black experience, how when a group is marginalized and stigmatized with certain stereotypes—like young black men as oversexed brutes—one way to deal with that stereotype is to embrace it, to exaggerate it to the point where it obviously becomes absurd. "You can have no reaction but to burst out laughing," he said, pointing out that on the tapes of our concert, the whole audience was laughing and singing along. There was never any threat of sexual violence or anything like that at our shows, because the whole thing was so ridiculous. "What you hear," Gates said of the tapes, "is great humor, great joy."

On cross-examination, the prosecution tried to badger Gates, mocking him for comparing us to Shakespeare, calling it ridiculous to put us in the same black creative tradition as James Baldwin and Ralph Ellison, but the professor was cool under fire. He'd already demolished their case, and by that point they were just fumbling along and trying to get this over with. They knew they'd lost. By the time we rested our case, the Vegas odds were 9 to 1 in our favor.

The verdict was set to come back on a Saturday. We made our

way to the courthouse. Outside it was swarmed with TV cameras and news crews from all over the world. I was the focal point of it all, giving interviews and making comments, being filmed walking to and from my car.

The media barrage was everything Nick Navarro had wanted, only Nick himself wasn't there. In fact, he'd disappeared about halfway through the trial. He knew this wasn't going his way, and he didn't want to be there when it blew up in his face. The media event of the year, and the man who never met a camera he didn't like was nowhere to be found. Three other people weren't there that day: Mr. Mixx, Fresh Kid Ice, and Brother Marquis, which tells you a lot about where the band was headed at that point.

The jury only needed one vote to come to a decision. They'd have been in there for less than ten minutes but they ordered a pizza and took time to eat lunch. We were called in to the court-room and the foreman stood to read the verdict: not guilty, acquit-ted on all counts. I turned and hugged Bruce. I was thrilled. It was a total rush. I was judged by a jury of my peers. They came back and said, "This is art. This is free speech. This is a free country. This shouldn't be censored." It let me know the fight wasn't for nothing and that not all people were fucked up, just some, like Jack Thompson. I was happy not just that I'd won this fight, but that I'd made my bigger point: that a black man in America could have his day in court and see justice done.

The minute that verdict came back, it was like the fever broke, not just for us but across the nation and across the industry. The whole censorship frenzy that had consumed the twenty-four-hour news cycle went away. Our very next show in Gainesville, a hand-ful of Christian groups tried to stop us, but this time the police and the local authorities shut *them* down. Cops didn't harass us or intimidate us at all. What were they going to do? Arrest us and try us again in Gainesville? The legal precedent had been set. We just did our show, the fans had a great time, and everybody went home happy.

In the next months and years, the record-store owners who'd stood up for us all had their convictions overturned, including Charles Freeman. In May of 1992, the Eleventh Circuit Court of Appeals overturned Judge Gonzalez's ruling that *Nasty* was obscene, saying he'd imposed his own judgment rather than a fair application of community standards. Rappers, heavy-metal bands, sexually explicit painters and sculptors, they were now free to do their work. They might get protests from self-righteous nut jobs, but that's just more free speech from the other side and that's fine. The threat of official interference from the state was gone. I fought that fight for myself, for hip-hop, for black musicians, and for every creative mind in the country. Not a single musician or artist has faced an obscenity trial in America since that day. Not one.

Not only did we win, everyone who was against us lost. Jack Thompson wouldn't give up. He petitioned the judge to nullify the verdict on the grounds that one of the jurors hadn't told the truth in jury selection about how much college education he had, as if that mattered to the case. He harassed the judge so much that she filed a formal grievance against him with the Florida bar for obstructing justice and wrongly trying to influence an officer of the court. Thompson still kept going, after me, after the video-game industry, after anyone he thought was corrupting the morals of America's youth. He harassed so many people and had so many grievances filed against him that the state of Florida finally disbarred him a few years ago.

Everybody that hitched their wagon to Thompson's lunatic crusade got burned, too. In their next elections, both Bob Martinez and Nick Navarro went down in flames. They'd tried to make me their Willie Horton, and it blew up in their faces. Martinez became a one-term governor after losing in a landslide a few months later to his Democratic opponent, Lawton Chiles. Navarro lost right after that, too. His fifteen minutes were up. The cameras moved on and he ended up running a private security company—just another retired rent-a-cop working Christmas parties and the senior prom. Even Dan Quayle only got one term as vice president before the voters kicked him and Bush Sr. out of the White House.

That fall, MTV invited 2 Live Crew to perform "Banned in the U.S.A." at the 1990 Music Video Awards. Finally. I felt like it was the first real, honest recognition from the music industry of the importance of what I was doing. I always kept up my game face in public, being tough and a fighter and all that, but it was hard. I'd been through so much shit that year, the death threats and the public turning against me and the eyes of the world on me from New York to Japan. I let all of that go onstage that night. It was the deepest moment I've ever had performing. Public Enemy and other artists started coming onstage hugging us, so it was like the weight of the world had been lifted. It was nothing we'd rehearsed. It was totally spontaneous. They just felt it in the room. They just felt it and came out onstage. It was some deep shit. People couldn't tell because I was wearing my sunglasses, but I was up there fucking crying and singing my heart out and letting the world know how incredible it felt that I'd won the fight.

That was the best performance of my lifetime.

ROCK STAR

Back when we were starting out, 2 Live Crew never got any respect from our fellow rappers or from the major labels. We were too raunchy, too controversial. Coming off the Broward trial, after taking that hit and becoming First Amendment champions, I started to hope that we'd finally get our due, the kind of respect I got from Bruce Springsteen when he let me use his song. I was thrilled when I received an invitation to attend the Grammys. They said they were going to be giving out a special Freedom Fighter award in light of everything that was going on that year with musicians' free speech under attack. They intimated to me that it was something special, and that it would be a secret until the show aired, but that I'd want to be there for it. I couldn't believe it. I thought, damn, here it is at last, the industry acceptance that I've never received.

I flew up to New York for the show at Radio City Music Hall. I walked through all the interviews along the red carpet, flashbulbs everywhere. I went in there that night ready to be recognized for taking a stand and holding my ground. I took my seat and settled in for the show. Finally they got to the special award. Somebody gave this big speech about music being an art form worth defending and how the First Amendment had been under attack and so they were going to honor an artist who had been fighting for free speech and free expression all over the country. "Please join us in bringing onstage . . . Madonna!"

I was like, *Madonna?!* Get the fuck outta here.

I ain't been back to the Grammys since.

In hindsight, it was foolish of me to think that the mainstream music industry was ready to start recognizing independent black artists and labels. In the end, I didn't care. I was too busy to give a shit. I wasn't looking for their validation and I didn't need it. Thanks to *Nasty* and the trial, I'd become an international rock star all on my own. Our record sales had been taking off in Japan, so the first thing I did once I got out of that courtroom was book my first solo tour over there to promote *Banned in the U.S.A.*

Japan was wild. We played Osaka, Kyoto, Yokohama, and Tokyo. I'd never even left the country before, and the whole experience was pure culture shock. Even though the audience didn't understand the words, they still understood the music. It was crazy to see how music is such a universal language. It was amazing to see how far hip-hop had traveled around the globe. This was barely ten years out from the Sugarhill Gang and "Rapper's Delight," but hip-hop style and music and fashion were everywhere.

MC Hammer was touring Japan at the same time, playing fucking arenas. We were both a long way from when he slept on my couch and did a show at the Pac Jam II. We met up with him for his show at the Tokyo Dome. Hammer had his whole entourage up onstage, must have been at least a hundred people. He brought me onstage to close out the show with him on "2 Legit 2 Quit."

I remember being up onstage, doing our thing and looking out at the Japanese kids. They'd never seen somebody move like Hammer did, shaking his body at 130 beats per minute. They went crazy for it.

And those Japanese girls were *freaks*. Straight-up wild, nasty freaks. Every night they were jumping onstage and grabbing my crotch. Every night. The last night of the tour, I said to myself, "I'm tired of these girls grabbing my dick onstage. I'm gonna pull some Rick James shit tonight." One time Rick James was eating out Teena Marie onstage. I wasn't going to do that, but I decided I was going to be the first rock star to get a blowjob onstage. I was like, fuck it, by the time the police find out I'll be on a plane back home. A bunch of girls climbed onstage and I told them, "Y'all motherfuckers line up. Give me some head. Run a train, right in front of the band." They took my shit out and they all took turns giving me head during the last song.

When I got back from Japan in December of 1990, I didn't even pause to catch my breath before launching my next big venture, the one thing every rock star needs: my own marquee nightclub. I still had my first club, Strawberries Too, out in Hialeah, but that was just a local spot in a suburban strip mall. We had the Hurricanes players, some NFL guys coming out there. Mike Tyson came in a few times. But it wasn't a five-star celebrity joint. That's what I wanted to create.

While Liberty City had turned into a bloody battlefield in the war on drugs, Miami Beach had turned into a drug-fueled paradise. South Beach was turning into the jet-set playground we know it as today. Money was flooding in. All the old art deco hotels were being restored. Models were up and down Ocean Drive wearing next to nothing. Celebrities were buying mansions on Star Island

and Fisher Island: Madonna, Sylvester Stallone, Gianni Versace, all of them. Me and a lot of pro athletes and other rappers were hanging out there more, too. There was this one club we used to go to, Fatback Pussycat. Cocaine would be everywhere, just laid out in lines on the tables, people snorting it right out in the open. There were a ton of new clubs opening up—Liquid, Hell, Risk, Club Z, Club 1235—and the scene was crazy. These rich motherfuckers were flying in from the Bahamas just to party at the clubs and enjoy the five-star treatment.

South Beach was returning to its former glory as America's Riviera. As a businessman, I wanted to be a part of it. Opening a nightclub there was the next natural step for where my company was going. And as a black Miamian, I didn't think we should be left out of the part of Miami that was booming. Why should we be stuck in the ghetto while everyone else is getting rich and having a party? I started making plans to build the best club in town: Luke's Miami Beach. If everything went right, it'd be the first in a string of clubs in tourist spots around the country.

There was a strip club that had just gone out of business at 1045 Fifth Street, the Gold Club, right at the last intersection before the MacArthur Causeway that takes you back into the city. It had gone under because the city of Miami Beach had actually passed an anti-nudity ordinance to try and stop the city from turning into another Las Vegas. I spent hundreds of thousands of dollars gutting and renovating the space and turning it into Luke's Miami Beach. Everything was top of the line. I outfitted it with the best lights and sound system money could buy. My brother Brannard put together a killer menu. It had a VIP balcony, several members-only rooms for private partying, and a pimped-out DJ booth where I would occasionally spin.

From the start I wanted it to be both exclusive and inclusive. I wanted the high-end clientele. I made it twenty-five-and-over and had a fifteen-dollar cover, which was pretty steep back then. I didn't want it to be seen as a "black" club. Back then all the clubs were de facto segregated. Whites went here, blacks went there, Hispanics went someplace else. I always believed in one Miami. I wanted everyone to come to Luke's. For the opening-night bash, I put together my own personal guest list. It had 150 black people on it, 150 white people on it, and 150 Hispanic people on it. It sent the message that anybody was welcome at my club. I met every single one of them at the front door in a tux and red bow tie.

Luke's was an instant hit because there was no place like it on the Beach.

If you watch the video for my single "I Wanna Rock (Doo Doo Brown)," that's what Luke's Miami Beach was like all the time, one big party. We had celebrities in there all the time. Robert De Niro was in the club all the time when he was down here shooting *Cape Fear*. Eddie Murphy came in every time he came to town. Jamie Foxx, who at the time was only known for *In Living Color*, would get up and perform stand-up and do characters.

Everybody went to Luke's. We had all the professional athletes, too. After every Miami Heat game, all the players would be at Luke's. It was almost like their living room. The players even started a little tradition that rookies who signed to the Heat had to come to Luke's and take more shots than the rookie the year before. Keith Askins, Bimbo Coles, and I would sit up there and they would bring the new rookie in, and we'd be like, "Gotta take them shots." They would always pass out, but I made sure they were all right.

We had VIP sky boxes that all the NBA and NFL players would use. Lawrence Taylor would get on a flight after his Giants games in New York and be in the club for Sunday night. The Chicago Bulls loved to party down here, too. And of course I was still close with all the guys on the Miami Hurricanes. They'd come by every

Saturday after their games to collect the money they'd earned on the field that day. We had a blowout party there when the Hurricanes won the national championship again in 1991. I remember one time, when they were playing Florida State at Doak Campbell Stadium, I told them, "Y'all go and get the fucking Indian out of the middle of the field. Take the grass out the middle of the field, put it in a bag, and we gonna put it up on top of the club!" They went and beat the shit out of the Seminoles and all these guys came with bags of the actual Indian painted on strips of turf. We put it on top of the club like a scalp. It was a nonstop party in that place. Miami Beach was the hottest place in the country back then, and Luke's was the hottest place on Miami Beach.

Being a rock star was keeping me busy. If I wasn't at the club I was out on tour. In the summer of 1991, 2 Live Crew put out *Sports Weekend*, the follow-up album to *As Nasty as They Wanna Be*. The lead single and video was "Pop That Pussy." I came up with that one the same way I'd come up with songs like "Ghetto Jump" and "Throw the D." It's a dance song. I just put a name to a dance that everybody was doing. "Doo Doo Brown" was the name of the dance. It was girls popping their coochies and slapping their ass cheeks together. Now everybody is calling it "twerking." *Sports Weekend* hit No. 22 on the *Billboard* Albums chart and No. 19 on the R&B chart and was certified gold.

Since I was in the band and also ran the label, I had to be in Miami most of the time and we couldn't go on tour like a regular band. So during the week I'd run the club and the label, and on weekends we'd fly out and play shows. We were still selling out every night, and life on the road was insane. Since the first days I started my business, I made a vow that I'd never have a drink before six P.M. I've never broken it. But after six, it was anything goes. We had bottles and bottles of Hennessy backstage at every show, and the band, the crew, we'd drink it like it was water.

Ever since *Nasty*, girls had been jumping up onstage out of the audience and taking their shirts off, dancing around topless. It had reached the point where it didn't even surprise anyone. After what happened in Japan, I started to see just how far I could take it. A girl would hop up and take off her shirt, and I'd tell her to take off her panties and finger herself . . . and she'd do it! If two girls got onstage I'd say, "Eat each other out." And they'd do it. These were just normal girls from the crowd. I couldn't believe they were actually doing this shit onstage in front of thousands of people. But it was like they wanted to. It was like they were using our shows as an excuse to let their natural freak out.

What happened onstage was nothing compared to the groupies backstage. 2 Live Crew had the craziest, nastiest groupies you could possibly imagine. I'd been knocking down groupies going all the way back to the Ghetto Style days. At that point, I'd seen so many different vaginas I couldn't even keep track of them. I had to start being creative just to stay interested. I was doing whatever I could with pussy just to see what was possible. I'd do this with the pussy, I'd do that with the pussy. If I could have put some pussy in a skillet and fried it up, I would have tried that, too.

The girls, they'd do whatever you told them to do. If you told a groupie to jump off the balcony, they'd jump off the fucking balcony. Fame is a strange thing. When we'd get to the venue, there would be groupies lined up at the backstage door. After the show there would be even more. We would just pick the ones we wanted to take back to the hotel. The ones we didn't pick, they'd follow the limo back to the hotel anyhow, just to try and get in. Some nights we'd drive right past them, go in, and put on a college football game. Other nights, we'd have thirty of them come up to the suite and it'd be an orgy until dawn.

We had what we called Sacrifice Weekends, where we'd push things to the absolute limit. It was called Sacrifice Weekend because it was to see what a woman was willing to sacrifice to get with the band. If we wanted you to fuck five guys, that's what you had to do. If we wanted you to lie on a table and let guys piss on you, that's what you had to do. For these women, it was their chance to get close to fame and fortune.

Sometimes we'd just make up crazy shit to see if they'd go along. We'd be in Detroit or Chicago or Atlanta. We'd have girls in the back of the van, and we'd tell them, "You want to be with us? Okay, now here's what you gotta do. You gotta take off all your clothes except for this mink coat. Then you're gonna walk up to the front desk and ask for Luke's room." And this lady would walk in with her mink coat and nothing on underneath. She'd walk up to the counter. People would all stare. She'd go up, and we'd all be standing there laughing at the man at the front desk, because his eyes were as big as grapefruits. He'd give her Luke's room number, then she'd let the mink coat drop and walk to the elevator naked. She would be eating it up. She was all about it, and the front-desk guy would be racing to call security.

We were crazy. We were living like black rock stars. There was this one show in Daytona Beach. We were running through this hotel and fucking everything that moved. I decided I wanted to see how many women I could fuck in one night. It wasn't how many I could have long sex with. It was how many women I could stick my dick in. I lined up ten or twelve girls, three in each room. I'd fuck for a few seconds, boom, boom, boom! Jump on another one, fuck another one. Jump on another one, fuck another one. Go to the next room and fuck another one. All these girls thought this was the best. They thought it was kinky and real cool to be fucking this rap star and all that.

I remember that night as being the point where I decided this groupie shit was just too easy. I only like doing something if it's a challenge. Seducing a woman is a challenge, but with the groupies it just got tired after a while. The crew and the rest of the group and the entourage, they kept knocking down as much pussy as they could. Me, after shows I started sitting down and talking to groupies. I used to have conversations with them, where they were in life, were they in college. That was way more interesting. You can only have so much sex before it starts to get old.

Pretty soon after *Sports Weekend* came out, life with 2 Live Crew was getting old, too. Brother Marquis and Mr. Mixx filed a lawsuit against Luke Records and called a press conference where they stood up with their attorney, claiming that they were broke and that I'd screwed them out of over a million dollars in royalties.

They were broke. That much was true. The lawyer said in the press conference that both guys were living with their mothers, Mixx in California and Marquis in Atlanta. But the reason they were broke is because they spent their money on bullshit like cars and women. I wasn't responsible for the fact that they couldn't handle their own money like adults. As for me not paying them, that was ridiculous.

2 Live Crew never had a contract. There was no written agreement between the group and the label. We'd just started putting out singles and everything blew up so quickly that we never stopped to paper everything. It was only after *Banned in the U.S.A.* came out and went gold that those guys started getting worried that they'd get left behind. They came to me before *Sports Weekend* and said, "We want a contract." A short while later we drew one up and signed it. Eight months later, Mixx and Marquis turned around and sued. Fresh Kid Ice wasn't a part of

any of it. He stayed out there, promoting *Sports Weekend*. He signed with me as a solo artist and we put out his first album, *The Chinaman*.

It was the same thing that always breaks bands up: jealousy. One guy in the group starts getting a lot of attention. Everybody starts getting different crews, the hangers-on that come with success, the entourage, the girlfriend. Marquis had his own group of guys. Fresh Kid Ice had his own group of people. Mr. Mixx got his own group of people. Their friends and girlfriends were in their ears, saying, "You need to be doing this, you need to be doing that. You should be in charge. You shouldn't let Luke be in charge." On and on like that. Everybody gets egos. Everything falls apart.

Those guys were jealous, but if anyone had a reason to complain it was me, going all the way back to the start of the *Nasty* controversy. The trial was the thing that sent the album through the roof and made us all a lot of money, but they hadn't done one thing to help out on the legal front. They would show up to the studio, but never to the courtroom. I was always in there with Rogow by myself. They hadn't wanted to fight. They never put any money, not one fucking dime, toward the legal fees for the case. It blew my mind that they didn't want to fight when their own personal freedom was on the line.

Normally, if you're an artist and your work gets caught up in a legal problem, the label pays to fight it, but the expenses come off the top of the revenues from the album. It's a cost of doing business, no different from marketing and promotion. I never held the legal fees against their royalties. I just paid them out of the Luke Records general account. It was hundreds of thousands of dollars, fighting all these lawsuits, and they didn't get charged any of it. But they sued me anyway.

There was a bit of unpleasantness going on at the time, but if I'm being completely honest, the breakup of 2 Live Crew disappointed me simply because I don't like it when things don't work out—but it wasn't the end of the world. 2 Live Crew wasn't like other groups. We weren't best friends who came up in the hood together, spitting rhymes in Mom's basement, dreaming of the big time. It was always more of a business relationship. If the business wasn't working, we didn't need to have a relationship.

Because the *Nasty* controversy had pushed me into the spotlight as this spokesman, the media always portrayed it like I was the front man for 2 Live Crew. But it was never like that. From my point of view, I was always a businessman and a record label owner first, and I also played onstage with one of my bands because it was fun to be a rock star. 2 Live Crew was just one of the things I was doing, and it wasn't even the most important thing I was doing.

When I moved Luke Records from the office on Biscayne Boulevard into the office/warehouse complex on Second Avenue, we were the single largest business to move back to Miami's black neighborhoods since the riots. I had sixty employees working for me. I had about eight salespeople on the phone at all times, calling every record store in the country, pushing the product. I had marketing people dialing every radio station in the United States, talking up the artists. I had people pressing the product, people shipping the product, guys working the warehouse. What had started as me hustling LPs out of an old Honda had turned into a multimillion-dollar operation. I'd gotten so big, and the potential in southern hip-hop was so huge, that Atlantic Records came and offered me a pressing and distribution deal, similar to the one that Russell Simmons could have had with Columbia. I'd keep my own masters and my own autonomy, and they'd handle moving the albums.

It was a $5 million deal. I took it. I thought it would be my final step to the big time, a chance to be a part of the big machine, to jockey with the major players. But then I backed out of it. There was a woman at Atlantic named Sylvia Rhone. She wasn't directly involved in my deal, but she was the top African-American executive at the company. She didn't like me. She didn't care for 2 Live Crew and the kind of music we did, but she was going to play a major role in the marketing and promotion of our records. I wanted her to be okay with the deal and I wanted to show her that I respected her position at the company, so I went to her before I signed the deal and I asked her, "Are you okay with this?"

She said, "Yes, I am. It's not a problem. I'm willing to support the albums."

At the time I felt she was just being diplomatic, just saying it to say it. I signed the deal anyway. But then almost immediately I started to regret it. I didn't feel good about the marketing and promotion, didn't think the label was really, fully behind me. I didn't like working for other people. I started to get paranoid about it. The South was just on the brink of becoming a huge market for hip-hop, and I felt maybe the only reason Atlantic signed me up was to keep me from being their competition down here. I gave the money back and bought my way out of the deal; it was a mutual parting. After that I went back to being completely independent, answering to no one, which was the way I liked it.

Being the only black-owned label in the country was important to me. I was able to do things that no corporate label would do. After Public Enemy kicked Professor Griff out of the group for his anti-Semitic comments, I signed him. No corporate label in the country would have done that. I was willing to give Griff a second chance because I understood what his problem was. He didn't hate Jewish people. He was just a kid from the ghetto who didn't know anything about the world. Griff was like Mark Caesar, the Hurricanes player I mentored; he was a young guy, angry, who needed help.

I signed him and brought him down to Miami. He met with Jewish students who reached out to him with questions about his comments. He went with them to the Holocaust Memorial on Miami Beach. He educated himself and learned what he'd done wrong. Luke Records gave Griff the money and the studio time he needed, and he made a great album, *Pawns in the Game*. It sold well despite all the negative media about him; he moved around a hundred thousand copies. Without an independent black-owned label, somebody like Griff never would have had that chance.

I kept finding new and interesting performers, and together we put out big hits. I went and found JT Money & Poison Clan, signed them, and put out "Shake Whatcha Mama Gave Ya." That was a big hit, right up there with 2 Live Crew in record sales. Even to this day they play it on the radio, in the clubs. I kept my own music career going, too. I hooked up with a new producer, Fresh McCray, and called in a few friends like Jiggie Gee and JT Money to MC. Together we recorded my first true solo record: *I Got Shit on My Mind*. We had fun making it. The rapping was tighter and I was able to explore the Luke character more and do some spoken word. I was able to have my say about Kid 'N Play and all the other rappers who'd dissed us during the Broward trial. It had party songs, mellow songs, diss songs, and some good, raunchy adult comedy. I was proud of it. It went to No. 52 on the *Billboard* Albums chart and No. 20 on the R&B/Hip-Hop chart. I didn't need 2 Live Crew. I was a rock star all on my own.

I was putting out an album a year of my solo stuff. *In the Nude* and *Freak for Life* were next. But my main goal with Luke Records was I wanted to prove to the industry that 2 Live Crew wasn't a one-off or a fluke. That I wasn't only selling dirty rap. I wanted to defy expectations, hit people where they wouldn't even know where I was hitting them from. People thought all we did was cuss and scream, so I put out a gospel Christmas album, *Christmas at*

Luke's House. It had a big church choir and featured all the artists from the label. The cover had me in a Santa hat with my kids Lil' Luther and Lucretia next to me.

I wanted to show the world that I could put out a hit record just as well as Columbia or Epic or anybody else without using dirty lyrics or controversy or any of the rest of it. In 1993, Houston Oilers running back Lorenzo White introduced me and my road manager, Ron May, to this guy Pat Johnson, the manager of this R&B trio who called themselves H-Town. I wasn't really into R&B, but my road manager listened to the demo and he and JT kept telling me, "These guys are hot. They're hot. You should give them a listen."

I had to do a show with JT in Houston, and while I was out there Ron and Pat kept telling me I should stay and check the guys out. I kept saying no. I wanted to get back to Miami. Those guys intentionally took the long way to the airport and got lost so I'd miss my flight and have to go check out the band.

H-Town was twin brothers Keven "Dino" Conner and Solomon "Shazam" Conner and their friend Darryl "G.I." Jackson. They lived in the projects. I mean, these guys had nothing. They were dirt fucking poor. First thing I noticed when I sat down with them was the holes in the bottom of their shoes. I talked to them for a little while and asked them to show me their stuff. They started singing for me right there in their living room and I was like, "Fuck. These guys are beyond good. They're incredible."

When I flew them down to Miami to sign them, they had never been on a plane in their life. When they showed up at my house from the airport, they didn't have any bags. I asked them why they didn't have any bags. It was because they didn't have any clothes to bring. They didn't own suitcases. Literally all they came with was the shirts on their backs. In that moment I said to myself, "These guys need help, and they deserve to succeed." I decided I was going to bring them along and make them stars. I took them to the mall right then and bought them each three sets of shoes and some outfits. I took them to get their hair cut, to get a good dinner. I wanted them to stay in Miami and make a killer album, so the next week I bought them a house. I went all-in on these guys. If I never made a dime off them, I figured, I was at least trying to help some young people get out of a desperate situation.

We got those guys in the studio, and once we had an album I went to work using all the talent and expertise and leverage I'd been putting together over the past few years to make it a hit: sales, marketing, radio. All of it. Their first album, *Fever for Da Flavor*, was released on April 15, 1993. It was Luke Records' biggest hit since *Nasty*. It went platinum, sold through the fucking roof. The leadoff single, "Knockin' Da Boots," went to No. 1 on the R&B charts and No. 3 on the *Billboard* Hot 100. The next summer I got them booked on the Coca-Cola Summerfest Tour with Shai, SWV, Jade, Naughty by Nature, and LL Cool J.

H-Town proved to everyone that Luke Records was more than just a one-act label and a flash in the pan. It proved that an independent black label could compete with the majors. Between the success of that album and my own solo work, I was living the life of a high-powered executive and a high-flying rock star at the same time. One of the best things about it was that I finally started getting a little bit of the respect that rappers never gave me back in the eighties, when they went on BET and dissed me and said 2 Live Crew wasn't really hip-hop.

"How Can I Be Down?" was a black music conference that started in Miami in 1993. It raised the city's profile as a new center of hip-hop, and my position as its OG. The younger generation of guys—Puff Daddy, Jay Z, Biggie, Tupac—they came up listening to my music, seeing me all over TV as the face of hip-hop's fight for free speech. They'd always thank me for taking that hit for all of them. I got a lot of love from those guys. They were humble. It was Kool DJ Red Alert who first called me Uncle Luke. I was honored by it. Me and Biggie did a song together, "Bust a Nut." When those guys started making real money, they were coming down here more and more. First thing they'd do when they got off the plane was ring me up: "Yo, Luke. Where I meet you at?" I'd meet them down at my yacht, we'd get some girls, some catering, some booze, have a party.

I couldn't imagine life being any better than I had it at that point in time. To celebrate H-Town's *Fever* going platinum, I decided to throw the biggest party Miami had ever seen. I spared no expense. I rented a huge party boat to take out in the harbor. I invited all the top rappers and musicians in town, hundreds of VIPs, had cases of champagne, prime rib, two huge cakes made in the shape of platinum records. We took the boat out and partied all night. The best part of the evening had nothing to do with H-Town. Since losing reelection as sheriff of Broward County, Nick Navarro had started a company that did protection for private events. As luck would have it, the company I chartered the boat from had hired his company to do security for the night. I was out there in my custom suit drinking the best champagne, on top of the world with one of the biggest R&B acts in America, and Nick Navarro was nothing but a fucking rent-a-cop looking after *my* party.

STILL AFTER ME

The most frustrating thing about my success was that I wasn't left alone to enjoy it. The higher I've climbed in this country, the more racism I've seen. You think it's bad when you're a young kid on the corner and the cops are throwing you up against walls and rifling through your pockets to steal your money. But then you work hard and play by the rules and get ahead, and the harassment gets even worse. It's not as physically threatening, but it grows more intense because once you're a black person with a little bit of money, a little bit of economic leverage, then you're even more of a threat to the status quo, and that's when you really become a target.

When I opened my first nightclub in Hialeah, it was mostly as a side project, a place for my brother Brannard to run and a place for me to break singles. There was a club in a strip mall out there called Strawberries. I bought the owner out and renamed it Strawberries Too. I was still running the Pac Jam II as a teen disco, and wanted a more adult environment to go with the new direction the music was taking. I had problems with the city from day one. Hialeah is a predominantly Cuban area surrounded by black neighborhoods, and Cubans and blacks don't always mix. Everybody out there was Cuban, and they made it clear that they didn't want a bunch of black folks coming around every night, especially to a club owned by a notorious rapper.

They said it would attract crime, and of course if you have a hot nightspot, some kind of bad element is always bound to show up. That's why you have security. I always had off-duty cops at all of my shows. But the city wouldn't let their off-duty cops work the club. When we did call the police for problems that came up, the cops would take forever to show, or sometimes they wouldn't show up at all. They deliberately made it an unsafe environment so they'd have an incident they could use as a pretext to get rid of me. Eventually, it happened. In July of 1990, some guy sprayed the parking lot with an AK-47 during a drive-by. A few months later there was another shooting that left one man dead, and they tried to hang the whole thing on me. I realized I'd never be able to run a safe club out there, so that's when I decided to get out of Strawberries Too and make the move to Luke's Miami Beach. The harassment I got on Miami Beach made my experience in Hialeah look like a walk in the fucking park.

You wouldn't think that opening a nightclub counts as a political act, but when you're a successful black businessman, everything becomes political whether you want it to be or not. When I was growing up, I was down on Miami Beach all the time because of football and the friends I made down there. But most black people would never go, even though the law gave us every right. Miami Beach is a public beach. But they didn't feel welcome, didn't feel comfortable. A lot of blacks still went to Virginia Beach, if they went to the beach at all. By the 1990s, it hadn't much changed.

Black folks I knew were still stuck in this mind-set of "We don't go there." I wanted to change that mind-set. I wanted a high-end, upscale establishment on Miami Beach blacks felt comfortable coming to.

The summer before I opened the club, in June of 1990, Nelson Mandela, just months after being released from prison in South Africa, came to speak at the Miami Beach Convention Center. The city's leaders had refused to issue a proclamation welcoming his visit because of pressure from the Cuban political lobby; Mandela was on friendly terms with Castro, and so a bunch of Cuban politicians had made a bunch of noise about refusing to honor his visit, and black civil rights leaders had responded by calling for blacks to boycott Miami Beach. I didn't see much point in boycotting a place that didn't want us there in the first place. The right response was to bring as much black business to Miami Beach as possible. I ignored the boycott and went ahead with my grand opening.

The harassment started right away, because Miami Beach didn't want blacks on the island, and because I refused to play ball with the powers that be. Miami Beach is a corrupt town. It has been since the days of Al Capone and bootlegging during Prohibition. If you wanted to do business on the Beach, you paid the kickbacks to the right people. The mayor of Miami Beach at the time was Alex Daoud. He eventually went to jail on forty-one counts of bribery. So that tells you something. Even months before I opened I had problems with food inspectors, fire inspectors, you name it —because I wouldn't pay. They weren't even subtle about it. I can still remember a guy from one of these boards coming in and telling me what I had to pay him. I told him he could go fuck himself. I said, "We've been paying for two hundred years in this country. What the fuck am I going to pay you off for?"

He didn't flinch. "Well, I'm going to be your worst nightmare."

The harassment was nonstop. I had every regulatory board and agency imaginable all over me, fucking with me, every week: the fire marshals, the food inspectors, the zoning commission. You're over capacity. You need a sidewalk variance. This, that, and the other. I'd fix it, they'd come back, ding me for something else. Everything I did in that club was legal and aboveboard, because I knew they were watching me. I kept the underage crowd out. Anybody was caught using drugs, the bouncers tossed them. I ran a legit club, but I was harassed constantly.

It was the same hypocrisy I ran into with my music: Andrew Dice Clay can get away with it, but Luther Campbell can't. Some of the other clubs on the Beach were upscale like mine, but some of them were like Studio 54 on steroids. All kinds of crazy shit went on. Despite the anti-nudity ordinance, people would be in there dancing on the bar butt naked. Drag queens would be simulating sex on top of pool tables. One club had a four-hundred-pound stripper. There was a gay club with a guy on a trapeze who would blow himself. There was a fetish club where a guy put a saddle on his back and crawled around naked while women rode him and spanked him like a pony. This one club had a naked woman lying on a table with a pool of chocolate in her belly button; you could dip strawberries in the chocolate and eat them—that had to be some kind of major health-code violation right there. And of course drugs were everywhere. Models would be passed out on heroin in the back rooms. Clubs installed showers so their customers could go wild on Ecstasy.

Did any of those clubs get harassed and fined and closed down? Not one. The anti-nudity ordinance? Never enforced. Miami's nightlife was big business, and the city was happy to have the money. Just not mine. As the months went by, the harassment only got worse. I was actually called down to the city manager's office, and they said, "You've got to cancel this Cuban night." They didn't like having these young Cubans on the Beach. They were that blatant about it. I said, "No, fuck that. If I stop the Cuban night, you're going to turn around and say that *I'm* racist, that *I'm* discriminating, that *I* don't want Cubans in the club. Besides, those guys are my friends. They listen to my music and buy my music the same as everybody else."

When they couldn't get me on code violations, they turned to the old standby complaint about blacks: crime. The cops were all over the club with raids, looking for underage drinking going on, and nothing kills the vibe of a club faster that a bunch of damn cops everywhere. The city even paid to have regular police surveillance of Luke's, like I was running a dope ring out the back door. You'll never keep all the drugs out of a nightclub on Miami Beach, but I wasn't condoning their use out in the open, because I knew they were watching and waiting for any excuse to bust me. I remember one night they had this van parked across the street. They weren't fooling anybody. You can't park some raggedy old van on the main drag of South Beach next to Jaguars and Ferraris.

I turned to my bartender. "Y'all do this," I said. "Go in the kitchen and make some fried chicken and cut up a bunch of watermelon. Take it over there to those motherfuckers in the van. I'm sure they're pretty tired and hungry."

My guys come out with piles of chicken and watermelon on a big serving platter and they walked it across the street and banged on the back door of the van. *Boom, boom, boom, boom, boom!* No answer. I yelled across the street, "No, no, they in there. Keep knocking." *Boom, boom, boom!* Finally the cops opened the door and busted out laughing. They knew I'd nailed them.

The thing that finally got me was the Nuisance Abatement Board, this board of old ladies who pursued citizen complaints. The thing about where Luke's was located, right there by the bridge, meant that every single person coming or going from the beach passed within a block of my club to go back to the mainland. It felt like this board started pinning any crime complaint in that area on the club, saying I had inadequate security and I was attracting a bad element, even though the crime had actually nothing to do with me or my patrons.

A year after we opened, there was a fatal shooting around the corner from Luke's. It didn't even involve people from our club, but the papers splashed it all over the front page: MURDER AT LUKE'S MIAMI BEACH. I agreed to close the club for a week and add more security, which I did, but even after that the harassment never let up. Finally I decided, Fuck it. I threw in the towel. It was the first time in my life I'd ever given up on a fight. I didn't like doing it, but I just came to the realization that it wasn't something worth fighting for. There was no upside. Nightclubs are an unstable business; you can only stay hip for so long, and it was always a side interest for me anyway. People knew I was having trouble. I got an offer on the lease that let me get out with a little bit of profit and wash my hands of the whole mess. I didn't need to waste my energy fighting over bullshit with the Miami Beach Nuisance Abatement Board anyway. I had a much bigger fight waiting in the wings.

After I beat the conservative, moral-majority wing nuts in a court of law, they pretty much disappeared from the headlines, but they never went away. Jack Thompson and the rest of them, they were like a bunch of yappy dogs that kept nipping at my ankles everywhere I went. They were obsessed. They never stopped writing their outraged letters and faxes. They sent them to everyone I did business with or was associated with: to the Miami Hurricanes, to George Lucas, to concert venues where I played, you name it. If they couldn't get me on obscenity, they were going to get me on something else.

Finally, after hundreds of these letters had gone out, one of them hit its target, landing on the desk of some litigious asshole at Acuff-Rose, the publishing company that owned the rights to the song catalog of pop crooner Roy Orbison. One of the tracks we'd done on the non-explicit version of *Nasty, As Clean as We Wanna Be*, was a parody of Orbison's "Oh, Pretty Woman." We took the song, cut it up, made the woman trashy and low-down instead of pretty, and just riffed on the different shit men might say to her. "Big hairy woman / You need to shave that stuff. . . ." "Two-timin' woman / You'se out with my boy last night. . . ."

Technically, you don't need permission to do a parody of something, but it's nice to have just to make sure you don't run into any issues later; "Weird Al" Yankovic always gets permission to do his because he wants everything to be friendly with the artists. I'd reached out to Acuff-Rose with a request long before the album even came out, but they never got back to me. We just went ahead and did the song. For a year after the song came out, Acuff-Rose didn't say a word. It was only when the conservative, wing-nut letter writing started that Acuff-Rose decided their copyright had been violated.

I was about to get another dose of America's racial hypocrisy. At that exact same time, Orbison's company had licensed "Oh, Pretty Woman" for a Julia Roberts movie about a prostitute. Nobody at Acuff-Rose seemed to have a problem with that. In 1982, Van Halen covered "Oh, Pretty Woman" for their album *Diver Down*. The video they made for it was so disturbing and offensive that MTV banned it from the airwaves for years. It featured a woman, tied up to a pole, being groped and fondled by dwarves. (I'm not making this up.) Were there any lawsuits filed there? Nope. But when the nasty black guys down in Miami wrote a parody of it, *now* the song's reputation had been damaged, and it was time to sue.

There was nothing malicious about the song. It was just a random thing we did for fun. It was bawdy and racy, but it was on the clean version of the album, so it wasn't even that explicit. In fact, we put it on the clean version specifically because we didn't think it should be associated with the nasty stuff. But that didn't matter. Acuff-Rose sued the band, sued the label, and Luther Campbell was headed back to court to defend the same rights that other musicians take for granted. I called in Bruce Rogow and we got ready to fight.

Unlike the Broward case, this fight started out going in our favor. The federal district court in Nashville ruled that our song was fair use under the Copyright Act of 1976 and did no harm to the market for the original song. Nobody who was thinking about buying the Roy Orbison single would ever turn around and say, "No, I'd rather listen to 'Big Hairy Woman' instead." But Acuff-Rose appealed the decision and we moved up to the Eleventh Circuit Court of Appeals in Atlanta. The judges on that bench were very conservative and had a very different point of view. They said that it was copyright infringement. We had borrowed too much from the original material, and the commercial nature of our parody had in fact damaged the market value of the original.

I was pissed when we lost, but Rogow calmed me down. He said we should appeal to the Supreme Court. He said it was a long shot and it would cost a lot of money, and they might not even agree to hear the case, but if we went all the way and won it could be not just a victory for me, but a landmark case in the history of intellectual property law. Rogow explained to me that there are two kinds of parody. The first is where you take a song and use it to make fun of something else totally unrelated. That's what "Weird Al" Yankovic does, like when he takes Michael Jackson's "Beat It" and makes it about food. The other kind of parody is where you take a song and rewrite it and use your version to mock the original work, which is what we'd done with "Oh, Pretty Woman."

That's the more controversial kind of parody, and there was no major Supreme Court precedent addressing it. When he told me that, I said, "Let's go. We're not stopping this fight. Let's fight again. They're going to have to knock me out cold before I stop getting up off of the mat. I've gone too far to stop now." Months went by as Bruce filed all the papers and petitions, and then in the spring of 1993 the Supreme Court agreed to hear the case.

Arguments for the case of *Campbell v. Acuff-Rose* went before the Supreme Court on November 9, 1993. Bruce Rogow and I got up early that morning and headed over to the court building. Our limousine pulled up to a mob of spectators and journalists who had lined up around the courthouse waiting to see Luther Campbell have his day in court, but the day was really all about Bruce. It was his turn in the spotlight. Arguing before the Supreme Court, for guys like him this is the big show: it's the Super Bowl. My only job that day was to sit in the gallery as a spectator and look good—and I looked *good*. I had a custom-tailored Armani suit, Armani sunglasses. Everybody was expecting this crazy rapper to get out of the car, but I played it totally conservative and classy and respectful.

We climbed up the steps to the court with this throng of reporters following us. When we got inside, the security was insane. They search us, damn near made us get naked, gave us a locker to hold everything, can't take nothing in with you. The clerk of the court was this no-nonsense guy, a former major general of the army in the Judge Advocate General's Corps. He drilled me on all the court rules and etiquette. Nobody is allowed to say anything in the chambers besides the lawyers and the justices. When Larry Flynt had been before the court over a case with *Hustler* magazine, as the justices entered—the eight men and Sandra Day O'Connor—Flynt yelled out, "Eight assholes and a cunt!" The federal marshals had to come and drag him out. I think they were worried about the dirty rapper making some kind of outburst like that. But I was a gentlemen and I told him he didn't need to worry. He warmed up to me a bit and gave me a great seat in the front row.

The place is intimidating. I'd been in plenty of courtrooms—no windows, shitty fluorescent lights, bureaucratic and depressing—but nothing prepared me for this. Cameras are forbidden in the room, so it's very secretive until you get there. I just sat in awe, looking around at all of the polished mahogany and big white columns and American flags. Before that case, I didn't know that much about the Supreme Court. Mostly because never in my life had I imagined that a black kid from Liberty City would find himself sitting in that room, making an argument about free speech and liberty, with a chance to make a real impact on how the law is applied in this country. Growing up in the ghetto like I did, seeing Arthur McDuffie's killers go free and watching friends get locked up every day, you just assume that the law will never be fair, that justice doesn't exist for people like you. But here I was in the same room where nine white men decided that Jim Crow was the constitutional law of the land, where Thurgood Marshall had argued the case of *Brown v. Board* to end the unjust segregation of schools, and *my name* was on the docket. I had a seat in the front row. Unlike the Broward case, I wasn't even angry this time. I was actually proud that my life and my struggle were going to be a part of something this important.

The justices made their entrance, which was dramatic, all of them stepping out from behind these dark red curtains like they were in some kind of Broadway play. I knew who they all were because I had bios written up on all of them that I'd studied. Of course I knew all about Clarence Thomas. I'd followed all his drama with the porno videos and the pubic hair on the Coke can. I watched him closely, wondering how he was going to treat a brother. But he just leaned back in his chair and glowered at everybody and didn't say shit the whole time.

The first thing they did was announce the briefs that had been filed on behalf of both sides, and that right there really reinforced to me just how big of a deal this was. All these major songwriters and copyright holders had filed on behalf of Acuff-Rose: Dolly Parton, the Songwriters Guild of America, the estates of George and Ira Gershwin, Michael Jackson. (It hurt a little bit that Michael came out against me, I have to admit.) There was big money at stake for these people if the case went my way. Filing briefs on my side were all the biggest comedy shows and satirists in the country: *Saturday Night Live*, *In Living Color*, *Mad* magazine, the *Harvard Lampoon*. If Acuff-Rose won the case, those places would practically have to shut their doors for fear of getting sued every time they did a parody, whether it was for a song or a TV show or whatever.

To this day, people always confuse the Broward case with the Acuff-Rose case. They think I went to the Supreme Court to defend dirty lyrics, but that was never the case. This was about parody and copyright and fair use and what kind of satire is protected by the First Amendment. The court's decision would have the biggest impact on comedians, but it had implications for hip-hop, too. Hip-hop is an art form built on taking existing material and breaking it down, reusing it, and commenting on it. Any ruling that limits free speech has a chilling effect on artists working in every kind of business.

As the petitioner, we got to go first. Bruce stood up in his little bow tie and walked up to the podium to face off against the nine justices for the oral arguments. That's when the shit really got going. For the next half hour, the justices all took turns grilling him. It was a nine-person firing squad. They would ask questions from all sides, and each question would be on a totally different issue than the question before it. Nobody was piggybacking off the last guy's question, so Bruce had to shift and pivot and tackle

complete new trains of thought and call up all this new information each and every time. It was like watching someone have nine
different simultaneous conversations that are all loosely about the
same thing. Me, I would have been lost up there, but Bruce, the
whole time they were coming at him he was firing back. *Boom,
boom, boom, boom!* I was like, *Damn*, Bruce. You are a fucking
beast. Win, lose, or draw, you handled that shit.

Then it was time for the lawyer for Acuff-Rose to take his turn,
and he just melted under the pressure. He cracked. He choked. He
was stumbling through his answers, turning red. The justices were
merciless, same as they'd been with Bruce, and this guy looked
like he wanted to crawl under the table and die. His arguments
were weak to begin with, and then he just blew it trying to defend
them. Watching him choke made me realize just how much of a
badass Rogow really is. To go into that high-pressure situation,
with so much on the line and one chance and one chance only to
get it right? I was glad I'd picked the right lawyer, and as soon as
the oral arguments were over, I had all the confidence in the world
that we were going to come out on top. I wasn't even sweating it.

It takes months for Supreme Court decisions to come down, so
after the hearing we went back to Miami and I went back to work
and waited. In March of '94 the ruling was announced: Nine to
zero in our favor. A commercial parody can be considered fair use.
Justice Souter wrote the opinion. What makes something a parody,
the court said, and not just a rip-off, is that it has to be transforma-
tive: You've taken the original source material and said something
new and different with it. That's what we'd done with "Oh, Pretty
Woman." We didn't realize we were doing it at the time; we were
just riffing in the studio and having fun. But we'd take this song
that was all innocent and naïve about attractive women, and we'd
brought it down to the street and made it about the negative and
dirty ways men really talk about women walking down the street,

and by doing that we were mocking the naïveté of the original lyrics.

It was thrilling to win. I was overjoyed, exhilarated. I'd like to be able to say that winning at the Supreme Court was my victory lap, that I dropped the mic and walked off on top, never to be bothered again, but of course that wasn't what happened. I had exactly two months to enjoy my success before I was back in the headlines with another controversy to endure, another battle to fight. The world wouldn't leave me alone.

The administration at the University of Miami had been trying to get rid of me for years. The players and the fans loved me, loved partying at my clubs, loved all the free Luke Gear I gave out. But as my notoriety as the King of Dirty Rap got bigger and the school kept getting pestered by the Jack Thompsons of the world for being associated with me, they kept trying to distance themselves. They banned me from the sidelines. At one point Sam Jankovich, the athletic director, talked about banning the players from coming to my clubs, because they didn't want the school associated with my image, but he realized that legally he couldn't stop the players from coming—at least the players still had some kind of freedom.

Then on May 20, 1994, the *Miami Herald* put out a huge front-page story from sportswriters Ken Rodriguez and Dan Le Batard: EX-CANES: WE PLAYED FOR PAY. It was a big bombshell, blowing the lid off the "scandal" of Miami players getting money from me and some other former teammates who'd gone on to the NFL and had come home to spread around a little of their good fortune. I knew the article was coming: Le Batard had been hounding me for weeks, running up alongside me at the golf course, yelling questions. "Did you pay them?" "How much did you pay them?" They got some of the facts right, like how I'd pay each player for a touchdown or a tackle. They also talked about a pool of money people had put together to reward the most violent hits, hits to take opposing players out of the game, and the article made it seem like I was a part of that, which was completely wrong. The biggest problem was the tone of the piece and the tone of the coverage it got (and it got a lot). All the outrage was directed at me and at the players, as if we were the ones in the wrong, and not the NCAA, which was getting rich by making all these rules that denied those kids a chance to earn a living or even pay for the food they needed. Everybody made it out that Luther Campbell had done something unethical.

I knew I hadn't done anything wrong. I took care of those players. I mentored them, looked out for them, and kept a little food money in their pockets when they were hungry. The NCAA carried out this big investigation and sent a couple of lawyer types to my house to question me. I didn't take it seriously for one second. When they arrived at my condo downtown, I opened the door and, to fuck with them, I had about a half dozen naked women there in the apartment. Just hot, naked women, walking around, hanging out on the couch, reading the newspaper.

I asked the guys to come in, sat them down. Every time one of them went to ask me a question, another naked woman would walk by. These guys couldn't focus on anything. Finally one of them said, "Uh, could you do something about that?"

"What do you mean? Do something about what? Aren't you here to talk about football? Let's talk about football."

I was having a ball. The whole thing was a big joke to me. They hit me with all their questions: Did you pay anybody? Did you pay for play? How much did you pay for the Notre Dame game in 1991? What's your affiliation with the school? Why were you on the sidelines? One thing I can proudly say is that I didn't tell them one single lie. They'd ask me, "Did you pay anybody?" And

I'd just reply, "Huh? Pay a college football player an honest wage for an honest day's work, why would I do something like that?" I just answered every question with another question, showing them how ridiculous the whole thing was.

They never proved that I'd committed any NCAA violations, but the investigation dug so deep it did turn up a whole bunch of other problems at the school, the biggest of which was the abuse of federal Pell Grants: the school took in a quarter million dollars for the team through bogus applications. The Luther Campbell "pay for play" scandal always get lumped in with the Pell Grant violations as a part of the whole "culture of corruption" of the school, because it happened around the same time. But I had nothing to do with that. I had nothing to do with bounties encouraging kids to be violent on the field or anything else. The real scandal is players not being compensated for their labor.

College sports have grown into a huge industry, in large part because of the swagger and popularity of teams like the Miami Hurricanes. In basketball, the NCAA has a fourteen-year, $11 billion contract with CBS and Turner Sports just for the March Madness playoff alone. That's *one* tournament. We're talking billions and billions of dollars a year, all of it coming in on the unpaid labor of young, mostly poor, mostly black athletes who have no leverage to change the situation or demand fair treatment. The schools say the kids are getting scholarships, but we all know with the amount of time they have to dedicate to playing, they're not getting an equal education. The kids are getting nothing. And if they don't make it in pro sports, they're done.

It's taken a while, but the public consensus is finally coming around to where I was when I first sat those Miami players down in my office and listened to their stories nearly thirty years ago. Every season we get more articles and editorials calling for students to be better compensated, and the tone is completely different than the *Herald* article from 1994. All the outrage points in the other direction, at the NCAA. Football players at Northwestern University are voting to unionize. Federal courts have ruled that college players can be paid for the use of their own likenesses. The tide is turning, and pretty soon people won't look back on the "Luther Campbell pay for play" story as a scandal or a scheme or another chapter in the crazy life of Uncle Luke. They'll see it for what it really was: the beginning of a very long struggle for the fair treatment and compensation these students deserve.

We think it's bad for young black men on the streets, and it is, but the higher up you go, the more racism you encounter. Whether you're upsetting some city councilman in Hialeah or Miami Beach with your nightclub, or you're threatening a multibillion-dollar athletic industry with the truth, if you're a black person who challenges the status quo, they'll come after you with everything they've got. Ever since *Nasty* took off and went platinum, I'd been rolling. Nearly every business I touched turned to gold, and I won nearly every fight that came my way. But I was so consumed with fighting off all the attacks, I took my eye off the one area that I should have been focused on. Soldiers in combat say you never hear the shot that gets you.

BANKRUPT

If there was one thing I was constantly vigilant about—even paranoid about—it was getting screwed. I'd heard all the stories about black artists getting fucked by the industry: all the old blues and R&B songwriters who had their work stolen with no compensation; all the rappers who signed terrible deals in the early days of hip-hop, who went out and had one hit single and then ended up back in the South Bronx projects without a dime.

When you run a successful entertainment company, there's vultures everywhere, guys on the make, guys trying to get in your spot. I'd hire somebody to handle a legal case and all he'd want to do is hang with the talent, go to strip clubs, and drink champagne. Next thing you know, that guy's trying to be a producer or some shit. I'd dealt with a dozen of those types of guys, and I'd always protected myself from them. Allen Jacobi, the lawyer who recommended Bruce Rogow to me, was one of the first entertainment lawyers I worked with. Allen was actually a stand-up guy, but he *looked* like one of these sharks who'd bend you over and fuck you sideways. I didn't trust Allen from here to the other side of the street. I didn't trust anybody.

But as Luke Records got bigger, I couldn't do everything myself. I was running a label, running a club, launching my solo career. I had to find somebody I could trust to watch the operation and keep everything running. I had a lot of legal shit going on, issues related to the business, on top of the First Amendment battles I was already fighting. Like every record company, I had distributors who owed me money; distributors are always late in paying, holding back your money for some bullshit reason or other, and you have to keep lawyers on retainer just to harass them and get what you're owed. There were also a lot of legal issues related to sampling; hip-hop DJs had built this whole new art form based on sampling other artists, but it had all been done on the fly, not thinking about how to make it work with existing copyright law. So the courts were now catching up, developing new legal standards for fair compensation to the original artists, and at that point in time every major hip-hop label had a lot of ongoing cases to settle what was owed for the songs our acts had sampled over the years. Plus the record business is one of the most corrupt, crooked industries on the planet; if you're not being sued, you're suing somebody else. It's constant.

In 1991 I was working with the Miami law firm Bailey & Hunt to handle my taxes, and there was a lawyer there working on some of my business named Joe Weinberger. He was a University of Miami Law School graduate, a specialist in tax law. I thought he did good work. More importantly, I liked the vibe he gave off. He wasn't like all these slick motherfuckers you find in the record business. He wasn't some hip-hop guy. He wasn't even into the music. He was just a tax nerd. I'm talking about the nerdiest nerd you've ever met. Short little Jewish guy with the dorky khakis and

THE BOOK OF LUKE | 217

the thick glasses. I thought, This is the kind of guy I need watching the farm, just a straight numbers guy to dot the i's and cross the t's. And Bailey & Hunt was one of the most reputable firms in Miami. I asked Weinberger to join Luke Records as my in-house counsel and chief financial officer, and he came over and joined the company.

For a while everything went great. I was a rock star on top of the world. The money was coming in, and the legal issues were being handled. The only major issue I had at the time was the breakup of 2 Live Crew. Since Weinberger was a tax attorney, he said we should bring in a litigator to handle the settlement. He recommended a guy he knew, a Cuban lawyer named Nicolas Manzini. Manzini didn't have a background in entertainment law, but he was a skilled negotiator, which is what Weinberger said we needed. I trusted his opinion and brought Manzini on for a $10,000-a-month retainer.

Manzini did a great job with the case. All the issues with Mr. Mixx and Marquis and Fresh Kid Ice, they were all settled pretty quickly. It was amicable, too. Marquis went and said some shit about me in the press, but that was just trying to stir up beef to promote this solo project he was trying to do. The truth is that we all walked away from the table on good terms. We just agreed that the ride was over and it was time for each of us to do his own thing.

The 2 Live Crew catalog was a huge piece of my business, and if that settlement had gone badly I might have had problems, but Manzini had done such a good job with it I agreed with Weinberger that he should handle another problem I had: MC Shy D. MC Shy D, also known as Peter Jones, was one of the first acts I'd signed to Luke Records. His albums sold okay in Florida and in the Atlanta area, but he was not a huge success. I dropped him after his first two albums, *Got to Be Tough* and *Comin' Correct*, and had paid him $95,645 in royalties on the two records, which was exactly what my records showed I owed him. But same as with Mixx and Marquis, Jones felt he was entitled to more. He went and hired an entertainment lawyer, this guy Richard Wolfe, and in June of 1990 they sued me, saying I owed an additional $180,000.

The whole thing was a nuisance. This was coming right in the middle of the Broward trial and I had much bigger concerns, like not going to jail for obscenity. I felt like, even with the most generous interpretation of the contract, Jones was owed maybe another fifty grand, and I was willing to settle for something in the mid-five figures just to make it go away. That case had been lingering for months when Manzini and Weinberger came on board, and I put Manzini on Wolfe to try and settle it.

Those guys were going back and forth when Jones went and did some typical thug-rapper bullshit: he got in an argument in the parking lot of a club in Atlanta and shot a guy in the leg. Jones ended up getting sentenced to a year in jail, and Wolfe realized his leverage was slipping away. He offered to come down thirty grand and settle for $150,000. I'd have taken that deal in a heartbeat— but I'd never told Manzini I was willing to go that high, and he never brought me the offer. He rejected it out of hand because I'd told him, ideally, I wanted to pay about fifty grand. But he could have at least *told* me about the offer. It was a costly mistake. In the meantime, Manzini was taking home $10,000 a month, costing me almost as much as it would have taken to settle and take the whole thing off my plate.

Was I paying as much attention to this as I should've been? No. I was bunkered down with Bruce Rogow, worried about taking Acuff-Rose to the Supreme Court. I was putting all my mental energy over there, going to circuit court in Nashville, to the appeals court in Atlanta. It was costing me hundreds of thousands just to fight that case, and if I'd lost it would have cost me hundreds of thousands more. That was a big fucking deal. Compared to that, the MC Shy D case was nothing. It was nickel-and-dime shit, just some minor piece of business that I'd delegated to Manzini. I figured at some point he'd come back with a settlement for eighty, ninety grand or something and that would be the end of it.

Manzini rejected four other offers from Wolfe, and by the time Jones was out of prison, Wolfe refused to lower his offer and decided to go to trial in December of 1992. The only thing at issue was the accounting practices of Luke Records, whether or not they accurately reflected what Jones should be paid. Wolfe's contention was that the records were wrong. My contention was always that the records were spot-on. I wasn't running my shit out of a shit house. I wasn't hustling records out of my mamma's utility shed anymore. I'd hired professional CPAs, the best tax attorneys in town. As far as I knew, we had a record of every sale. We have catalog numbers. You go to the manufacturer and say, "How many copies of XR-102 did you press?" Then you go to the distributor, "How many XR-102 did you purchase?" Then you add and subtract. It's not difficult. I had all that information because that's how I kept track of what I was owed. You don't just lose stuff like that.

But Manzini made what turned out to be a crucial mistake. He tried to make a counterargument against Jones by saying that Luke Records had overestimated the number of records sold, so Jones had actually been *over*paid, that he owed money back to the label. But in making that argument, Manzini had agreed in principle that the records were not accurate, that my company had not been keeping its own books properly. Since Manzini wasn't an entertainment lawyer, he didn't know about a key legal precedent in the history of the record industry. It's the case of *Thomas v. Gusto Records*, which came out of Nashville in 1991, right around the time Jones first sued me. It's now considered a landmark case in the business, but Manzini wasn't an entertainment lawyer, he was a Florida litigator, so he wasn't familiar with it.

B. J. Thomas, who wrote "Raindrops Keep Fallin' on My Head," sued his label and the court decided that whenever there is doubt about a record company's accounting of its sales, the artist is allowed to present expert testimony to determine the real sales figures. With his counterargument, Manzini had opened that door. Wolfe and Jones were able to bring in their own accountants to plow through my files and present the court with their estimate of what they thought the sales were, as well as what Jones's royalties ought to be based on that estimate. In October of 1994, after nearly four years of depositions and hearings and filings, the judge ruled that Luke Records owed this guy $1.6 million. By the time they added legal fees and punitive damages, it was $2.3 million.

When I heard that, I was shocked, floored. I said, "This is the craziest shit in the world." $1.6 million in royalties? You have to be doing 2 Live Crew–level sales to make that kind of money. MC Shy D never even came close to that. I knew Wolfe and his team had to be doing creative accounting of their own. First thing I did was call Weinberger and Manzini and say, "Let's fucking appeal." Manzini wanted to. He said we'd win. But Weinberger said we didn't have enough cash on hand to do it. To appeal a civil case in the state of Florida, you have to post a bond of 124 percent of the judgment just to start the process. I'd have to take $3 million in cash and set it aside to post the bond. Then there'd be years of legal expenses on top of that. I didn't care. I'd never shied away from a fight when I knew I was right. I said, "Fuck it. Put up the $3 million."

But I couldn't. I didn't have it.

While all this MC Shy D stuff was going on, 2 Live Crew had come back. They weren't gone but a year or two when they realized shit wasn't working out for them on their own. Mixx was jumping around, producing on different albums, doing work-for-hire-type shit. Brother Marquis had moved to Atlanta and started a group with DJ Toomp called 2 Nazty. That bombed. The solo album that Fresh Kid Ice did for Luke Records, *The Chinaman*? Horrible. Probably the worst record we ever released.

It didn't look like those guys were going to make it with solo careers, but there was still a lot of demand out there for new music from 2 Live Crew. We had an offer to do a single for the soundtrack of the new Ice Cube movie, *Friday*. Seemed like it'd be a fun thing to do, and there was no bad blood between us. We decided to put the group back together and re-sign them with the label. I asked Weinberger to work up the contract, and I thought what he came back with was terrible. The way I read it, I felt like it was loaded in favor of the other guys against me with rights and conditions that no other artist on the label had. It didn't make any sense to me.

At the same time, I was involved in signing a new distribution deal with Sony/Relativity. I'd had a bad experience with Atlantic, but now I was expanding into R&B. Back then, in R&B you needed a big machine behind you in a way that you didn't for hip-hop. Rather than keep working with all these independent distributors, I was in negotiations with Sony/Relativity to take over and consolidate that part of the business. I had a big New York law firm handling that deal for me—Grubman, Indursky, Schindler, & Goldstein, one of the most powerful firms in the business.

There was one sticking point in the deal over the subject of bar codes. Switching from one distributor to another, it would have been beneficial to Luke Records to change the bar code on the inventory, so that we could separate the returns coming from the old distributor from the returns at the new distributor. Any losses coming from the independent distributor wouldn't count against the money we'd be owed from Sony. We were insisting that Sony change the bar codes, and Sony didn't want to.

It was a Friday morning, maybe a week or so before Christmas. The MC Shy D decision had just come down six weeks before, and I was wrestling with how to resolve that. I was on my way to Canada to do a show that night. The way I recall it happening was that Weinberger came to me and told me that the lawyer from Grubman had called to say the contract was ready to sign. So I said, "Great. I'll stop off in New York on my way to Canada and sign the deal." And that's what I did. I swung by Sony's offices and signed the contract, but I should have reviewed it, or at least double-checked the bar code language, and I never should have signed it since it didn't come to me straight from my law firm. Monday morning I called Grubman to talk to my lawyer and tell him the contract was done. First thing out of his mouth was, "You did *what*? I didn't say the contract was ready to sign." The problem with the bar codes was still in the language of the deal, and I wasn't able to back out once I'd signed. What the hell had Weinberger done, telling me Grubman had okayed the contract to sign? Did he have some miscommunication with them? Did he deliberately have me sign a bad deal? Whatever was going on, between that and the contract he'd drawn up for 2 Live Crew, I started to get a bad feeling. I fired Weinberger. But I was too late.

A few days later, right around New Year's, my assistant Nikki got a call from Jose Armado, who ran Caribbean Cassettes, one of the local pressing plants I used to make my records. Armado was one of my best and oldest vendors; he'd built his business on the work that I brought him. He called that day looking for me, but I was out. He told Nikki that he'd received a disturbing phone call from Weinberger. He said that Weinberger had called him and told him that Luke Records was broke, that I was never going to pay him on the invoices that were outstanding from the past few months, and that he should join Weinberger in forcing me into bankruptcy. In Florida, if you have unpaid creditors, all it takes is three of them to band together and they can force you into what's called a Chapter 7, an involuntary bankruptcy, in an attempt to recover their debt. Armado said he told Weinberger, "No way." He never liked Weinberger. He called him a snake on the the phone call with Nikki. That's how he phrased it, "Tell Luther this snake just called me . . ."

The next couple of days, we started to piece together what was happening. We started reaching out to clients and vendors. A lot of them hadn't been paid properly, and they were getting calls from Weinberger trying to band them together to put me in Chapter 7. Why would my former CFO and in-house counsel be trying to force me into bankruptcy? It turned out that Weinberger had put himself in a position where he could say that Luke Records owed *him* money, too. A lot of money. I'd never asked Joe Weinberger for money in my life, as a loan or anything else, but he'd gone and put a few hundred thousand dollars of his own money into the company account, calling it a loan to help cover expenses. He insisted later that Luke Records had needed the cash. It didn't make any sense to me. You're the CFO and you see a cash flow problem, but you give the company a secret loan and you don't actually tell the head of the company that there's an issue? Whatever his motivation, this "loan" meant that Weinberger was now a creditor to the company, and since he was no longer an executive employee owing the company any kind of fiduciary duty, the door was open for him to come back around, find some willing partners, and drive me into bankruptcy.

Now don't that sound like some devious shit?

I sued Weinberger for tortious interference. On January 11, 1995, the court held a hearing on my request for an injunction to stop him from contacting anyone doing business with me. The court found that Luke Records' reputation and ability to do business had suffered "irreparable harm" due to Weinberger's actions, and that there was "a substantial likelihood of success on the merits for a claim for interference." In plain English: the facts of the case were in my favor and I had a good chance of winning if I took him to trial.

The injunction was granted. But, again, I was already too late. One week before I filed for the injunction, on January 4, Weinberger had gone and filed incorporation papers for a new company: Lil' Joe Records. He was starting his own record label? Dude was a tax attorney. He didn't know the first thing about music. What acts was he planning to sign? How was he going to make money? All those questions would eventually be answered.

Despite the injunction, Weinberger had already made enough phone calls to convince a handful of my creditors to file for Luke Records to go into involuntary bankruptcy. As I recall, it was one of my distributors, a sound engineer who was owed about a thousand dollars, and one other guy. They filed the petition on March 28. At the same time, I was still trying to figure out what had happened with the Sony/Relativity deal. The new H-Town album, *Beggin' After Dark*, had just dropped. It was blowing up, already well on its way to being certified gold, and the money from that could have helped me take care of a lot of my problems. But Sony/Relativity wouldn't release any of the money from the album. They said there were too many losses being reported from previous distributors— the bar code issue.

Once the Chapter 7 petition was filed, I had to go and find a new lawyer to clean up the mess. She told me if I filed for Chapter 11, a voluntary bankruptcy and reorganization, I could preempt the involuntary bankruptcy, renegotiate the bad contract with Sony, and have at least some control over what was happening. So that's what I did. On June 12, 1995, Luke Records filed for Chapter 11.

When you file for bankruptcy, the first thing the court does is send in an accountant to go through your books and establish what's what: every asset and receivable you own, every outstanding debt that you owe. What this accountant uncovered was that my accounts were in terrible shape. The artists on my label, groups like Poison Clan and H-Town—they'd stopped receiving royalty statements. They were getting angry, wanting to know where their money was. The pressing plants and other vendors I worked with, they hadn't been getting paid, either. Their accounts were falling behind, 90 days in arrears, 120 days in arrears. I'd never even been notified about it, and I had brought Weinberger in as CFO to oversee this kind of stuff. This whole time my focus had been on launching H-Town and fighting the Acuff-Rose case. I trusted that the person I hired to handle it was handling it.

This accountant also uncovered a paper trail of checks that Weinberger had written to himself from the company. As CFO, Weinberger was allowed to write checks on the company account up to $3,000. The safeguard I had in place was that all checks had to be countersigned by myself or my office manager, Debbie Bennett, but there was no limit on the number of checks he could write in a given period. Weinberger had been making these checks out to himself, sometimes a stack of them in the space of a month, and taking them to Debbie—and she'd countersigned them. All of them. She said Weinberger had told her these checks were for reimbursement on the "loan" he'd given me—the loan I never asked him for.

I don't recall exactly the number of checks, but it was a lot. I confronted Debbie about it. I thought she had to be in on whatever was going on. She put it back on me. She said I'd given Weinberger too much authority and too much say in the company. I'd been so busy that whenever legal or financial issues had come up I'd gotten in the habit of saying "Ask Weinberger. Talk to Weinberger. Check with Weinberger." She'd grown accustomed to taking Weinberger's word as mine. If he said it, she assumed it was either coming from me or it was something I knew about. So she'd deferred to him without question.

She wasn't wrong about the blame being on me. I trace it back to one terrible, regrettable decision on my part. Back before I hired Weinberger, my accountant was this guy Sharpton, from one of the top black accounting firms in Miami. After Weinberger came in, he was always coming to me with complaints about Sharpton: Sharpton didn't use the right bookkeeping system, this and that. Weinberger kept saying he couldn't work with the guy and he wanted to bring in a new accountant he had a good working relationship with.

I never went to business school. All my decisions on how to run Luke Records came from instinct. My approach to the label came from my background in sports. I thought of that company like a team. I was the coach, and my management team was my coaching staff. When you're a head coach and you bring in a new offensive coordinator, you usually let him bring in his own guys, the people he works best with, his own quarterback coach, his own running back coach. So when Weinberger said he'd work better with someone else instead of Sharpton, I said, "Okay. You're handling the money. That's your crew. You staff it however you think is best."

Because I was thinking of my company like a team, I wasn't thinking about checks and balances, having competing forces to keep tabs on each other. I still believe if I'd kept Sharpton, he would have served as that needed counterbalance and notified me of all the financial trouble spots that were later revealed in the bankruptcy court. By the time I was stuck in the middle of the bankruptcy, it was too late. I'd spent thousands on lawyers. My money was tied up in mortgages, recording studios, all the things I used to run the business. I couldn't believe it, but it was true: Luke Records was broke.

I spent the next year in bankruptcy court, my assets being picked over and divvied up by lawyers from all my major creditors. My yacht, gone. The nightclub I'd bought in Pensacola, gone. The property I owned, with the exception of my house and my parents' house, gone. I'd also started a real-estate development and mortgage company to develop housing in black neighborhoods. They took that, too.

Then came the final twist. Weinberger did more than just collect on his so-called "loan" to Luke Records. I came to find out that Weinberger and Richard Wolfe, MC Shy D's lawyer, had gone to law school together. They were friends. Was another conspiracy going on there, or was I just paranoid? I know what it looked like to me at the time. Because of the court judgment, MC Shy D was my biggest single creditor. Wolfe was appointed by the court to serve as a liquidating trustee; his job was to oversee the dissolution of the company's assets. As part of that, he approved the sale of most of the Luke Records catalog, including 2 Live Crew and all my masters, to his old friend Joe Weinberger for $800,000. I'd say that's maybe a tenth of what it was worth, but no one came to the table with a better offer and the court signed off on the sale. My catalog was now the property of Lil' Joe Records—the new label Weinberger had conveniently thought to incorporate while forcing me into Chapter 7. Sony ended up breaking off the rights to H-Town and taking that. I got to keep my office, the Luke Records name, some of the publishing rights, but my business was gutted.

The bankruptcy judge approved the final settlement on March 22, 1996. As part of the final settlement, in addition to the $800,000 paid to the bankruptcy trustees for the rights to 2 Live Crew and the Luke Records catalog, Weinberger did make a payment directly to me to close the transaction. Per the agreement, he paid me $10. The largest independent, black-owned record label in America, the biggest piece of black-owned intellectual property in the history of hip-hop up to that point, and all I got for it was ten lousy bucks.

But when Weinberger bought the rights to my catalog, he didn't buy the rights to me. I wasn't signed as an artist to my own label. Luther Campbell never had a contract with Luke Records, because why would I need a contract with myself? If Weinberger thought he could own me he was dead wrong. I'll never let anybody own me. While the bankruptcy was being settled, I couldn't use the Luke Records name for anything, so I formed a separate company, Luther Campbell Music, and made a one-off distribution deal with PolyGram. I wanted to put out an album right away so the world would know: Luke ain't dead.

I went into the studio angry and came out with my biggest album yet: *Uncle Luke*. I brought in the best talent in the country: Ice Cube, Trick Daddy, Verb, the Notorious B.I.G. The single from the album, "Scarred," blew the fuck up. Hottest record in the damn country. Some new Luke shit. You couldn't walk into a club anywhere in America without hearing it. *Uncle Luke* hit No. 8 on the R&B/Hip-Hop Albums chart. "Scarred" went to No. 64 on the *Billboard* Hot 100 Singles and to No. 7 on the Hot Hip-Hop Singles. Even with everything they threw at me, I could still make a hit record as good as anyone in the business. It was a testament to the fact that even though I was hurt, I was gonna get better because I was tough.

The producers and rappers who worked with me on that album, they stood by me in a tough time. When you go through something like what I went through, you find out who your friends really are. You lose your money, people are out trashing your reputation, and you see who stays and who runs for the exit. H-Town left and went with Sony. A year later they were on BET, talking about how Luke put chains on their legs and now they were free. But I bet they never got the love over there that they'd had with Luke Records.

Within a couple years, H-Town's career dried up and they went nowhere.

I've never been more wrong about a human being than I was about Joe Weinberger. This guy I'd pegged as the nerdiest nerd on earth, after he bought out my catalog he went and took Lil' Joe Records and he started signing up groups. He was driving around Miami in a pimped-out Jaguar. This little Jewish tax attorney, riding around Miami with a baseball hat turned around backward, wearing all this jewelry, big gold chains, a blinged-out, diamond-crusted Rolex watch, all these fat gold rings. It was crazy.

The other guys from 2 Live Crew, they didn't stick around. Mixx and Marquis and Fresh Kid Ice, they signed with Lil' Joe, and it must have been pretty terrible for them because they all ended up suing each other to try and get out of the deal. They've never come close to the level of success we once had, and they can't perform together or even use the name 2 Live Crew without Joe Weinberger's say-so. He owns them.

After it was all over I did a lot of soul-searching. Should I be mad at myself? Should I kick myself? No. Most musicians who go broke, they don't pay their taxes, they blow it all on cocaine and hookers. I made an error in judgment. I wish I'd done things differently, but I sleep easy knowing I made the best decisions I could with the information and experience I had at the time.

To this day Weinberger insists he did nothing illegal. But even if he never broke the law that doesn't mean he didn't do me wrong. At a minimum, when I was in a bad spot he turned on me and took advantage of the situation. My whole career I'd been fighting— against the racist cops who tried to shut down the Ghetto Style DJs, against the moral majority wing-nuts who tried to censor me, against the sleazy record executives who wanted to screw me. I'd been so busy looking for sharks in the water I hadn't kept an eye out for snakes in the grass in my own backyard.

At the time all the shit came down, I was seeing red. I felt the same as I did after Handsome Harry was killed and I shot up that car. Weinberger, Wolfe, Manzini, all of them, I wanted to blow their fucking heads off. I wanted to go chop them up into little pieces. I still had that thug voice going in the back of my mind, but I had to think about my kids, what a stupid waste it would be for me to spend my life in jail because of anger over what somebody else did.

I did feel like I had a claim to pursue in court. As the judge in my tortious interference case said, I had a "substantial likelihood of success" based on the facts. Between the $3,000 checks, the calls to my creditors, what if anything had gone on with the signing of the Sony/Relativity deal, I believed if I pressed it I could prove what I believed then and still believe to this day: that there was a deliberate attempt to sabotage my business and drive me into bankruptcy, a hostile takeover from start to finish. I'll never know for sure because I decided to let it go. By that point I'd been dragged down in court proceedings for five years, ever since Broward. I'd thrown good money after bad, easily a million dollars, paying lawyers for this, that, and the other. My resources were already strapped. Did I want to pour those last remaining resources into another lawsuit and spend another five years in court with a whole bunch of other lawyers, or did I want to take what I had left and get on with the things that are important to me in life?

It wasn't a difficult choice. As part of the bankruptcy settlement, I signed a General Release and Hold Harmless Agreement, releasing Joe Weinberger and Lil' Joe Records from any and all future claims, damages, or demands. The same with Sony and everybody else. I washed my hands of the whole thing. I paid my creditors what the court said I had to pay, I took my $10 check from Joe Weinberger, and I never looked back. Today, I'm fine with it. I really am. Whatever Weinberger did, he knows he did it, and he has to live with that for the rest of his life. He has to live in an eternal hell, knowing that the food on his table is there because he's a vulture. To this day, the money he makes comes from exploiting assets he has no business owning. Every day he's out there selling my merchandise. Every day he's got to eat off my shit. Knowing that he has to live that way, that's justice enough for me.

LUTHER CAMPBELL V. UNCLE LUKE

Right before I filed for bankruptcy, I discovered Trick Daddy during a rap contest at my Pac Jam disco. I told the crowd that night, "Whoever wins, I'm gonna sign you to a contract." Trick Daddy was a kid named Maurice Young who'd just got out of prison for cocaine possession, carrying a concealed weapon, and violating probation. He had these razor-sharp rhymes he wrote while he was locked up. He intimidated everyone else onstage.

Trick won the contest hands down. His father was somebody I knew from the neighborhood. He was still in a prison, and he asked me to look after his son. The kid had no place to stay, so he was living with me. He was a hell of a cook. He'd cook breakfast every morning. He was staying with me while all the bankruptcy shit was going on. Watching all these people fuck each other over, he thought maybe he didn't want to be a rapper after all.

But Trick was too good. Kid was going to blow up. That's why I brought him along to the studio and featured him on "Scarred." It was the first time the world heard of Trick Daddy. The only catch was I couldn't sign him. At the time all of my money and assets were tied up in the bankruptcy proceedings. The money I made from *Uncle Luke* and "Scarred" was being used to keep the lights on. I told Trick that as soon as I sorted some shit out, I was going to sign him and produce his first record. After "Scarred" came out and people realized he was unsigned, the kid was getting offers, and he didn't wait around for me.

When Luke Records started to liquidate, all my best people got picked up by these other local producers looking to be the next Luther Campbell. One of these guys was Ted Lucas, who started Slip N Slide Records. He staffed it up with former Luke Records guys and started signing artists, convincing them that I was done and he was the heir apparent. Trick Daddy didn't want to wait. Even after I'd mentored him, had given him a place to live, put him on this hit single, he went and signed with Slip N Slide. I wasn't mad at him. I put him in touch with great producers, helped him in every way I could. But I was disappointed. I wish that he'd waited for me. I was out of bankruptcy just a couple months later.

I once had a conversation with Russell Simmons about the music business. He said, "Don't fall in love with no fucking artist. They're a catalog number. There's going to be a time when the record don't work, and you gotta let it go. There's going to be a time when the artist don't work, and you gotta let it go. Make sure it's all business and not personal, because if you make it personal, then these guys will fuck you. They always blame their mistakes on you."

I didn't run my label in a traditional way. I'd always made it personal. I signed 2 Live Crew because I was frustrated nobody would give them a chance. Poison Clan, I got those motherfuckers out of jail and put them on their feet. I bought H-Town a house and put clothes on their back because they came from nothing. I looked after Trick while his dad was in prison. I always ran my label and saw my business as having a purpose beyond just making money. I was about wanting these guys to succeed and giving them a voice. I was about giving opportunity to people who otherwise wouldn't have had anything. I always felt about my artists the same way I felt about my University of Miami guys; I wanted to mentor them, help them. Russell was right: the business doesn't work that way. When you make it personal, it's nothing but heartbreak. Because things don't always work out, and at the end of the day the artists just don't care about you. Artists are about themselves. It's always the label's fault when the albums don't work. They always fuck their own money up, and they'll always come back to you for more. After I lost Trick Daddy to Slip N Slide, after all the betrayal and backstabbing that went on with the bankruptcy, I started to ask myself, Is this a business I really want to be in anymore?

I kept going for a little while. I made a deal to bring my label to Island Records. I wasn't up to being fully independent anymore, and Island's founder, Chris Blackwell, had a lot of respect for me and let me do my own thing. I did two more solo albums, *Changin' the Game* and *Somethin' Nasty*. I did "Raise the Roof" with No Good but So Good. The single was a huge hit, went to No. 26 on the *Billboard* Hot 100 and No. 1 on the Hot Rap Singles. We did a killer video with Diddy, Ice Cube, Stuart Scott, tons of people. I could still put out a hit, but my heart wasn't in it. Breaking records, always trying to follow up and top the last hit, holding artists' hands, it no longer appealed to me.

The last artist I discovered at Island was this young guy named Armando Perez. I found him by sitting at home and reading the newspaper and looking at the new census report. The report said that Latinos were the fastest-growing demographic in this country. I'd always known that a large part of 2 Live Crew's fan base was made up of Latinos. Mexicans, Cubans, Puerto Ricans, they all loved our music because of the Latin rhythms and the bass and the energy we put out. I thought it was fucked up that they didn't have their own big-name hip-hop artist. All they had was Fat Joe and Big Pun from New York, who were known more for being fat than for lyrical ability or for being Latino. I looked at it this way: I'm from Miami. It's a predominantly Cuban demographic and culture here. I can't say I'm a Miami label and not have a Cuban artist. My career won't be complete until I sign one. I told my guys on the street, "Go find me a Cuban artist." One of them came in with a videotape of the rap battle. Out of all the guys on the tape, this one guy caught my attention. He was as relentless as his stage name: Pitbull. I said, "Go find that motherfucker. I like him."

Pitbull came in. He was a tough guy. He was a little Cuban kid, but he was living like a black guy. He had the cornrows and all that shit. We hung out, went for a ride. I spent a few days getting to know him. His parents had come over in the Mariel boatlift. He was living in the streets, going hard. He was out in Opa-locka, Cal City, Hialeah, slinging, getting his money the best way he could. But he wasn't a bad person. He was trying to help his mom; she couldn't make ends meet. I saw a lot of me in him.

I knew he could rap. I knew he could battle. I got Lil' Zane, who was hot at the time, to do a record with me and Pitbull, "Lollipop." We laid down the track. I took the track to Power 96, which is the Cuban station in Miami. I took it over there personally, told them, "Look, this is a no-brainer."

They came back the next day and said, "We can't play this song."

"This is a fucking Cuban rapper that I'm giving y'all, and y'all can't play this song?"

"Naw, we can't play it."

I took it to 99 Jamz, the black station. They played it. Pitbull started blowing up all over Miami. He was going hard in the studio. He was a great freestyle battle rapper, but he had to learn how to be a great studio rapper. It's a different challenge, but he was ferocious going after it. He wanted to be the best. I did all I could for him. I'd take him on tour with me. I'd introduce him to crowds, hazing the shit out of his ass to teach him. Just like how I did all the rest of them. I would show him: this how you deal with the fans, this how you deal with radio stations, this is how you deal with retail-store appearances.

I was going out all over Miami and all over the South, hyping him and his music. I put him on a few tracks on *Somethin' Nasty*. But even as I was doing it, even as I was all excited about this kid's potential, I could tell my heart just wasn't in it. I'd lost my appetite for the record business. I'd been headed that way ever since the bankruptcy, but now I was sure of it: I didn't have the appetite for it anymore. I knew Pitbull was going to be huge. Everything he has today, millions of records sold, No. 1 singles, I knew back then that he was going to be that huge. I loved him like a son, but I also knew he deserved a mentor and a label that was going to give his career 110 percent, and I wasn't that guy at that time in my life. I told Pit, "You're going to be a star, but I'm not the guy to get you there." I called around, talked to people I knew, and I got him on the right label with the right people. One of the biggest rap stars of the new millennium, and I sent him down the road to take a different path. That was my million-dollar ticket back to the big time, and I didn't take it. But it was the right decision—for him and for me. I was ready to put my days as record label owner behind me.

The history of Luke Records is one of the most important stories in the history of rap. It was the first black-owned hip-hop label to challenge the dominance of white corporations. It was the only label with the independence to take the fight for free speech all the way to the Supreme Court. For many music writers, the history of black entrepreneurship in hip-hop starts with Puff Daddy and Bad Boy Records, with Master P and No Limit, with the Wu Tang Clan and Wu Wear.

I inspired the generation that came after me. After Luke Records blew up in the early nineties, all the young guys were coming down to Miami and hanging with me: Puffy, Biggie, Jay Z. They came down and had nothing but questions. How did I do it? What kind of deals did I make? Who are the best distributors? All the things I learned on my own in the beginning, I shared it all with them. They read my interviews in *The Source*, talking about how I own my own record company, manufacture and sell my own product, and they took all the information and used it as a blueprint. They took it back to the major labels and said, "We want to own our own label. We want to call it Bad Boy. We want to call it Roc-a-Fella. We want to run our own A&R units. We want control over producers." And they started getting it. To this day Jay Z calls me the Michael Jordan of hip-hop, because I was the first one to show everybody how to make serious money.

Part of the reason I get no respect from these writers and journalists is that the South itself gets no respect, and I'm the father of southern hip-hop. I'll never forget going to the New Music Seminar in New York back in the early 1990s. I was on this hip-hop discussion panel, and Hank Shocklee from the Bomb Squad started dissing 2 Live Crew and my label. He said southern rap was nothing but a fad. I got pissed off. I stood up in front of all of these people in this Marriott Marquis ballroom, about 1,500 people, and I said, "That's some bullshit. Mark my words: when it's all said and done, the South will run hip-hop. No disrespect to New York and California, but we're bigger. We have North Carolina, Memphis, Houston, Charleston, Georgia, Florida, Alabama. Once we fire up, you're gonna eat your words. Right now, I'm selling a half million records a month, not including New York. I'm doing the same numbers that you're doing in one town, but I'm doing it throughout the South. Imagine what will happen when more Luther Campbells come on." There was so much untapped potential in the South, and by the end of the decade it had taken off—and it all flowed from one place: Miami.

When I signed MC Shy D, he was the first rapper in Atlanta to get a record deal. There was no Atlanta scene to speak of back then. There were no southern labels there. L.A. Reid and Babyface's LaFace Records and Jermaine Dupri's So So Def Recordings hadn't come along yet. There was no southern radio, even; all of Atlanta's urban stations were playing New York music. But what we did in Miami, creating our own sound, that then flowed up to Georgia. Georgia artists got inspired and started saying, Damn, we want our own sound. We want to do something different than Miami, but we don't just want to imitate New York. Lil Jon pioneered crunk music, an evolution of Miami Bass. T.I., Usher, Ludacris, Goodie Mob, Outkast—they all started to blow up.

I signed the first rapper out of New Orleans, this kid named Bust Down who had a hot song, "Nasty Bitch," that I loved. Pretty soon after that, Ronald "Slim" Williams and Bryan "Birdman" Williams were setting up shop down there as Cash Money Records, which they did because they were having a hard time getting me to sign them. Birdman tells a funny story of how they were trying to get to me through Bust Down to sign them up. He told me, "We were young guys and you signed up fucking Bust Down. We begged him to hook us up with you, because you were the only brother that was in the game." For guys in the South, there was only one place to go, Luke Records. And it wasn't just the South. Even Sir Mix-a-Lot sent me a demo, a guy doing bass music out of Seattle.

I couldn't sign everybody, so these guys took the initiative and started doing their own thing. Pretty soon Cash Money was blowing up with Lil Wayne, Drake, and DJ Khaled. It had been the same in Houston with the Geto Boys years earlier. I'd brought them down to the Pac Jam for a few gigs, they went back to Houston and started Rap-A-Lot. Then it was Three 6 Mafia in Memphis. Then it spread to Charlotte, North Carolina. Then to Virginia Beach. The next thing you know, Outkast is taking home the Grammy for Album of the Year and Three 6 Mafia snags the Academy Award for Best Song from the soundtrack for *Hustle & Flow*. The South took over hip-hop, just as I predicted it would.

Every one of these guys who started at that time, I met them at some point down the line. Either they called me in Miami for advice, or I'd play a show in their town, do a radio interview and give them a shout-out on the air. It's a rite of passage. You show respect when you come into their territory, and they return the favor by linking up with you when they at your home. And whenever we'd meet, they'd tell me the same thing: "Hey man, I read about you in *Source*, man. I saw that shit in there. I started selling my own little mixtapes. I got hot. Radio station start playing my stuff, and then I start selling my own records." It was always the same story, and I never got tired of hearing it.

It wasn't just the inspiration of Luke Records that spurred these guys on. I'd built the infrastructure that they used to get their music out into the world. In 1986, when I was going around hustling copies of "Throw the D" and *The 2 Live Crew Is What We Are* out of the trunk of my car, there was barely even a hip-hop section in the record stores. There were no southern venues putting on rap concerts, no program directors looking for independent southern rap to play on the radio. By the time the younger guys came along, all that was in place. There was a network of DJs, promoters, distributors, and radio stations ready to promote them. I built that network, by hand. I created all those relation-ships, going town to town, meeting with promoters, shaking hands, selling them on my product, getting them excited. I paid all those college kids in all those towns to get the records in the hands of club owners and DJs. Then, a decade later, I'd be sitting with CeeLo Green and the Goodie Mob in Atlanta, telling them, "This is the distributor you should talk to in Memphis. Here's the guy to talk to in California."

The best part was, by the time the major labels figured out how much money and how much talent there was in southern hip-hop, black artists and label owners had already made it their own. I can't take credit for the artistic talent and the musical genius of all of those groups, but I can say I poured the foundation they built their success on. If you read the "history" of rap, you won't find one word about it.

At the end of the day, there's one simple reason why hip-hop historians and journalists don't give me the credit I'm due. It's because of Uncle Luke: the cartoon character I invented onstage, the loud-mouthed hype man, the King of Dirty Rap. Thanks to the 2 Live Crew controversy, Uncle Luke's crazy nonsense overshad-owed everything that Luther Campbell ever accomplished. Uncle Luke makes it rain at the strip club. Luther Campbell gives lectures at law schools on the First Amendment.

I could blame the media for that, and I do, to an extent—they love to sensationalize and twist everything. The truth is that I have to accept at least some of the responsibility myself. I didn't see any point in trying to change the media's point of view, so I embraced it, played up the man in the black hat. Uncle Luke was popular. He sold records. If I was out in the club or at a concert, that's who the people wanted, and I gave it to them. When I was getting tired of running a record label, Uncle Luke gave me a lucrative second career. The King of Dirty Rap became the King of Dirty Videos.

Adult entertainment was the logical next step, the only place for Luke to go. Luke would be the black Hugh Hefner. There wasn't anybody filling that niche for black audiences. I started seeing these *Girls Gone Wild* videos advertised on TV, and I thought to myself, "Man, I can do *Girls Gone Wild* times a thousand." Little blonde girls flashing their tits on camera? Shit was tame. Ever since the days of 2 Live Crew, my stage shows had been out of control. Bob Johnson and BET had just bought the Action Pay-Per-View network, and they needed programming. I pitched them *Luke's Peep Show*. I'd interview rappers and R&B artists, talk to Tupac, Foxy Brown, whoever was in town. We'd do these interviews, and in between there'd be a little peep show, freaky stuff going on. One show I interviewed Jay Z with one hot girl eating out another hot girl on the couch right next to us. Show was a hit. Thousands of guys paying ten dollars a pop to watch. The market for direct-to-DVD sales was blowing up at the same time. On DVD I could be even more explicit. I turned my stage shows into full-on live sex shows, filmed everything that went down and packaged it as *Luke's Freak Show*. Sold like crazy.

Between 2 Live Crew and the Freak Show videos, I was defined as Uncle Luke in people's minds. When I was doing those videos it was all a performance. Luke was out there on camera leading the show, but as Luther, as myself, I was detached from it. I was mostly just watching the whole phenomenon take place, and I was usually confused by it, to be honest. The thing is, people thought my music was explicit. It was *mild* compared to what I saw other people, regular people, doing out on the road. The freakiness was always out there. *They* came to *me*, wanting to be in the videos. People got up onstage and did things I never in my wildest imagination would have thought to ask someone to do. Girls would come and audition and show me their crazy sex tricks to get on the road. One girl came in and put fucking aluminum foil in her pussy, stuck a lightbulb in, and lit the motherfucker up. I was like, "Get the *fuck* out of here. I gotta take you on tour!"

During the shows I'd have these girls onstage and we'd sing "It's Your Birthday" and guys would volunteer to come up and join them. Then the girls would strip them naked and lay them down on their stomachs and start fingering their ass. Then the girls would spray styling mousse on their ass and light it on fire while everybody cheered. This was all live onstage, *on camera,* and guys loved it. Everyone signed the video release. They wanted to be a part of the show. It was almost like I was an anthropologist, dong a study in human nature. "What will these people do tonight?" I'd go onstage and say, "Everybody get fucking naked!" And they would. I'd say, "You, sit on his face. You, give her a golden shower." And they'd do it.

There was this one girl that toured with us named Jasmine. Jasmine had the biggest fucking vagina in the world. Like, Jesus Christ. I never auditioned girls in the hotel room, always live onstage. Jasmine said she got a fucking trick for me: she was going to have a baby onstage. I got her up there, completely naked, and she started dancing and pulling out these fucking beads from her vagina. Just this long chain of beads. Beads for days, like, get the fuck out of here. Just beads, on and on. At the end of the beads she yelled, "I'm fitna' have a baby!" Then she pushed . . . and pushed . . . and pushed . . . and this plastic baby doll popped right out her pussy. Like a full-size doll. I played it off like I knew it was going to happen. I was up there going, *"This is what the fuck I'm talking about! Luke's dancers ain't no motherfucking joke!"* In the back of my mind I was thinking, Damn, why'd she do that? That was fucked up.

I'd embraced the Uncle Luke persona because it made money,

and it was fun for a while. But then it wasn't anymore. In 2002, I was hired to host a party in North Charleston, South Carolina. It wasn't an official Luke concert or a Freak Show. I was just there to MC a dance party, sign autographs, and take pictures with the crowd. The promoter who put the show together was pretty slick. He didn't want to pay my fee to put on a whole Luke show, so he just paid for my appearance fee and then went and hired a bunch of girls to get onstage and do a bikini contest and strip and get freaky. He staged something that was similar to one of my regular concerts. I showed up for the event, did my MC bit, and then I stepped off to do my autographs and shake hands. This whole strip contest was going down and the girls started getting people out of the audience to come up onstage just like a Luke show, but I didn't have anything to do with it. The guys started getting naked, the girls were getting naked, and I just sat on the side of the stage, watching the shit.

Next day the cops called. A woman from the concert was alleging that I had raped her during this explicit sex show. I said, "What? I raped somebody? You're out of your fucking mind."

Lucky for me, I was videotaping all my public appearances, in case I wanted to use the footage for any future videos. My boy Lucky, he followed me with a camera, shooting me for the whole show. I turned the video over to the cops, and it clearly showed me offstage signing autographs and shaking hands the whole time. It also showed this woman voluntarily getting onstage, joining in the show, and then getting off. Cops apologized and dropped the case and filed a felony charge against the woman for making a false report.

I thought I was free and clear of it, but this part of South Carolina where the club was? It's white, rural, and conservative. It's fucking Ku Klux Klan country, come to find out. The district attorney there, he decides to get all Nick Navarro with me: he's going to make me an example so he can look good crusading for his white, rural, conservative voters. He files an obscenity charge against me for promoting a lewd and lascivious act onstage.

I wasn't doing anything. Wasn't even my show. My first reaction was, Fuck this. I'm going to fight this motherfucker, but my lawyer told me, "Luke, you'll probably lose."

I said, "How? These motherfuckers don't have no case. The rape was thrown out. I'm on the video not doing nothing wrong."

He said, "But there probably ain't but two blacks on the jury rolls in this whole county. It's all white, conservative Christian. They'll hang you for it."

The DA offered a deal. I took it. Growing up, my father had always taught me: "Don't ever say you're sorry for something you didn't do just to keep other people happy." But I did it anyway. I just didn't feel like fighting it. Thousands of dollars in legal fees, going back and forth to South Carolina to defend myself, the whole thing becoming another media spectacle, I didn't want any part of it. I pled guilty to the obscenity charge. In exchange for the plea, a suspended six-month sentence and an agreement not to make any paid appearances in South Carolina for five years. Fine with me. I didn't ever want to go back there anyway.

After South Carolina, I lost my enthusiasm for the stage shows. The guy I'd been producing the Peep Show videos with, he'd moved to California to do hardcore adult films. The industry was taking off, making a lot of money. I thought it might be the next move. I saw an avenue that was open. There was nobody doing good black porn. It wasn't really done the way that Playboy and Vivid did it. Their porn is upscale. Black porn is always done in some fucking roach motel, and the whole shit is cheesy. So I was like, "I'm going to do some high-class, top-of-the-line shit." That would be the next big step for Uncle Luke.

We did a movie. *Luke's Bachelor Party*, we called it. There was a concert going on, but in the back rooms during the show there'd be all this wild sex. I was in it to sort of walk around and introduce the couples and get the party going. Then we went to shoot the film, and while we were shooting it I was walking around watching all the blowjobs and fucking—and I hated it. Hated every second of it. I kept saying to myself, "I don't like this. I don't want to be doing this. Get me the fuck out of here."

The stuff I did with the stage shows was all spontaneous. It was a party, people just getting up onstage and letting their inhibitions go. This was just a business, the girls negotiating what they will and won't do. It was all a transaction, they'll do this for this much, that for that much. They'll work with this guy, but not that guy because his shit's too big. I thought doing that video would be the same kind of raunchy fun we had at the 2 Live Crew and Luke stage shows, but it was a totally different vibe. Being there, watching it, listening to it, I couldn't stomach it.

It was a mistake.

The fight for 2 Live Crew's explicit lyrics was never really about the lyrics. It had been about the principle of fighting for the right to do the same thing white artists did without legal harassment and censorship. It had never been my dream to be the King of Dirty Rap or the black Hugh Hefner or a guy who made porno films. But here I was. I'd lost my way. I'd let myself get wrapped up in the fun and excitement of being a rock star. I'd lost track of who I was, the mission I was on, what my life was really supposed to be about.

When the media played me up as this caricature, I went along and played the part to the max because I got a charge out of provoking people and breaking down parameters of what black men were allowed to be in this country. But I'd won that fight . . . fifteen years ago. Since my company went bankrupt I'd just been stuck in the same place, doing the same shit. I was becoming the cartoon that the media made me out to be. I wasn't challenging myself. I wasn't living up to what my father or my mother or Uncle Ricky had wanted for me. I wasn't doing anything to make the world a better place. I knew I had to change something. I had to find a new path and a new purpose. I went back to the place where I started. I had to go back to Liberty City.

OPTIMIST

After I walked out of that Broward County courtroom back in October of 1990, after all the attacks I had to endure from politicians like Governor Martinez and Sheriff Navarro, from so-called do-gooders like Jack Thompson and Focus on the Family, it was never lost on me that their attacks on me had been a huge distraction from what was really important. The whole trumped-up controversy over dirty rap was so trivial compared to the actual problems that were going on in black Miami at the time. Jack Thompson said his whole crusade against me was to protect the children. In Liberty City, black children were going hungry. In Overtown, black children were getting shot in the streets. Jack Thompson never talked about them. The moral-majority types went on and on about the safety of kids who bought cassettes in suburban record stores, but they never talked about the kids being fed to the meat grinder of the inner city every single day.

The Arthur McDuffie riots destroyed Miami. You'd think

maybe the cops would have learned something and changed their way of doing business. Not a chance. In January of '89, a twenty-three-year-old black man named Clement Lloyd was riding his motorcycle through Overtown. An officer in the area radioed in that Lloyd was "driving erratically." His only alleged crime: driving erratically. An officer nearby, William Lozano, heard Lloyd's motorcycle roaring up the street, reportedly fleeing the first cop. Without warning, without calling for the driver to stop, Lozano stepped into the street with his gun drawn and fired a single round, a fatal shot to the head that killed Lloyd instantly and sent his motorcycle careening into a second young man, Allan Blanchard, who was also killed instantly. They were shooting black men off the backs of motorcycles like it was cowboys and Indians. Riots broke out again, raged for two days, leaving one dead, buildings in flames, and millions in damages. Convicted of manslaughter at trial, Lozano won acquittal on appeal and walked away scot-free.

A decade had passed since McDuffie, and nothing had changed. If anything, it was worse. Like Trayvon Martin or Michael Brown today, Clement Lloyd's shooting was just the one black death that caught the media's attention. Miami's inner city had become a war zone. Crack cocaine brought gangs to Liberty City and Overtown in a major way. They were some of the most notorious in the nation: the John Does, the Boobie Boys, Cloud Nine. The violence quickly spread beyond Liberty City and Overtown. Opa-locka, North Miami Beach, Little River, Allapattah, Model City, West Perrine, Carol City, Coconut Grove, Florida City—they all had their own gangs and their own problems. The violence of the crack era brought the War on Drugs to Miami's streets, but militarizing the police only made the problem worse. The Reagan and Bush administrations were hell-bent on fighting a war against the cocaine cowboys with no regard for the victims who were the most in need of help; SWAT teams were storming into people's homes with tear gas and body armor, arresting innocent bystanders and low-level players in a futile attempt to root out the drug trade.

By the early 1990s, Miami had the fourth-highest percentage of residents in poverty out of all major US cities. In parts of Liberty City, 68 percent of families were living in poverty. The child poverty rate was higher than it had been thirty years before, under Jim Crow. To make matters worse, Miami also started seeing a massive surge in immigration from Haiti, just like we did with the Cubans after Mariel. Thousands of Haitians descended on Florida trying to escape the torture and killings of the Duvalier regime back home. New Haitian gangs like the Zombie Boys, E-Unit, Zoe Pound, and several others exacerbated the problems. Unemployment, homelessness, crime—all the bad indicators went up, and they'd been way too high to begin with.

For the drug gangs, it was all business, and business was good. When young black men went looking for jobs, the gangs were the only ones hiring. Fourteen-, fifteen-year-old kids were dropping out of school to work the corners while the gangsters sat inside, counted their paper, and carried out the hits. The murder rate soared. It was the same bullshit that killed my man Handsome Harry: drive-bys, revenge killings, executions. If you weren't killed in a gangland beef, then it was probably the cops that got you. Or, like Trayvon Martin, you were killed for the crime of being black and walking down the street near some idiot with a gun—and the whole state of Florida is nothing but idiots with guns.

At the time, Saddam Hussein had just invaded Kuwait, setting off the first Gulf War. For a young black man from south Florida, statistically it was safer to be an enlisted soldier in Iraq than to be on the streets of Miami. Every month brought a new funeral with some kid's sophomore yearbook picture next to an open casket. Whenever the murders grabbed too many headlines, the police would start on the "weed and seed" arrests, make a big show of going after "the bad element." They mainly targeted loitering, public drinking, and graffiti. Judges were handing out prison sentences like door prizes. Nonviolent offenders and petty crooks were filling the jails and getting criminal records while the real problems went unaddressed.

The response from the city of Miami to all this was basically nothing more than a big PR campaign. The important thing was not to save the children of Liberty City, but to keep the tourists and their dollars from being scared away. The art deco renaissance of South Beach got splashed all over the national media: fashion models in bikinis, boutique hotels, celebrities on Ocean Drive. It's what the rest of the nation saw while the problems of black Miami were swept under the rug. Miami needed police reform and better schools. Instead, Liberty City got SWAT teams and private prisons while Miami Beach got glossy brochures and tax breaks for tourist hotels.

Part of the problem was with the black community itself: we didn't have a community. Our institutions had been broken up by the destruction of Overtown, and had slowly eroded in the decades since. We didn't have leadership. The black politicians who represented us at the county and state level, some of them were good men and women, but too many of them were crooks, garden-variety hustlers. They'd come out to Liberty City, tell black voters what we wanted to hear, then go back to City Hall and do nothing but line their own pockets.

Because of the broken education system, you didn't have many successful blacks making it out of the inner city, and the blacks who were successful, they all left because they didn't feel there was any opportunity for them here. My older brothers, the successful college graduates, every one of them moved away for jobs they couldn't find in Miami. You go to the major banks and office buildings downtown, you won't see many black faces, and the ones you do see, a lot of them moved here from somewhere else. Twenty years out from the end of the civil rights movement, and black Miami was trapped in a cycle of unemployment, poverty, and crime—the invisible chains my uncle Ricky had taught me all about. It was time to break the cycle, time to break out of the chains.

I was one of the few who made it. In 1990, I had more money and more fame and more influence than any other black man ever born in Liberty City. I was smart and I'd worked hard, but I was also just lucky. A stray bullet or my temper getting the best of me in a bad situation, and my whole life might have been different. I had my chances to leave. At the pinnacle of my success, I had offers to do TV and film and music projects in New York and Los Angeles, and I could have made a lot more money going that route. But I never thought about leaving. It never crossed my mind once. I was born in Liberty City. This is my home, the place that made me who I am.

I couldn't go off and live the life of a rock star while the people around me got left behind. I always knew I had a responsibility to help, to reach back and use the money and influence that I'd gained to lift up the next generation, the kids who deserved a chance to follow their dreams and better their lives. I knew the way to do it was through the one thing that got through to these kids, the one thing that spoke to them louder than the gangs or any of the other negative influences in their lives: football.

When I was with the Optimist program on Miami Beach, I loved my coach, Alex Medina. He was a good man. He always looked out for me, gave me tough love at a time when I needed it. But the way the program itself was set up, I felt the poor black kids were being used. Our talents were being exploited to put points on the board, but we weren't getting everything we needed outside of football. And then in school, when you're bused to the other side of town to play, you're coming home at eleven o'clock at night. Your focus isn't where it should be: on homework. I got summer jobs and free shoes and boat rides on Miami Beach just because I played football. It was fun, and I felt lucky: "I'm good enough to play where the rich white kids play." But I didn't get an education. I was the least educated one in my family. I had a family of five brothers, all of them physics majors and scientists and college graduates, and me, the football player, and I'm the damn dummy. Going into my senior year of high school, I could barely read or write. It was the same for a lot of other black athletes bused over to those schools.

If you wanted to play, there was no choice. You had to go to neighborhoods like Miami Beach or Suniland, because there were no organized youth teams in our area. After what I had been through, I'd made a vow that if I ever got two cents over my lunch money I'd go back and start an Optimist program in Liberty City. I'd build it based on what I went through. It would be a program in our own neighborhood, right in the heart of Liberty City, so that kids wouldn't have to ride the bus home at 11:30 at night; the only bus they'd ride would be to away games. It would be a football program, but football wouldn't be the point: we'd be using football to teach the kids discipline and hard work and commitment. It would be a means to improve their education; we'd have academic requirements, strict ones, and use that as an incentive for kids to keep their grades up. It wouldn't be about playing ball to make other people look good; it would be about kids getting an education, becoming responsible adults, and having fun.

As luck would have it, right around that same time, this thirty-six-year-old Miami-Dade bus driver named Sam Johnson came looking for me at the Luke Records office. He coached a Little League baseball team that played at Charles Hadley Park in Liberty City, and he wanted to talk to me about sponsoring it. I told him, "I'll help you. I'll sponsor your baseball team, but I also want to start up football."

"I don't know anything about football," he said.

"Well, I do. I know a *lot* about football. I have a bunch of friends that I played football with at the Optimist program at Miami Beach. They'll be more than happy to help us out."

"All right, let's do it," Sam said.

It was a perfect partnership. I was busy running the record label, but I could provide the money and the ideas and Sam would be the guy to execute the program. We started the program as a 501(c)(3), a nonprofit. In the fall of 1990, I made an initial donation of about $80,000. With that, we were able to charter the Liberty City Optimist Club.

I did it the same way I built my record company. I just did it. I was going into an enterprise and learning how to build it from the ground up with common sense. I placed a call to a guy named Charlie Brown who ran the football program for the Boys Club. I knew Charlie from my own days of playing ball. I went down to the Boys Club and got some advice from him. He walked me through the whole process of setting up an Optimist program, the proper forms and all that. With the money I'd put in we bought uniforms, helmets, shoulder pads, everything we'd need. I started calling up all my friends who played ball at Miami Beach High with me. I said, "Yo, I'm starting football over here. Would y'all come out and coach?" Everybody was on board. It was a real team effort from day one.

I even called up my old coach, Alex Medina, to help organize everybody. He helped put the whole coaching program together. Before we knew it we had enough gear and volunteer staff to field eight teams in all the different weight divisions. Coach Medina also helped us get into the Pop Warner league, which is by far the biggest and most popular league for youth football in America: it has 3,000 teams and 350,000 kids. Originally, Sam had wanted me to sponsor his baseball team, and so people wanted to call this new organization the Luther Campbell Optimist Club, with the teams named after me, too. I vetoed that. I wanted it to be the community's program. I wanted everybody to be a part of it, the local bank, the local stores, the community police—everybody needed to put his hand in this and support it. We ditched my name and picked a mascot: the Liberty City Warriors were born.

It was exciting. We thought it would be big, but we had no idea how big. When registration opened up, the response was crazy. Hundreds of kids registered. The word was out and people came from everywhere. At that time, I didn't realize just how much weight I carried in the community. I'd been off doing my albums and my tours, and now I came back and I'm this big-time guy. I'd unknowingly tapped into something really big. We had way too many kids. We eventually had to close registration because we could only have thirty-five kids on each team based on the rules. We took them on a first-come basis and promised the families who didn't make it that we'd expand the program as soon as we could.

Our first game was against this team from Richmond. When we started the program, I believed our kids had the most talent, the most drive, the most grit of all the other teams in the area. I was ready to get on the field and show Richmond what we could do. They beat us so bad. They just killed us. I remember sitting in the dugout saying, "God, when is this going to be over with?" That first year we got beat up all over the place. I thought we were ready, but after that Richmond game, I realized how much work we really had to do. Still, I told all the coaches, "We're going to be the best thing in Pop Warner." I believed in those kids—we just had to build them up into champions.

Making them champions wasn't just about what happened on the field. From day one, I made sure that academics were a core part of the program. One of the things we liked about Pop Warner as a league is that you have to have a 2.0 GPA to play. Before you can sign up, you have to bring your report card from last year. If you're below a 2.0, you can still register, but you're going to be put on a progress report throughout the nine-week season. If you had a bad progress report, you were not going to play. If you fell below a 2.0, to stay on the team it was mandatory that you register in a tutoring program. It made kids want to get the grades.

For the tutoring, I reached out to the teachers at Allapattah Middle School, where I used to DJ dances back in the Ghetto Style days. Allapattah is right next to Charles Hadley Park, where we played. I went over there and spoke to Ms. Jerkins, the same principal who'd let me DJ the school dances there years before. All the teachers at Allapattah knew who I was long before I became vilified as the King of Dirty Rap. I was the guy who played at their dances and owned the Pac Jam, where their students could hang out drinking Coca-Colas instead of hanging out on the corners and getting into trouble. In Liberty City, in my community, I wasn't the bad guy. I wasn't the one hurting kids; I was the one looking out for them. Ms. Jerkins knew that. I went over to her and said, "Hey, Ms. Jerkins, how you doing? I'm putting this football program together over here. Can I use a couple of your portable trailers to do some tutoring and get some teachers who want to volunteer some time?" She was thrilled to help. It was a mutually beneficial arrangement. We got some wonderful teachers who stayed after school to help out our players, and we were helping the school identify the kids who needed the extra tutoring.

We had volunteer teachers helping out with the kids' academics, and we had volunteer coaches teaching the kids not just about the game but about life. All my guys coached like Coach Medina did back in the day. They were mentors, surrogate fathers, always available to drive a kid home or lend an ear for a kid who had a problem. They understood that's what these kids really needed. These guys knew how to treat the kids off the field as well as coach them on the field.

Our coaching was one of our secret weapons. Liberty City

coaches watched tapes of the other clubs. We put together college-level playbooks. We weren't messing around. By our second year we started winning. We started winning big. We were stomping on established teams that had been dominant for years. We were beating the wealthier suburban teams that had budgets for new uniforms and private buses. Pretty soon, the crush of kids registering to play was nothing compared to the crush of fans that came out to watch them play. Youth football in Miami is serious business. You're talking about a town where even high school football exists on the level of a religion. Regular-season high school games down here can draw anywhere from ten to forty thousand fans a game. We didn't have quite that many, but the games were always sell-outs, the bleachers packed, two and sometimes three thousand people, parents running up and down the sidelines with their kids, cheering them on.

Some of the coaches of the suburban teams started referring to Charles Hadley Park as Little Big Horn—it was where you went to get slaughtered. And that was the reputation I wanted to have *on* the field, but from the start I was concerned about Liberty City's hardcore reputation. I knew those suburban families were scared to come here because of the riots, because of the crime, because of what they saw about us on the five o'clock news. The first thing they probably expected to see was black people going crazy. I was determined that when white kids and their parents came from other communities that they would have the best time they ever had at any park in the city. Our program was built on respect and sportsmanship. Not one of our kids ever set foot on that field acting like a thug. I wanted those white families to go back to their neighborhoods and say, "We went over there and enjoyed ourselves. We were in the heart of Liberty City and we had a great time! Those kids are great kids, just like ours. They're no different from us." It was a big piece of what I wanted to do. We were counteracting all those negative images of us portrayed in the media.

As those first seasons went by, the teams and the organization kept growing. I did everything I could to use my celebrity and my clout to get people behind the team. I knew the team wouldn't survive if it was dependent on only me year after year. It had to be self-sustaining if it was going to succeed, so I did everything I could to create the awareness and support that would keep it going through thick and thin. We did celebrity softball games and golf tournaments and raised thousands of dollars. Every year we had a full-fledged training camp with kids running around and learning fundamentals. I called up my friends that I met through the entertainment world and said, "Hey, come out to my camp and have some fun. Come play in my golf tournament and help raise money." We had everybody out there. We had University of Miami players like Edgerrin James and Bennie Blades and Melvin Bratton and Michael Irvin. We had guys from the Miami Heat like Alonzo Mourning and Dwyane Wade. We had national stars like Dominique Wilkins from the Atlanta Hawks showing up. I would have all those guys participate in raising funds for the Liberty City Warriors.

My name and my celebrity gave the club the push it needed to get off the ground, but the real heart and soul of that program was Sam Johnson. Sam passed in 2011, far before his time, but when he was alive he fought for those kids like nothing else mattered in the world. He fought for Charles Hadley Park, too, a place that has so much significance both to the club and the community. Like so much of Liberty City, the park had been ignored by the city for so long. Even as we were using it, the municipal government had let it fall into total disrepair. It didn't have modern facilities. The benches were cracked and splintered. The irrigation system hadn't been replaced in fifty years. The frustrating thing was that a $6.5 million renovation had been approved for the park, but the funds were tied up in bureaucratic red tape over planning and development. It wasn't a priority for anyone in City Hall. That languished for years, and Sam haunted the city commission and parks department meetings, fighting for the funds to be released. Back in the 1980s, when Charles Hadley Park had just the one Little League team, Sam had two adult volunteers and twelve kids. Ten years later, he had one hundred adult volunteers and over six hundred kids—and he could tell you the name of every single one of them, because he cared that much.

The parents were pleased with the program, too. They were all just so happy. They volunteered in huge numbers, because it was something their kids looked forward to, to go and play organized sports and be a part of something bigger. There were no after-school programs for them, no organized summer camps in the park. Nobody had given them something like this before. After the riots, this program was needed so badly. The spirit of Liberty City had been broken down by all the crime and the unemployment. There was a lot of anger and frustration. Nothing was being done by the city to bring that spirit back.

This program, like hip-hop, was ours. We started it from nothing, built it from the ground up into a major presence in Miami. Everybody in town knew about the Liberty City Warriors and what a great program it was. The kids on these teams were playing for everybody in Liberty City. Their success was everyone's success. They became a symbol. They brought so much pride to the community, which in turn brought out our competitiveness, our will to work hard and not give up. It brought us together toward a common goal: keeping these kids off the streets, keeping them alive, and showing them what they could achieve by working hard and believing in themselves.

The biggest challenge in running the program was that there was still so much violence. Sometimes, a kid would go home and not come back the next day. Their high school got shot up, their older brother was killed, something happened to them. We prayed every day that our kids would make it home safe. Our program created a safe space in Liberty City. Thanks to the Warriors, Charles Hadley Park was sacred ground. There was a lot of killing going on, but nothing ever happened at the park. It was always a place where everybody could go and enjoy themselves and know that their kids were protected. During that period, Miami had one of the most notorious gangs in the world: the John Does. They were responsible for a lot of the violence and killing that was going on in the neighborhood. But they knew not to start trouble at the park. You didn't even have to have a conversation with them about it. There was an understanding: don't go out there with that bullshit at the park.

A majority of those kids in these gangs, they knew me. They grew up fans of the Ghetto Style DJs. When we used to drive around in our rap van with the shorties following us and jumping in the back of the van, half of the gangsters had been the crazy kids jumping on the back of the truck. They knew me, and they had too much respect for me and the music to bring that nonsense around the park. A lot of these gang members, they had little brothers and nephews on the teams, and when they came out to watch the games, that would be a time of peace. If anybody from outside the neighborhood came around trying to start trouble, the gangs took care of it and kept them away. That was their park; it was their little brothers and sisters out there.

We had a lot of cops coaching teams, but the cops and the gangs left each other alone at the field, never bothered each other when they were out there. The gangs protected the park while police officers coached the kids. It was a strange arrangement, but it worked. The crazy part was that these gangsters were betting on the kids, laying down thousands of dollars to bet on youth football games. The coaches would be shaking in their boots; they didn't want to lose for fear they were going to get killed. But nobody ever got hurt. There were no shootings, no fighting, none of that.

The success of the Liberty City Optimist Club had a ripple effect that went far beyond Charles Hadley Park. The demand for youth football in Miami had always been big. Now it exploded. You had all these inner-city neighborhoods where organized sports were needed the most, but there had never been resources to put together the teams. We showed other parks how it could be done. We started inspiring other teams. We were having babies all around us. The police union wanted to sponsor a team. The longshoremen wanted to sponsor a team. The first program to follow ours was in Gwen Cherry Park. They were the Gwen Cherry Bulls. Then came the Overtown Rattlers and the Inner City Jaguars. A lot of coaches who came through our program went to those parks and built teams over there. Everything started to spread out.

Northwestern, Central, and Jackson were the three main high schools serving the black community. Back when I played for Miami Beach High, we used to beat the crap out of them. It was a joke when we played them. Their athletic programs were a joke because the suburban teams were taking all their good players and the inner city had no feeder system of youth leagues to teach kids the fundamentals of the game. The players didn't have the back-ground of playing real organized football. They played sandlot ball, no pads, no tackles, a lot of reaching and all that.

The Liberty City Warriors changed everything. All of our kids had been coached in the fundamentals, how to tackle the proper way, how to play with pads on, how to run an offense. It took a few years for those kids to trickle up through the system, but once they did, they turned Northwestern, Jackson, and Central from jokes into national powerhouses. The whole center of gravity of high school football in Miami shifted. After we started the Warriors, the football program at Miami Beach fell apart, and it hasn't come back since, because they could no longer take our kids. College recruiters started looking more closely at Northwestern, Jackson, and Central, always looking to get a kid who played for the Liberty City Warriors. When we founded the club, we didn't know what we'd started. But once we started slaughtering the teams at Palmetto Bay, Kendall, and Miami Beach, we started realizing we were getting good and the kids were really understanding what we were trying to teach them. The effect of us starting that program was huge. We changed the whole athletic landscape of south Florida.

In 1998, the club won its first national championship in the Junior Pee Wee division at the Pop Warner Super Bowl in Orlando. It was such a great feeling. It was better than a gold record. It was one thing to galvanize the community and beat a bunch of other local teams in your area, but you go win a national championship? That's a hell of a deal. It showed the world that kids from Liberty City could compete at the highest levels.

They weren't writing about the Optimist Club giveaway turkeys at Thanksgiving or toys at Christmas, because that didn't fit their agenda. They were going to write that I was this misogynistic pig, that I hate women. Fine. If people are ignorant enough to believe certain newspaper stories, then that's on them.

Once the Optimist program took off, I stopped performing in Miami entirely. I don't think I set foot on a stage in Miami for over twenty years. I separated those two parts of my life completely, because I didn't want the image of me from the national media overshadowing the work I was doing with these kids. On the road I was Uncle Luke, the Black Hugh Hefner, the King of Dirty Rap. In Liberty City I was Luther Campbell, local businessman and community leader. I kept both sides going for over a decade, but eventually I reached the point where I had to decide which of those guys I wanted to be my legacy. Did I want to be remembered as the guy with the dirty lyrics, or as a guy who did his part to leave the world better than he found it?

COACH LUKE

I never expected my music career to last forever. If you're Bruce Springsteen or the Rolling Stones, you can play stadiums well into old age, but for everyone else in that industry, fame comes and goes.

By the late 1990s and early 2000s, guys like Jay Z and Kanye and Pitbull, they were the new voices, and the stage belonged to them. After that last obscenity charge in South Carolina and working on that porn film, I knew the whole Uncle Luke thing had played itself out. It wasn't a challenge anymore. It wasn't fulfilling. After fifteen years of being the villain, the nasty rapper, the freaky bad boy of hip-hop, I was just as tired of that persona as the public was. I had a best-of album I was working on. It would be my last record, a look back at my career, at my favorite collaborations with Trick Daddy and Pitbull, but other than that it was time for me to start the next chapter, to dedicate myself full-time to the thing that was really important: my community.

Football had always been a big part of my life, and my son Luther Jr. had inherited the same passion for the game. Once he was old enough for Pop Warner, he wanted to play. He and his mother lived near me in Miami Lakes, and she didn't want him playing in Liberty City. She felt it wasn't safe. I knew that it was; Charles Hadley Park was probably the safest place in Miami *because* of the football program, but it wasn't worth arguing about. I also wanted my son to be able to play the game as himself, not as "Luther Campbell's son," which is exactly how he would have been seen in Liberty City. In the fall of 2003, we registered him with the Miami Lakes Optimist Club. It couldn't have been more different from Liberty City. These were suburban kids, a mixed group of white and black, most of them from pretty well-off families.

At first, my attitude as a father was that as much as I knew football, I wasn't going to get involved in any official capacity; again, I didn't want my celebrity or my role in Pop Warner having any influence on the way my son was treated, for good or for bad. I'd coach him one-on-one at home, I cheered from the sidelines, but I resolved that I wasn't going to be one of those parents yelling at the ref, or always complaining to the coach about playing my son. I just wanted to go to the games and watch from the bleachers and be a proud dad.

Right from the start, however, the team had problems. The guy who was supposed to coach the team had pulled out at the last minute, and they'd started the season without a real coach, just a couple of dads and assistants trying to keep the team together. They lost their first game. The team was a mess.

The other parents knew I'd started the Liberty City Optimist Club, and they asked me to step in. Reluctantly, I told them I'd help out until a regular coach signed on. Everybody looked at this team like they were the Bad News Bears, and nobody wanted to coach them. I ended up coaching this team for the entire season. To prove there would be no favoritism toward my son, I worked him as hard as any of the other kids. I put him on the second team to make him earn a starting spot. I benched him when he needed to be benched. I made him do what everybody else had to do.

Same way I am with everything, once I was out there, I was out there 100 percent. Practice was every day from 6:00 to 8:30. I always got there early and I always stayed late. I learned a lot that year, about how to coach and how not to coach. The guy before me, who'd put the team together, he'd recruited a lot of really good players from outside the neighborhood, but the parents of the kids inside the neighborhood were complaining: they felt that all these kids from outside the area were playing while kids from the neighborhood were sitting on the bench. I heard about that from the parents sitting out there in the bleachers, and it made me mad. My feeling was that every kid who came out deserved to be coached and deserved a shot to play. Winning is great, but the focus should be on the kids learning. If they came every day to practice and if they came to every game to play, my job as a coach was to get them ready to be a good player.

There was this one kid in particular. He was overweight, kind of a nerdy kid with glasses. Some people were ready to go ahead and kick him off the team, because he couldn't make the weight. When I eventually took over, I did the opposite. I refused to cut him. I went and told the kid and his mother, "Look, you gotta make the weight, because it's a weight-driven league. But you stay on the team, I'll work with you on conditioning, and you'll make the weight and you can play."

I gave him a goal and made him work for it. The kid ended up losing the weight. He made the cut, and became eligible to play. It was one of my all-time favorite moments of coaching, seeing that kid get on the field. He was a smart kid, a 4.0 student. Teaching him the techniques and fundamentals of the game wasn't difficult, and once the weight issue was dealt with, he became a great player. He went from being the last guy you wanted on the team to the first guy you wanted on the team. After nearly every game his mother told me, "Thank you, thank you, thank you."

The kid inspired me. He made me see what kind of impact I could have if I really put my heart and soul into coaching. After a rough start, I worked the team hard, we won the last five games of the season, and we secured a berth in the playoffs. We ended up losing in the first round, but every kid on the team made progress during the year. They all made valuable contributions to the team, and in youth football that's the definition of a great season. It's not your win-loss record. It's how much you help each kid grow and improve. What was really great was that, even though this was a suburban team, I never heard a single complaint that a "dirty" rapper was coaching the kids. All the parents, white and black, looked past that. They only saw my dedication to the team and to the kids.

I'd tried to keep my coaching gig quiet; I didn't want any media attention for it, because I knew the media was going to put their spin on it, comparing my music to my being a coach. But some reporter at the *Miami Herald* heard I was doing this and came down wanting to do an article. I said, "Yo, I'm not out here for that. This is about the kids." They did the article anyway. Once the people at Liberty City Optimist found out I was coaching for another team, a few of them got really upset. They called me up to complain. I knew if I was going to keep coaching, it had to be for the Warriors. I talked to my son's mother, she agreed to let him start playing in Liberty City, and at the end of the season with Miami Lakes, I went to coach for my own club.

I became a coach the same way I became a record executive: by accident. I was frustrated that the job wasn't being done right, so I stepped in to do it myself. I was trying to stay on the sidelines, but once I got into it I was hooked. The best-of album I was working on, I put it on the shelf. It wouldn't come out for another two and a half years. It could wait. I wanted to focus on what was in front of me. I am a perfectionist. In the music business, I was responsible for other people's lives, careers, and dreams, and if I wasn't going to be the best, I didn't need to be doing it. It was the same thing with football. I couldn't ask the kids to do their best if I wasn't prepared to do the same.

When I started coaching in the Liberty City Optimist program, I went to Sam Johnson. "Give me the team that doesn't win. I don't want some ready-made group of kids. Give me the worst team you got out here." I wanted the kids who needed the most help, because I wanted to be able to have an impact in their lives.

I took over the Junior Midget team, which was the ninety-pounders, about ten-to-twelve-year-olds. As a coach, on the field, I wanted to be Jimmy Johnson. I wanted to be the absolute best. I used ten position coaches for my team, the maximum allowed by Pop Warner, because I wanted each kid to get as much attention as he needed to excel. I went to all the guys from the neighborhood who were the best high school players when I was a kid. Some of them had kids on the team like I did. I went to those guys and said, "Hey, look, let's get together and coach this team on a higher level. Let's get them ready for the next ten years of football." And that's what we did.

First thing I did was go down and visit my friend Randy Shannon, the defensive coordinator at the University of Miami, to ask him for drill tapes to give the kids. My guys were a bunch of middle school kids, but I was determined to teach them some college-level football.

These young black boys from the inner city, a lot of them don't do well in school because they're not given the support they need, at the institutional level or at home. So people write them off. Nobody challenges them, and they fail. But kids are smart. Their minds are like sponges. If they're exposed to the wrong information at a young age, it gets more difficult to root out bad habits and plant good habits later. If you challenge them and support them, they can do anything. At that age they know nothing, so whatever we instill in them, they'll take it and learn fast.

I'd sit and talk X's and O's with Randy. My coaches and I would get together before the season. We would talk about the drills and what we wanted the kids to do both in training during the summer and as the season went on. Once the season started, we watched tape and ran those drills with the kids religiously. I made them memorize playbooks. They had to know the Power 1, the Cover 2, the Gap 8, and the Split Back. Randy would come down to the park and watch my practices and correct me if I got something wrong. I learned a lot from him.

I ran a controlled practice that would end with an eleven-on-eleven scrimmage. After the scrimmage, we had conditioning: sprints and drills and calisthenics. I was hell-bent on conditioning, and they took it like champs. I'd condition more than anybody. When the kids would protest, "Man, Coach. Why you doing this?" I'd tell them, "I have to set the bar high for y'all. I'm not getting you ready for JV. I'm getting you ready for varsity. I'm not getting you ready to be redshirted. I'm getting you ready to start."

They came to accept my philosophy and work ethic. By the time they went off to high school and college they were running the other teams into the ground. To this day my players come back from college and say, "Coach, you ran us to death. Everything in high school and college is a piece of cake compared to playing for you."

Along with the conditioning, the other thing we provided was quality food. We practiced nearly two hours a day, four times a week, and many of these kids were undernourished. A lot of them were coming from families where there was no good food in the house, or not enough food to feed everyone properly, so we always had food at practices and pregame meals. These kids were young and growing and needed as much as we could possibly offer.

My responsibility to the kids on the field was nothing compared to my responsibility to them off the field. Part of being a coach is mentorship. Even during the off-season, you have to be a phone call away at all times, especially in Liberty City. Down here, that means more than just giving the kid a ride home because his mom works late. Some of these kids are coming from terrible situations. I've had players who can't afford cleats or a decent meal, players who've seen their relatives sent to prison, who've seen friends die. A lot of them need a father figure because they don't have a father at home. Some of them don't have any parental figures at all: Dad's gone and Mom's in jail and they're staying at a cousin's house. I've had kids sleep at my house on nights where they literally have no other place to go. One time a player came over and he stayed for days. He'd seen a dead body in the street near his house and was afraid to go home. Coach Luke's house was the safest place he could think to be.

As a coach, I would start every year with a greeting, talking to parents. Some parents are in difficult situations, and some are not, and when you get to know them you know the situation the kid is going through and what he's dealing with. It gave me an idea of how to deal with each kid. Every kid is different, and I had to approach each one as such to bring out his best. I had one kid we called the Professor. His mother and his dad were educators, professional academics, but they brought their son back to the neighborhood because they wanted him to understand his own people. They didn't want him to lose his culture. The Professor had a 4.0 all of his years of playing, just a really smart kid, but he had insecurities about being in this new environment. I had to treat him completely differently from how I'd treat a kid from a disadvantaged, broken home. Some kids were a bit more rough around the edges, and when you met their parents, the parents were a bit more rough around the edges, too. That kid may need some tough love where the Professor needed some nurturing and coaxing to feel a part of the group.

I had two goals. One was to teach these kids football, *real* football, the more intellectual, problem-solving side of the game. The other was to use football to give them life skills that they weren't getting in the difficult situations they were living in. I wanted to teach the kids that sports was a means to an end, not an end in itself. Many of these Liberty City kids grew up thinking that it was either sports or jail or death. They couldn't imagine a successful and useful life beyond that.

The first thing I did, before we even gave out the uniforms, was identify the kids who were struggling academically. Typically, we'd make kids go for tutoring if they were anywhere below a 2.0 GPA. I made it 2.5. If they had anything lower than that, I would automatically send them to get help, and I would make them bring in progress reports on a weekly basis to show me they were keeping up, because I knew during the football season a kid has the tendency of concentrating more on football than his academics. The ones who needed additional tutoring, they would come in before practice and put their thinking caps on before they put their football helmets on. In my first year as coach we had one kid who went from being an F student to an A student over the course of the season. I always told my kids, "I don't care nothing about you playing in the NFL or anything like that. I just care that you get your diploma. Send me a copy when you graduate." Years later, many of them did.

I used the game to give these kids structure and purpose, to

teach them accountability and responsibility. I would give moti-
vational speeches and teach them life lessons. Often their parents
would sit in and build on what I was saying. I would tell them, "We
got too many black men not taking care of their kids and not being
held accountable and responsible." I would tell them that football
is a team sport. In life, you have to work with a team of people,
whether you work from home, or a shop, or work in an office
building with other people. Some days you get the things that you
want, and some days you don't, but it's not about you. It's about
the team, the community.

I was straight with them and I made damn sure they knew the
rules. I would tell them this sport is like a job, and we're going to
treat this like a job. If you're a linebacker, you're held responsible
for taking care of the job of being a linebacker, just like your parents are responsible for putting a roof over your head and doing
the things a parent has to do. You're expected to be on time. When
you're not, there's consequences. If you don't show up for the class,
you're going to fail. If you don't show up to your job, you're going
to lose it. I would tell them, "I'm not getting y'all ready for football, I'm getting y'all ready for life. You have to be accountable and
responsible for whatever your job is."

As a coach, I knew I was responsible for these kids, and I took it
very seriously. I didn't even let my players curse, if you can believe
that.

I knew the problem for most of them was that they just didn't
have any money. They're surrounded by all images of rich people
on Miami Beach living the high life, and they don't even have
money for a sandwich or a comic book or a pair of sneakers without holes in them. Some of them were trying to help provide for
their own mothers. That's what drags so many of these kids into
petty thieving and drug dealing; they just don't see any other way.
There's no jobs in their communities, no malls where they can go

sweep up the movie theater for minimum wage, even.

With these kids I was in the same position I was with the Miami Hurricanes guys. I could have given them money—here, here, and here—but that wouldn't have taught them how to work for things. I didn't want to teach them to be beggars. I would say, "Look, when you need something, don't ask nobody for nothing, no dope dealer, nobody on the corner, nothing like that. Because they want something in return. Anytime you need something, come to me and I got work for you. You can wash the cars, you can cut trees in the yard, you can paint houses, you can wash windows. My neighbors and I got thousands of windows in our houses that need cleaning. Come by my house and do some work." After they worked, I'd pay them and let them relax and swim in my pool, because they'd earned it. I always taught them you've got to work for everything you want in life.

I've mentored dozens of kids over the years. They're all important to me and have incredible stories, but some of them stand out because they've achieved so much in the years since. Devonta Freeman was one of the nicest, sweetest kids I've ever known. He was well mannered, soft-spoken, just a lovable kid. He was also one of the most gifted athletes I've ever seen. He wasn't tall, but he was strong. He played baseball and football. He later went on to be a running back, but in middle school we had him at quarterback with the Liberty City Warriors.

Devonta was the oldest of seven brothers and sisters being raised by a single mom in the Pork N' Beans area of Miami. His father was in prison for his entire childhood. They had nothing, but he always had this sunny, happy-go-lucky way about him. These kids in the hood, they look at the TV and see guys riding around in Bentleys living in nice houses—things they'll never have the opportunity to experience. Then they go home to shootings and killings. They're mad. They're angry. They're frustrated. That was the thing about Devonta, he wasn't mad. I had a lot of kids who were mad, but he wasn't one of them.

I knew Devonta had the potential to take that attitude and do great things, but these kids, even the good ones, are always at risk. The violence is random. You don't have to be caught up in the streets to catch a stray bullet. In addition, the temptations are always present. Simply being in this environment you're around potential danger because you can always make a few dollars here or there doing something shady. If you see your mom struggling to feed seven kids, you might do anything. I took it on myself to be a father figure to Devonta. I'd tell him, constantly, "You're the man of the house. You mess up, you're not just messing up your life, but you're going to mess up the lives of all of your brothers and sisters, because they're depending on you." He took it to heart.

Durell Eskridge played tailback for the Warriors. He was Devonta's best friend. Durell's father was gone, too, and his mother, Margaret, was selling sandwiches from a cart at the airport. She couldn't make ends meet. There were times when they'd be homeless, Durell and his mom and his two sisters living in their car, or staying in a shelter for weeks at stretch. He might show up for practice having slept in the backseat of a sedan all night. During one particularly hard time, the family had nowhere to stay, and Devonta's mom invited Durell to come and live with them. She already had seven kids in that cramped little Pork N' Beans apartment, but Durell was like family. He went to live there and his mom would send food stamps to help with the meals.

Devonta and Durell were inseparable. If you saw one of them, you saw the other. They hustled for everything they could get. They'd hang around the gas station, pumping gas in exchange for tips. They'd hang around at the grocery store, carrying people's bags for spare change. They were at my house, working, almost every weekend, mowing my lawn and cleaning my pool. They'd take the money I paid them and buy clothes that they'd share on alternate days.

Like all the kids in Liberty City, Devonta and Durell went to bed hearing gunshots every night. They walked past dead bodies and homicide crime scenes on the way home from school. I worried about them same as I worried about all the kids, but I knew they had each other for support. "You boys keep each other close. Watch each other's back. Protect each other," I told them. I was more worried about the kids who had no one. Imagine being twelve years old and seeing all this violence on the streets, and not having anyone to talk to.

Rakeem Cato was one of seven kids, too. His mother Juannese raised him and his siblings in a five-bedroom house in Liberty City and worked two jobs, at the hospital and as a clerk at PetSmart, to support them. Rakeem's father had been in prison since before he was born, for armed robbery and second-degree murder. Devonta and Durell first brought Rakeem around when he was about twelve. I would have loved to have him on my team, but he was already playing quarterback for the Gwen Cherry Bulls, and we didn't need any quarterbacks.

Rakeem's situation wasn't ideal, but his mom worked day and night to take care of him and his siblings. In April of 2005, right after he turned thirteen, his mother died of pneumonia. She was only thirty-nine. Rakeem's eighteen-year-old sister took custody of him and the younger siblings and they moved into the projects in Overtown, but Rakeem was rarely there. After his mother died, he was lost. The kid walled himself off. He was drifting through school. He'd stay at his older brother's, at friends' houses, anywhere he could find a couch.

He wound up staying a lot of nights at my house. He wasn't

even one of my players, but that never mattered. He was a kid who needed direction, a hot meal. He was pretty much on his own, raising himself. He had this idea that he had to be a man. He'd always refer to the other players as "kids," even thought they were all the same age. If some other players were horsing around, he'd say, "You kids need to stop playing." He'd say, "Y'all got mammas and daddies at home. I gotta find my own food. I got to provide for myself. I'm a man." But of course he wasn't a man, he was just a kid with this idea that being a man meant being tough. He was mad at the world, at everything. He missed his mom. The kid needed a hug more than anything, but he hid the pain behind this gruff persona.

For Devonta, Durell, Rakeem, and the dozens of other kids like them, football was a sanctuary. It was the place they belonged, where they had a family, where they found father figures. Their dedication and concentration was phenomenal, because they used the game to block out all the hell they experienced on the streets and at home. When they suited up and stepped on the field, they brought everything they had. Most kids in youth sports, they're doing it for fun, or because their parents want them to do it, but for the kids from Liberty City and Overtown, football provided a dream and a mission and a purpose in life. It was that passion that they brought when they absolutely destroyed every team they encountered.

My first year of coaching for Liberty City was, hands down, one of the most amazing years of my life. We had a team that was coming from a losing record. The year before they were 3–7. Nobody believed in them, but I knew I could turn them around and make them better. By the time we hit the field those kids had so much confidence, their skill level was so high, their fundamentals were so strong. They were ready. People would say, "Y'all coming out here like the University of Miami." That's how my guys played. They had that same swagger.

It's competitive and all the other teams were gunning for us. When you go out to the field for a Pop Warner game in Miami, it's crazy. It's standing room only. There's two thousand people in the bleachers, at the fence. It was even more so because Luther Campbell was coaching. Everybody wanted to beat the rapper's team. People were coming out and talking trash. Many people thought, The rapper can't coach. The kids were too young to even know what 2 Live Crew was, but I explained it to them: "You've got a bulls-eye on our backs because of who your coach is, but don't let it bother you. You're out here playing for yourself and your family, and that's it. You concentrate on yourselves and each other."

Those kids got out on the field and they just crushed it. My kids played at such a high level that people accused me of bringing in ringers from out of town, which I thought was hilarious. "Luke is paying the refs! Luke is paying the refs!" parents from the other teams were yelling. They couldn't believe it. Game after game, we walked all over the competition. We won the city championship. We won regionals. One year out from a losing season, and we were going to the national championship at Disney World in Orlando.

Taking the kids to Disney World was an incredible experience because a lot of them were just like me when I was a kid, they'd never been past the Dade County line. Some had never even left the neighborhood. The whole trip was so foreign to them that it didn't even seem possible. I made sure they knew it wasn't a vacation, though. The other teams went to Space Mountain and rode the rides. We ran drills and studied tape. We bulked up at the Ponderosa Steakhouse for the games ahead.

We won our first two games, which put us in the national championship for our division against the Oak Grove Red Devils from San Jose, California. Looking back on it, the whole national championship game is a blur for me. I was so wrapped up in emotion the whole time, the adrenaline, the excitement, the anxiety. The Red

Devils were a great team. It was neck and neck down to the last play. With less than a minute left we had possession. It was fourth down, we were down 20–14, and we were within passing distance of the end zone—one completion away from a tie, one extra point to win everything. We called a halfback pass across the middle. Our quarterback, Raymond Lee, stepped up to take the snap. Everybody in the stands was yelling, "Ray-mond! Ray-mond!" It was a perfect pass. Raymond drilled the football straight to the receiver. Kid was inches away from the goal line. He caught the ball . . . and then he dropped it. Incomplete pass. The other team took possession of the ball, took a knee, and won the game.

I cried like a baby. I literally fell to my knees and cried. It was the first time in any kind of football game that I had ever shed a tear. I had so much hope for those kids because they'd worked so hard and they went up there and accomplished so much. In the end, it didn't matter. On the bus home there were still smiles all around. They were happy just to have played the game and gone as far as they did. And besides, we knew we'd get em next year.

The following season, after that first championship loss, most of my kids moved on to the next weight group. Normally, most coaches follow their group up to the next weight class, but I liked the age group I was working with. A few of my key players didn't move up in weight, and I wanted the chance to make them team leaders and whip a whole new group into shape. We got the new kids in, and it was the same story as the year before. We rolled through our division like a steamroller. We mercy-ruled everybody. It was a massacre. Referees would ask me, "Can you put your second team in?" I would respond, "That *is* my second team." We were beating teams 35–0 in the first half. I think we still own a Pop Warner record for points scored in a season. We went through the whole state of Florida blowing everybody out, and before long we were in the national championship again.

Back in Orlando again, we were a better team. The year before, as good as our players were, we were not as close a team as we could have been. There were some personality issues. But this year, the kids all banded together to form a perfect unit. When we arrived back at Disney World that December, I had no doubt that we were the best football team in the nation for our division. Miami had been battered by a terrible hurricane just a month before. All of my kids were scattered all over the city, commuting to different schools to finish out their terms, but we kept it together and stayed focused.

We beat Mesa Eastern of Arizona in the semifinals in a close game that took us to the championship against the Cedar Town Comets from Texas, a team that had previously won a national championship. Texas and Florida are the two biggest powerhouses in the country when it comes to football talent. This game was about bragging rights, and everyone knew it. The Comets were a great team, but the Warriors came to play. I told my kids that this was their game, that this was their year, that I had never coached or even seen a team this good before, that I was proud of every single one of them. Those kids were yelling their heads off as they hit the tunnel onto the field. Then they went out and beat those Texas boys 33–0.

Over the next couple years I dedicated myself more and more to the Liberty City Optimist Club. I was Luther Campbell, youth football coach and community organizer. Uncle Luke the rap star, I kept that guy around, too. He pays the bills, which is what allows me to dedicate myself to the program as much as I do. I put out my best-of album, a three-disc box set called *My Life & Freaky Times*. I starred in one season of a reality show for VH1, *Uncle Luke's Parental Advisory*, starring me and my wife Kristen and two of my kids. I'd make personal appearances at clubs and festivals, but more and more my life centered around the young people of Liberty City.

After my two trips to Orlando, I started getting frustrated with the Pop Warner organization. The whole league was becoming commercialized. If you went to the national championship, Pop Warner required you to stay at Disney hotels on Disney property at astronomical Disney rates, and inner-city programs like ours didn't have the money. I was talking to guys from Baltimore, Washington, Philadelphia, all over the place, and they would say, "It's hard, man. We need somebody like you to step out there and start something where we won't be getting licked by Pop Warner."

I started a new league, the National Youth Football League, in affiliation with the Orange Bowl Youth Football League, which is the main competitor to Pop Warner. We set up branches mainly along the East Coast, North Carolina, Virginia, Baltimore, and the Washington area. I used my leverage to bring a lot of rappers and professional athletes in to help. I called P. Diddy, Rick Ross, Nelly, T.I., Trick Daddy, Flo Rida, and Snoop Dogg. I enlisted NFL players like Chad Johnson, Warren Sapp, Vernon Carey, Edgerrin James. A lot of those guys have children in youth football, too. They all agreed to coach teams, donate money, make appearances, do whatever was necessary. A lot of teams left Pop Warner to join us. We always have the championship game in Miami, and all those teams come down here to play at Dolphin stadium. We didn't become as big as Pop Warner, but we have thousands of kids in south Florida alone, players and cheerleaders, and we've made it into an affordable alternative for parents and groups who can't foot the bill for a trip to Disney World.

The success of the National Youth Football League capped off nineteen years of strong community work with the Optimist Club. I was proud of what so many kids had accomplished, and proud of the work we'd done.

CHAMPIONS

On January 23, 2009, a bunch of kids in Liberty City were doing what they always do on Friday night, hang out on the corner. They were out in front of a grocery store at NW Seventieth Street and Fifteenth Avenue with a dice game going on. One of the kids out there that night was Durell Eskridge. Even with all the mentorship we'd given him with the Optimist program, he was still struggling, falling under some bad influences. He'd stopped playing football and had skipped around to a bunch of different high schools because of his mother's unstable living situation. He wasn't into any trouble, but he was out on the corner when he should have been home with his schoolbooks.

Durell and his buddies were hanging out when, out of nowhere, this dude came up, pulled out an AK-47, and fired into the crowd, spraying bullets everywhere. Everyone screamed and scattered, bodies dropped, and the shooter turned and ran. Police found forty-five shell casings on the sidewalk. Two dead and seven wounded.

Six of the nine victims were high school students. Durell, just a scared, frightened teenager, survived by diving and clutching the pavement behind the dead bodies of two of his best friends.

That shooting was so horrible that I made a public statement about it: that this had to change, that we had to fight on the front lines of this problem, and that I was personally going to do something about it. My frustration had been building up for months. We worked hard at Charles Hadley Park to keep kids safe and to put them on the right path. Some were doing well. They were starting to graduate, to go to college. But we were losing too many of them when they went to high school. The year before one of Liberty City's star running backs got picked up on a murder charge. Then one of our cornerbacks got picked up on a gun charge. When those two boys were in the park, they were the nicest kids in the world, respectful, well behaved. Something had gone wrong.

Devonta Freeman had started working weekends at Richardson Funeral Home, which is owned by Dwight Jackson, one of the coaches in the neighborhood. Devonta worked as an usher, carrying flowers and escorting the families to their seats, but he also saw the bodies laid out on the slab, being embalmed and stitched back together for the open caskets—the bodies of people he knew, of kids his own age. Devonta wasn't mixed up in anything, but he narrowly escaped some close calls himself. Running away from one shooting, he had one bullet clip his sneaker—not good for a running back counting on his feet to earn him his way to college.

Despite everything we did at the Optimist Club, the violence and the shooting didn't stop, and these kids kept getting caught up in it. Sam Johnson and I would sit and talk about the change in the kids when they went to high school. These kids were getting to high school and they started dealing with so many different things: girls, sex, dealers, gangs, guns. They were struggling with their identity and losing their way. I was hearing story after story of kids being picked up by the cops. Kids getting shot. These were my kids and I didn't want to lose them to the streets. I decided I was going to follow them all the way to the finish line and make sure they crossed over it.

My record in Pop Warner was strong, with back-to-back trips to the national championships in Orlando. Word got out that I was looking to move up to the high school level. I had interest right away. Coach Telly Lockette at Central reached out to me. Of the three high schools serving black Miami—Northwestern, Jackson, and Central—Central was by far the worst. It was a failing school on every level. The building had gone up in 1959 and was in disrepair. In athletics, the Central Rockets were the perennial stepchild to the Northwestern Bulls. Northwestern won all the titles, and Central could never get over the hump to even get in the playoffs. In academics, Central was rated an F school by the state. It was in danger of losing its accreditation and being closed down. Where kids were in the most trouble, that's where I wanted to go. I arrived in the fall of 2009 at the same time as the new principal, Doug Rodriguez. Coach Lockette had come over the year before from Northwestern, where he'd been the offensive coordinator who helped bring home two state championships in consecutive years. There was a sense of a breath of fresh air in the place, of things beginning to turn around. Lockette respected my knowledge of the game and liked the analytical, tactical way I had of looking at the game, always making players watch tape and memorize playbooks. He called me "Information Man" because my head is full of everything anyone would ever want to know about the game.

Lockette hired me to be an assistant defensive coordinator. I was going to be a position coach, running the linebackers. All of the coaches and teachers in the Miami-Dade school district have to have certification from the state. They're the only county in the state that requires it; in all the others you can be an assistant coach just by volunteering. In Miami-Dade you can hire guys like me who aren't professional teachers, but there's a three-year certification process. You're given a temporary certification, and at the end of the three years, the state decides whether or not to award you a permanent certification. I took my temporary certification and got to work.

Moving to the high school level, I really had to humble myself. I was starting at the bottom in what was basically a volunteer position. I hadn't worked for anyone else since I'd left the kitchen at Mount Sinai hospital twenty-five years before. I was always the boss, and whenever I hired employees, I always expected them to be team players and work up under me. If I had an employee with no respect for the business, no respect for the boss, I'd fire him. So when I went into high school football, I couldn't be a hypocrite. I was very aware that I was working up under another guy's business. I just wanted to be a good Indian and play my part. I'd set up the field for practice. I'd clean up gear in the locker room. Anything the team needed.

My first day on the job I saw exactly what was going wrong with our kids. They'd changed. They behaved differently. They'd been the nicest, sweetest boys in the world when we had them in the park, but now they were in this high school environment, trying to act like men, and their ideas of what it meant to be a man were all about being tough, acting like thugs and hard-ass gangsters. I'll never forget, I was in the locker room that first week and this kid, a good kid who'd been in the Optimist program, was mouthing off to the wide receiver coach, being disrespectful, cussing, using every profane word imaginable. I was in shock. This was a kid, I'd never seen him act that way in my life. I walked right up to this kid and looked him in the eye, like, Are you *serious*? When he saw me he just shut down, because he knew. All those kids knew. Coach Luke don't play. If they stepped out of line with me, they were going to see me at their breakfast table the next morning, telling their moms about the problem. I still had the respect of these kids, because I'd brought them up. I put it out to all the other coaches: if there's a problem kid, send him to me. I jumped on them, got that kid back on the straight and narrow.

That first season at Central had its ups and downs. Devonta had transferred to Central from Miami Edison High School. He was coming off a broken ankle that had sidelined him for most of sophomore year, but he'd rehabbed it and bulked up to two hundred pounds. Durell had transferred in, too, to join his friend. The same night of that shooting back in January he'd resolved to get back to football, to stay off the corner. Devonta was running back and Durell was at wide receiver. Charles Gaines, the kid who'd picked up the gun violation, he was at wide receiver. He'd been proven innocent of the charges and, like Durell, had been scared straight by how close he'd come to losing everything.

I was confident about the talent we had on the field, but I felt like, as a team, we weren't living right with the football gods. You have to live right by the football gods or else there'll be a reckoning. We were letting discipline issues and morale problems get in the way of success. I didn't agree with a lot of the coaching decisions being made, but I was the new guy and could only assert myself so much.

Even with all the talent we had, when we got to the home stretch and we needed these kids to perform at a high level, they simply couldn't do it. We had a solid season and made it to the playoffs. We even beat Northwestern in the quarterfinals, but we lost to Miramar High School in the semis, even though we were the stronger team. We lost that game inside the five-yard line. We kept driving all the way down, and then the offense just couldn't punch through. We went down 21–14. The state championship should have been ours, and we blew it. The thing was, it was pouring down rain the whole game, only somehow it only rained when we had possession. Miramar would get the ball and the skies would clear. We'd get it back and it would pour again. It happened every possession. We were staring at each other in disbelief. It was the craziest thing. We weren't living right with the football gods, and that was their way of letting us know.

The disappointment of that first season was tough, but we managed to put it behind us because there was so much excitement for the next. Despite the problems, we'd gone further than any Central team had before. For the 2010–11 season, the expectation was that we'd go undefeated and win the state championship, maybe even be national champions. *USA Today* ranked us the No. 2 high school team in the country on the strength of our roster. We had twelve returning starters, including Devonta and Durell, and we had four all-star players transferring in, including Rakeem Cato.

I'd been keeping my eye on Rakeem through the years. He was over at Miami Springs, and he wasn't doing well. He wasn't getting the support he needed on or off the field. He was struggling academically, and Miami Springs was close to kicking him out. Even though Rakeem's numbers at varsity quarterback were good, the team around him wasn't performing, so he wasn't getting the chance to show his stuff to recruiters. That summer I told Rakeem, "If you really want to come to Central, you need to come right now before the season starts. But there's going to be a lot of discipline over here. We're going to work you and you need to be ready for it."

It didn't take much convincing. Rakeem wanted to be with his buddies Davonta and Durell, and he wanted to play for Coach Luke. We brought him over from Miami Springs to start at quarterback and we got him set up with a tutor to pull up his grades. For the preseason we cracked down on all the kids. We ran them hard, pulling two-a-day practices in the August heat. My goal that year was to root out all the favoritism and lack of discipline. There was no doubt that these kids were all incredibly talented players, but they still needed to learn how to play together as a team, and the coaches needed to learn how to get them there. It was the only way to fix the mistakes of the season before.

Despite the high expectations, or maybe because of them, we stumbled out of the gate. We lost our first away game in Kingsland, Georgia, against the Camden Wildcats, the previous year's state champions. Rakeem played beautifully, but those Georgia boys were beasts. Their defensive line was a wall of pain, and they were shutting down Devonta and our running game on nearly every play. Rakeem wanted Durrell in at wide receiver, but there was one coach refusing to play Durrell. Durell is six three and runs the 440 under fifty seconds, but this coach was playing another kid who was five five and who, in my opinion, couldn't even carry Durrell's jock strap. Georgia kept answering every touchdown and Rakeem had to watch Durell just sitting there on the bench with a towel over his head, begging to get in the game. We lost the game 45–42. There went the chance of going undefeated and winning a national championship.

I decided I had to stick up for my kid. I went to the head coach's office and laid it out. "Look, I think you guys are showing some favoritism in not giving Durell enough opportunities." Telling a coach something like that is like spitting in his face, accusing him of doing his player wrong. "I'll tell him to leave and go play for Jackson if you guys keep doing this to him, because it makes no sense." I gave them an ultimatum: either they play Durell at wide receiver or I send him to Jackson or: they could give him to me on defense.

Under my charge, I put Durell at strong safety, and he did well there. The bigger problem was Rakeem. Rakeem was stubborn. He was a hard case. He'd been living pretty much on his own since he was thirteen. He didn't deal well with discipline. He was so desperate to prove himself a man, to be the leader of the team, that he started acting out. Rakeem wanted Durell at receiver. When this coach wouldn't play Durell at that position, Rakeem started going off on him, launching into him with profanity. I agreed with Rakeem's position, but no player has a right to go off on a coach like that. No player can be bigger than the team, even the quarterback. Some of the coaches wanted to kick Rakeem off the team. I put my foot down. I knew Rakeem had too much potential to waste, not just as a player but as a young man. I understood his background, the trouble he'd been through. I knew what he needed. I told the other coaches, "No, I'll take Rakeem and he'll be with me. I'll handle him. I'll coach him. If he does anything else wrong, you can fire me. I'll take responsibility for it."

For the rest of that season I took Rakeem under my wing. Even though I was the defensive coordinator, I'd take him through his quarterback drills every day, and then he'd run over to the offense when it was time to scrimmage. I worked him hard. A word out of line or the slightest bit of attitude and I'd punish him. Extra drills, extra sprints, extra conditioning. When I punished him, I was teaching him. "I'm doing this because one day you're gonna have a kid and you're going to have to discipline him, too. You can accept it and take it like a man, or you can rebel. But if you do, that ain't tough, that ain't character, that ain't taking it like a man."

After a couple weeks, his rebel posture started to drop. He wanted the discipline. He wanted the structure. He needed it. He needed a parent to show him that tough love. Pretty soon he was coming to me and saying he wanted more punishment. He said, "I want punishment every day." He knew the extra hardcore coaching was making him better. It was rough. He would be cramping, running drill after drill, flipping tires, but he knew the hard work would pay off when he was in the pocket or scrambling around a crumbling offensive line.

The team started to pull together. We were living right, and the rest of the season we just slaughtered everybody. In Desoto,

Texas, we killed Dallas Madison 48–6. We beat my old team Miami Beach 41–6. We destroyed Miami Springs 70–0; Hialeah, 42–0; Miami Lakes, 63–0. Devonta and Rakeem were rushing and passing at record-setting levels. Durell was returning punts 85, 90 yards for touchdowns. We blew past Miami and Northwestern in the early rounds of the playoffs and faced off against Cypress Bay in the semifinals. It was the roughest game we'd played since Camden mauled us at the beginning of the season. Devonta ran for 354 yards with three touchdowns, and it was still neck and neck going into the fourth quarter.

We were down by three with two minutes left and we drove down to the five-yard line. We were in the exact same spot where we'd been against Miramar the year before. I went to the head coach. "Hey, just give me a time-out to talk to these guys." I went into the huddle. "Remember what happened to us last year? We couldn't punch it in on the goal line. That's why we did not go to the state championship! Don't let that happen again!" The kids ran out there on that field and pushed that team to the back of the end zone. We scored the touchdown and advanced to the state championship. Everybody was crying, the kids, the coaches, all of us.

For the state championship game we went up against the Phillips High School Panthers out of Orlando, one of the best teams in Florida. They came out strong, and suddenly we were down 17 points just minutes into the game. Rakeem and Devonta stepped up, together scoring three unanswered touchdowns before the half. From that moment on, it was all over but the shouting. Devonta had 36 carries for 308 yards in the game. With the numbers Rakeem put up that day, he became the top passer in the history of Dade County football, with 9,412 yards in his high school career. We beat the Panthers 42–27, capturing Central's first-ever state championship trophy.

For most coaches, winning that game would have been the pinnacle of their careers, but not me. My goal was to see Devonta, Durell, and Rakeem on their way to a better place, and now that they were I didn't waste any time turning my attention to the next group of kids coming through.

That winter, I got a call from the head coach at our rival, Northwestern, offering me a job for the 2011–12 season. I didn't hesitate to say yes. During my two years as a high school coach, I'd helped some of the coaches from the Warriors move into jobs at Jackson and with me at Central. But we didn't have anybody at Northwestern, despite the fact that a lot of Warriors were going there. It was where I needed to be, plus it would be a promotion to defensive coordinator, a new challenge for me as a coach.

I went right to work. The season was solid. We went 8–2 and put up some incredible numbers. Spring, after the end of the season, the expiration date for my three-year temporary certification came up, and I started the process to get my permanent certification. On May 15, 2012, the administrative judge overseeing my application recommended to the Education Practices Commission of the State Board of Education that I be approved. "Petitioner does not pose a risk to the safety of the students entrusted to him," he wrote in his evaluation. "For the past seven years, Petitioner has had significant direct contact with vulnerable youth without any reported problems." That should have settled it, but two weeks later the state rejected me. Somebody up in Tallahassee had a problem with me coaching. The attorney for the State Board of Education, Charles Whitelock, appealed the judge's recommendation, saying that I lacked "the required good moral character" to coach students because of my "criminal" record.

Once again, Luther Campbell was back in court, defending my basic and fundamental rights. The way the system is designed, technically, if you have charges on your record from up to twenty-five years ago, you're not fit to be employed by the school board to work with kids. *Charges*, not convictions. Which is crazy. I grew up in a community where the cops threw everybody in jail and sorted it out later. They didn't care about anybody's rights. They just did a clean sweep, and my neighbors and I were swept up like trash. Fortunately, I'd always been self-employed, so my record never had an impact on my ability to work. But how many black and brown people are being kept unemployed because they had the bad luck to come from a place where police harass you all the time? It's an unfair policy. It's unjust.

I've never been convicted of a serious crime in my life. I've never been to prison. I've stood up in front of the Supreme Court of the United States and been found not guilty. How many people can say that? But all these years later, they were telling me I was unfit to coach kids. Did I make mistakes in my youth? As a performer? Of course I did. But that's all the more reason I should be a coach. If they denied my certification, they'd be sending all these young kids a message that you can't turn your life around and get a second chance, and these are kids who need all the second chances they can get. More than losing my coaching job, I was concerned about what kind of message my players would have taken away from it had I lost. I preach to my kids that they can change their lives and succeed, and nobody can ever take that from them. My kids believe it because I'm living proof that you've got to fight and work for what you get, but you can make it.

It's also not like there was a long list of people running in to help the kids at Northwestern High School in Liberty City. Why would you try and stop anyone who's genuinely committed to serving that community? Same as with the censorship trial in Broward, I wasn't just fighting for myself. There were a lot of guys like me who want to volunteer and contribute who might have made some mistakes at a young age. As a matter of fact, it's the people who've been through the bad times who are able to mentor kids the best. A guy who's squeaky-clean can't tell a kid anything, because he can't really understand what that kid is going through because he's never experienced it. If you've never sat in that jail-house holding cell, feeling stupid, how can you tell a kid what that experience is and how stupid you were for doing the stupid thing that got you there? Mr. Squeaky-Clean can't tell that kid, "Hey, I see a lot of me in you, and I know what's on your mind right now. You think you're superman. You think you're bigger than the world and smarter than everybody, but you ain't that smart, buddy." I felt like if I put up a fight, I might help set a new prec-edent for people to be able to go and coach and contribute. On top of my own desire to keep coaching, that was my big motivation.

After the state appealed the judge's recommendation, what fol-lowed was months of bureaucratic red tape, appeals and hearings, as I waited to see if I was going to be allowed to keep coaching. Given my celebrity, my case started attracting attention from the media, and who jumped in to join the fray but my old nemesis, Jack Thompson. Guy just doesn't know when to give up. He fired off more of his angry letters to the judge in the case, saying I was still a part of the adult industry, that I was still just a dirty rapper. Of course, by that point Thompson had been disbarred by the Florida Bar Association for making false statements and harassing litigants, so nobody paid him much mind.

Fortunately, a real Miami attorney was following the case as well. Mike Carney, a lawyer from one of the biggest firms in Miami, read about my story and reached out to me. I didn't even know the guy, and he called me up and offered to handle the case, no charge. He said, "I just want to do it because I think you're doing something great for these kids. I'd be honored to be your lawyer and defend you in this." I thanked him, and he dove right in to help me argue my case.

The Board of Education's only actual legal argument was based on my application, which was incomplete. I'd listed and chronicled most of the charges and brushes with the law I've had, but not all of them. I forgot to add the South Carolina thing and the display-of-firearms charge from 1987, mostly because the forms were confusing. It's not like I was trying to hide anything. I gave them my fingerprints knowing full well that they were going to run a complete background check. Besides, I'm Luther Campbell. Everything you could possibly want to know about every bad thing I've ever done is right there on Google.

Their case wasn't really about an incomplete application. It was the same moral hypocrisy that had triggered the whole censorship controversy twenty-five years before. In the deposition this attorney, Whitelock, grilled me for hours. It was worse than the criminal trial when I went to jail for performing onstage. In that case, I only had to defend one performance. This guy put my whole life on trial. He grilled me about every arrest, every late child-support payment. He grilled me about dirty lyrics, over and over again, lyrics that I didn't even write. He did everything he could to make me out to be some kind of moral degenerate. This wasn't some routine background check. I felt like the guy was out to get me, that he was just another Jack Thompson. Except that he wasn't some random nut job. He was a government official, representing the authority of the state, interfering with my mission to serve my own community.

I didn't take any chances. In the months I spent waiting for the hearing to take place, I made my own case in the court of public opinion. I gave interviews to the *New York Times*, to Andy Staples at *Sports Illustrated*, to Soledad O'Brien at HBO's *Real Sports*. All of them, the most mainstream of the mainstream media, came out in my defense, applauding the work I'd done for Liberty City youth over the years. When the hearing finally came, we flooded the court with character witnesses and letters testifying to my good works in the community: grateful parents, pastors, former players.

State senator Oscar Brennan wrote a letter. Jimbo Fisher, head coach at Florida State University, wrote a letter. Lance Moore from the Miami Dolphins. We had dozens of them.

By the time we'd made our case to the judge who presided over the hearing, there was no question about which way he would rule. He found that I was both fit and capable of coaching high school football. There were a few stipulations. I have to be on probation for three years, with a coach supervising me and filing progress reports to a probation officer up in Tallahassee. I also can't participate in any kind of adult-related concerts or activities during the coaching season. It wasn't a problem because I wasn't doing anything like that anyway. They also made me take an online ethics class, which was a joke.

The judge's decision was handed down in August, and after that, I was free to focus my attention back where it belonged, on the 2012–13 season and the kids who need me. I'm Coach Luke now, and that's the way it's gonna stay. In the course of my career, I've probably spent six months of my life sitting in courtrooms, fighting for what I believe in. I've spent over a million dollars in legal fees, easy, not because of things I've done or crimes I've committed, but because of attacks and harassments people have brought against me, trying to take away my First Amendment rights, trying to interfere with my ability to run a business, trying to stop me from helping high school kids that no one else is trying to help—trying to keep me trapped in those invisible chains. But every step of the way, I've fought for what I believe in. Same as my father before me, I refused to keep my head down and keep quiet. It's cost me. I don't have a mansion or a yacht or a private jet anymore. I don't have the corner office at some billion-dollar record company. But that's fine with me. I never cared about any of that anyway. What I have now is something far, far more important.

CHARLES HADLEY PARK

Before we won the state championship at Central, Devonta Freeman was being heavily recruited by Florida State University and made an early commitment to them. He led the team in rushing in his first three seasons in Tallahassee, and his junior year he took the Seminoles all the way to win the 2014 BCS National Championship Game, with career highs in rushing yards (1,016), receiving yards (278), and touchdowns (15). Last year he bypassed his final year of eligibility to enter the NFL draft and was picked up by the Atlanta Falcons.

Rakeem Cato graduated from Central and joined the Thundering Herd at Marshall College in West Virginia. Marshall's a smaller school, but they punch way above their weight. Rakeem's sophomore year he was Conference USA MVP, and he led the entire nation in passing yards per game. He finished his four seasons with a school-record 14,079 passing yards and 131 passing touchdowns, came up in a lot of conversations as a contender for the Heisman, and set an NCAA record by throwing touchdown passes in thirty-nine consecutive games.

Durell Eskridge went to Syracuse. As a redshirt sophomore at strong safety, he led the team in tackles and interceptions and has been one of their top defensive players every single year. As I write this, both Rakeem and Durell have entered the 2015 NFL draft and are waiting to see what happens.

It's not hard to imagine a different life for any of these guys: Devonta's foot blown off by that stray bullet, Durell lying dead in a pile of bodies on the corner of Seventieth and Fifteenth, Rakeem kicked out of high school because nobody cared to help a troubled kid learn discipline and self-control. The difference for all three of them was the Liberty City Optimist Club. Not just what Coach Luke did, but what all of our coaches did: looking out for them, teaching them, taking time with them, showing them the opportunities that are out there.

People like to talk about the Devontas and the Rakeems and the Durells because they're the big success stories, the superstars. Our program has dozens of them. Every year we have kids joining NCAA powerhouse teams and being drafted in the early rounds of the NFL. Duke Johnson from the University of Miami is one of the top running backs in the nation. He's one of ours. He'll probably go in the first or second round in this year's draft. Darryl Sharpton just went to the Bears as a middle linebacker; he's one of ours. The top middle linebacker in the NFL, Lavonte David, who plays for the Tampa Bay Buccaneers, he came out of our program as well. Chad Johnson, who played ten years with the Cincinnati Bengals, he was one of our first.

But like I've always said: this isn't about football. These success stories are just the icing on the cake. The real story is in the hundreds of kids who've come through our program and used it to get an education, to get further down the road than they would have otherwise. I've built up relationships with dozens of college recruiters nationwide, and I've got all of them on speed dial. Everybody focuses on the Florida States and the Notre Dames, the powerhouse schools in the SEC and the Big Ten, but you can find scholarship dollars in plenty of other places, too. I can tell you where every spare nickel of NCAA scholarship money is and how to get it. If there's $50,000 for a tailback at a Division II school in Ohio, I'm on the phone to that coach, telling him about my player's SAT score, telling him to give that kid a look. Last year we put thirty-two kids in major universities across the country. Next year, we'll do more.

There's success stories even beyond that. Not every kid can get a scholarship or play at the college level, but after coming out of the Liberty City Optimist Club, they've had years of tutoring and mentorship. They've acquired the life skills and the knowledge to make something of themselves. They've stayed off the corners. Every year we still lose too many kids, but every year more and more of them are finishing high school. Maybe they're working and doing community college part-time. Maybe they're in a vocational program. Whatever it is they're doing, they're doing it with drive and dedication. They have a sense of self-worth. They can see a path out of poverty where they didn't see one before. They'll never have to wear those invisible chains again.

Flying on the private jet, partying on my yacht, living in the mansion with the big Jacuzzi, I remember those days. Being a rock star is fun, but the truth is I'm happier now. I make $1,500 a year coaching football. That doesn't even cover the cost of the gas I use. I have the royalties from my solo career, my appearance fees and speaking fees. My wife and I have started a few small businesses, a local restaurant and a line of Uncle Luke imported rum. We lead a much simpler life than I used to. I coach my kids and write a column for the *Miami New Times*, our alternative paper.

I sold the big mansion in the fancy gated neighborhood, and I don't even miss it. The rich people there, they never acted like neighbors. Nobody talked to each other. They all just lived in their own worlds. Now I'm out in the suburbs—out in Broward County, if you can believe that—living in a nice area with middle-class families. The kids play in the street and the neighbors all say hello. It actually reminds me a lot of Liberty City when I was growing up, only it's not just black. It's all kinds of different people, living together.

I'm happier than I've ever been right now because I have something I never had before. I have a family. All my life, I looked at all the money and everything I had, and I always told God, "You can take all this stuff, just give me a wife and a family." You can have all the money in the world, but you come home to a house and lay in the bed with the wrong person, you're not happy. You know it's some bullshit. You go through those relationships and they don't pan out, but you learn things from them. They're preparing you for the real relationship that you're meant to have.

People's misconception of me is that I'm out there dating strippers. But that was never the case. I wasn't looking to marry some girl in my music videos. Like the saying goes: you don't get high on your own supply. When I was a rock star, most of the women I was attracted to and had serious relationships with were professional women, educated women I could relate to on my own level. Kristen was all of that. She's an attorney. Intelligent, confident, kind. She saw right past the Uncle Luke stuff right away. She started spending time with me out at the park, working with the Optimist kids, and she knew right away that that's the man I really was. And the fact that she liked sports helped a lot. We'll be married seven years this July.

Uncle Luke isn't gone forever. I still love music, still produce songs here and there and do appearances with other artists. I've got a couple dozen tracks in the vault that I haven't released, and I may do something with them at some point. The music business, it's like a drug. It's exciting and fun, and people always come back to it wanting that fix. Every now and then, when the vibes are right, I'll think about getting back out there and doing something. But every time that happens, I get pulled back in the other direction, back to the place that needs me most, back to Central and Northwestern, back to Charles Hadley Park, back to my community. As happy and as settled as I might be in my personal life, I know that I can't rest even for a minute, because the fight for Liberty City continues every day. I know that the fight isn't hopeless. I know that we can win, because I've seen it happen. I've helped make it happen.

In March of 2011, Miami voted to recall its mayor, Carlos Alvarez. He was a terrible mayor. He raised property taxes during a housing crisis. He gave his cronies in city government big fat raises in the middle of a budget crisis. Miami-Dade has been run like a banana republic for decades, and Alvarez was one of the worst we've ever had. After the recall, the city called for a special election to replace Alvarez, and the whole city, blacks, whites, Hispanics, suddenly we had an opportunity to take a clean, fresh look at our problems.

I've always believed in one Miami. I've seen it happen. I've seen it when everybody's dancing together at my concerts, when the whole city rallied around the Miami Hurricanes in the '84 Orange Bowl, when white and Hispanic families enjoy some Liberty City hospitality during football games in Charles Hadley Park. But then every time it gets to the level of politics and effecting change, everything falls apart. Many politicians and private entities have a vested interest in dividing us, playing us off against each other to enrich themselves. I've always believed that if politicians would stop dividing us, we could unite for the good of everyone.

Back when I was a DJ, I went downtown from time to time to get permits to play in different places. It was my first brush with politics. What I noticed every time I set foot in City Hall was that I didn't see anybody who looked like me. We had a few token representatives, but it was all white people and Cuban people. They were running the shit. Black people *built* Miami. Bahamians and Jamaicans cleared the tropical forests and filled in the swamps so that other people could get rich, and a century later we barely had a seat at the table. Our communities had been destroyed, first by "urban renewal" policies and then by the riots, and they've never really come back. The gang violence hasn't gone away. The violence at the hands of the police hasn't gone away. And because we have no real voice in government, the programs that are voted on and put in place do us no good or work against us.

Half of our problem is the one I've been on about my whole life, what my uncle Ricky taught me: ownership. Owning your own self, your own property, your own labor. In a capitalist society, money is power. Property is power. But we were denied that. Time and again our land and our wealth and our labor have been taken from us, leaving us with no economic leverage to demand the change we deserve. The other half of our problem is that black communities don't engage the way we should. If President Barack Obama's not on the ballot—and he never will be again—we don't vote in the numbers we should. We're apathetic about the process because we don't believe the system will work for us, which guarantees that the system won't work for us, which leads to a cycle of frustration and hopelessness.

The Cubans came in fifty years ago, just at the moment when we were supposed to finally secure our rights. They took Malcolm X's playbook and ran with it. They used their buying power and their wealth and their ethnic solidarity, they took all the government programs meant to help other minorities, and they built a political coalition that controls not only south Florida but that swings national elections. Eventually, they became the more solid race of people. We became the more disenfranchised and confused race of people—a divided community.

When the Alvarez recall happened, I wanted to use it as an opportunity to energize the black community, to raise awareness of the black community's needs in the places where our concerns never get addressed. I was using my weekly column in the paper to hold politicians' feet to the fire, but I felt like the only way I could really accomplish that was to put myself out there, to go out and say all the things that I wanted to say. I decided to run for mayor myself. Luther Campbell for Mayor.

My campaign slogan was "I'm dead serious . . . are you?" Because I was serious. I wasn't running as some novelty candidate. I was running to win, to have an impact. The theme of my campaign was One Miami. I wanted to energize African-American voters and raise awareness of the issues that affect the black community, but my main thing has always been bringing this city together. When I announced my candidacy, I got a few of the predictable jokes from the national media, but down here in Miami, nobody was laughing. They know that we've got serious problems, and they know that I've been working hard in the community for the past twenty years. They read my column and listened to me on the radio all the time, talking about housing and taxes and education. Joy Reid, the *Miami Herald* columnist and MSNBC host, wrote that I was "as credible a candidate as any" with "some serious ideas about things like policing, politics and community development."

I knew it would be virtually impossible to win the election, but my goal was to energize voters, wake people up, and change the conversation. I had Trick Daddy and NFL celebrities come out for fundraisers, exciting young people who probably never voted before. I sat down with the police union and the firemen's union and the housing authority and kept it 100 percent with them. I was brutally honest about issues like low-income housing, over-policing in black communities, failing schools. The two leading Cuban candidates, Hialeah mayor Julio Robaina and county commissioner Carlos Gimenez, were forced to respond, forced to address issues that otherwise they could have avoided.

For me personally, the single best and most rewarding part of the campaign was going into old folks' homes in Overtown, soliciting votes. I'd introduce myself. They'd say, "Yeah, I know your mamma. I grew up with your mamma." Or they'd say, "I know your granddaddy and your grandmamma. Your grandmamma, she loved to play cards." I started hearing all these stories that I'd never heard before, about my aunts and uncles, how my mom and dad really met, about the history of the community, how deep and rich that history is, how far back it goes. Running for office, I learned who I really am. I'm a better person for it, a much better person. I understand where I'm going and that I'm definitely going in the right direction. I'm not just a famous rapper and a successful businessman. I'm a part of a community and a history and a tradition. Working with the kids in Liberty City, running for office, I'm doing what my mother, father, and all these folks set out for me to do. In the end I got 11 percent of the vote. Not enough to win, obviously, but it represents a real constituency. My campaign accomplished what I set out for it to accomplish: it energized the community, in better ways than I ever could have hoped for.

Keon Hardemon grew up in Liberty City, in the Scott Carver housing projects. He spent most of his childhood living with his grandma while his mother was away in the army. He met his father only twice, once in fifth grade and again in high school. Like hundreds of other young black boys from the projects, Keon could have slipped though the cracks, but fortunately for him he found a constructive outlet: playing youth football with the Liberty City Optimist Club. The program gave him the discipline and focus he needed to stay out of trouble and stay in school, same as it did for Devonta, Durell, and Rakeem.

But Keon wasn't destined for the NFL. He graduated from Northwestern High School, got his bachelor's degree from Florida A&M, and earned his law degree from the University of Miami. Straight out of law school he landed a fantastic, high-paying corporate job with the pharmaceutical company Pfizer. They had him flying all over the world on business. He was living the good life, supporting his family. Then late one night he was in Shanghai, stuck at the airport because he'd missed a flight. He was browsing the Internet for news from back home and he saw a video about my run for mayor. Seeing that video reminded him of how important the Optimist Club had been to him, how I'd always stressed the importance of community and giving back.

It was a message that hit home for Keon in a particularly hard way. The Scott Carver homes where he'd grown up had been destroyed, bulldozed by developers with a promise from the city that the land would be used for better mixed-income housing, with new facilities and services to help the poor. The eight hundred families who lived there were evicted, scattered out to Homestead and other places out in the middle of nowhere, and the promised development never came through. Private developers and their political cronies used the money to line their pockets, embezzling millions while poor black families lost their homes and their community— the same script that's been playing out ever since they ran the I-95 through Overtown, ever since they took our beachfront land and handed it over to white folks to build hotels and resorts.

Keon could have stayed in his corporate job and made a lot of money for himself, but he didn't. He quit, came home to Miami, and went to work as a public defender, fighting on behalf of the young black men who got trapped in the cycle of poverty and violence and lack of opportunity, guys who weren't lucky enough to make it out like he did. In 2013, the city commissioner representing Miami-Dade's Fifth District was going to be stepping down. District 5 is the poorest and most crime-ridden district in the city. It covers Liberty City, Overtown, and Little Haiti. Keon called me up and reminded me of his time in the Optimist Program. He told me he was going to run for the city commission, and he asked for my help. His opponent was the establishment candidate. All the big-money people were backing him. He was going to win. Keon told me, "I don't have a lot of money, but I've been inspired by you and would like your support."

I saw in this young man the culmination of everything I'd been working toward. I couldn't say yes to him fast enough. With the political base I'd built, I wasn't going to be the king, but I could be the kingmaker. I brought out all of Miami to get behind him. I cut radio commercials for him. I staged a fund-raising concert with Trick Daddy and all the other local hip-hop artists. I tapped the network of donors and voters I'd built by running my own campaign, and we went hard to get his name out there and get people involved in the process—and we won. It wasn't even close. Keon was getting double and triple the usual numbers in the youth vote, and he ended up winning with 72 percent of the overall vote.

We celebrated with a big election-night party at Overtown's Jackson Soul Food restaurant. That night, Keon pulled out his phone and showed me a video he took of himself three years before at the airport in Shanghai. It was a testimonial he'd made, talking about being inspired to run for public office by my campaign and how he was going to dedicate his life to public service from that point on. I couldn't have been more proud. Now we had one of our own in office: the youngest city commissioner in Miami, just twenty-nine years old, a young African-American man from the hip-hop generation who knows and understands what our community needs.

Charles Hadley Park has been home to the Liberty City Optimist Club for the past twenty-five years. It's the place where our community has healed and come together, where we've launched dozens of young boys like Hardemon himself on to college and better lives. But the park itself hasn't done well. It's falling apart. When Sam Johnson was alive he fought the city commission year in and year out for the $6.5 million appropriation we were owed to bring the park back, to fix the drainage and add new facilities. Sam hit a wall of bureaucratic incompetence and indifference every single time. Then in January of 2014, Keon Hardemon, just weeks into the job, used his political capital and leverage to lean hard on the rest of the commission, and he drove the appropriation through with a unanimous vote.

We're getting the money. The facilities are being built. The park is being restored.

Considered against all the problems that African-Americans face today, it may not seem like much, just a simple park, but it couldn't be more important. That park was ours. In 1947, thirty-five black families owned homes on that land, and they were evicted by the city to make way for an all-white park. We lost our land, our leverage, our control. It was taken from us. But we rallied, we organized, and now we've taken it back. Today, Charles Hadley Park is a place where young kids come to get the guidance and tutoring they need to stay in school. It's a place that gangs know to stay away from, because it's too important to destroy with more violence. It's a place where cops mentor and coach young black boys, instead of gunning them down in the streets. It's a place where families can come together and enjoy a Saturday afternoon—and not just black families, but white and Hispanic families, too, who bring their children and see that our community is warm and welcoming and not so different from their own.

If you come down to Miami, you won't find Uncle Luke out on some yacht, drinking Hennessy, surrounded by groupies. You'll find Luther Campbell in Charles Hadley Park, making sure kids have a safe ride home from practice. You'll find me in the field house at Northwestern High, putting the defensive line through their hundredth round of practice drills in the hundred-degree heat. You'll find me on the phone, talking SAT scores with guidance counselors and teachers and college recruiters. You'll find me down at the city commission, raising hell about housing and education and changes in law enforcement. That's where you'll find me, because if we want to save our communities, that's what it's going to take—from me, from you, from all of us.

Twenty-five years ago, Sam Johnson walked into a millionaire rapper's office and asked for a check to sponsor a Little League team. Since that day, we've done things and helped kids and saved families in a way no one would have ever imagined in a place that most of the world would rather forget. Liberty City gave me everything I have. It gave me an incredible family. It gave me a love of my own culture and its music. It gave me the opportunity to take an amazing, unbelievable ride, and I could never turn my back on a place that has given me so much. Liberty City is my home, and I'll fight for it every day for the rest of my life.

ACKNOWLEDGMENTS

I would like to thank my family. I'm settled down and married now, to a wonderful woman, and we have an incredible son together. I love all of my kids equally: my daughters, Shanetris and Lutheria and Lucretia; my sons, Luther Jr. and Brooklyn and Blake; and I feel that they love me, too. I had my first daughter when I was twenty-one years old. I was young, and I wasn't ready for it. At times it's been difficult, a fact that the tabloids have always tried to sensationalize. But I've consistently tried to be the best father I know how to be.

What I am as a coach right now, and as a mentor to kids, is what Alex Medina was to me. He's the guy who's totally responsible for everything I do for kids today. Thanks for the inspiration.

Thank you, Tanner, for bringing my story to life and doing a wonderful job. Peter McGuigan, my literary agent, thank you for believing in my story; and to the *New York Times* writer that brought us together, Greg Bishop. And then there is Tracy Sherrod, my editor, and all the hardworking staff at HarperCollins, thank you for your commitment and passion.

Last but not least, I would like to thank my Haters—you keep me motivated.

ABOUT THE AUTHOR

LUTHER CAMPBELL, hip-hop's original bad boy, a pop culture icon, and consummate businessman, is one of the few American celebrities who has had an indelible impact on the worlds of music, sex, business, law, and politics simultaneously.

The first southern rap star to emerge on the Billboard Pop charts, with "Move Something," Campbell established Skyywalker Records (eventually renamed Luke Records), and made national headlines in the early 1990s as a part of 2 Live Crew, when he triumphed in one of hip-hop's most important cultural and political victories, protecting the right to free speech in rap. His highly publicized obscenity trial and Supreme Court parody case were First Amendment landmarks that still shape the entertainment industry today. In 2000, the Rock and Roll Hall of Fame honored Campbell's contribution to hip-hop by including him in its "Hip-Hop Nation: Roots, Rhymes and Rage" exhibit. In 2004, Campbell won the Free Speech Coalition's first Celebrity Freedom Fighter Award for his legal struggles against the federal government.

Today, Luther Campbell is known as Coach Campbell to students at Miami's Northwestern High School, a position he won with the help of a letter-writing campaign from area parents and community leaders, testifying to his positive role as a mentor and leader in Miami's black community. In addition to his work for the Miami public school system, Campbell is a coach in the National

Youth Football League through the Liberty City Warriors, a youth organization he cofounded in his hometown to keep wayward boys out of trouble.

The Liberty City Warriors won the Pop Warner National Championship in 2005, but Campbell considers the program's real accomplishment to be his players' academic progress.